MW01194036

SIDELOCKS AND BOXLOCKS
THE
CLASSIC BRITISH SHOTGUNS

SIDELOCKS AND BOXLOCKS
THE
CLASSIC BRITISH SHOTGUNS

GEOFFREY BOOTHROYD

SAFARI PRESS INC.

P.O. BOX 3095, LONG BEACH, CALIFORNIA 90803

SIDELOCKS AND BOXLOCKS copyright © 1991 by Geoffrey Boothroyd. All rights reserved. No part of this publication may be used or reproduced in any form or by any means, electronic or mechanical reproduction, including photocopy, recording, or any information storage and retrieval system, without permission from the publisher.

The trademark Safari Press ® is registered with the U.S. Patent and Trademark Office and in other countries.

Boothroyd, Geoffrey

Second edition

Safari Press Inc.

1998, Long Beach, California

ISBN 1-57157-118-3

Library of Congress Catalog Card Number: 90-20424

10 9 8 7

Readers wishing to receive the Safari Press catalog, featuring many fine books on big-game hunting, wingshooting, and sporting firearms, should write to Safari Press Inc., P.O. Box 3095, Long Beach, CA 90803, USA. Tel: (714) 894-9080 or visit our Web site at www.safaripress.com.

To my Daughter, Susan Mary, who transferred material from one disc to another, researched all the photographs and was of immeasureable help to her aged parent throughout the birth of this book.

CONTENTS

FOREWORD

"It is a well-known fact that Americans are not by any means partial to guns manufactured in their own country, and will always buy in preference an English gun." So wrote Cadwallader Waddy in the August 1872 edition of *Belgravia Magazine* in which he described the methods and gunmaking facilities of W. & C. Scott in England. His statement, although a bit overenthusiastic, did capture the status of British-made guns in the eyes of American shooters. For more than a century and a half, British double guns have been held in high esteem by shooters around the world. Nowhere, except perhaps in Britain, are these guns more highly valued than in America. Since the perfection of the muzzle-loading gun during the first half of the 19th century, British guns have represented the highest level of materials and workmanship, features always sought by discerning shooters. As efficient methods were applied to breech-loading guns during the last half of the 19th century, British gunmakers became known for more than just their best guns. A number of makers produced a wide range of qualities, which in most instances were very well built guns. Consequently, so-called plain quality British guns often were better made, more reliable, and longer lasting than their more highly decorated American and Continental counterparts. Further, and less related to the nature of the guns themselves, is the fact that a lot of Americans view many things British with a certain degree of reverence. There is a mystique about the finest products of the land from which many Americans trace their ancestors.

The factors that influenced the reputation of British gunmakers included the quality of materials and workmanship of the guns, innovative designs, marketing strategy, and the successes of shooters who used particular makes. Several London makers, such as Purdey, Boss, Woodward, and Holland & Holland, established world-wide reputations by focusing on production of the very highest quality guns and by obtaining royal appointments throughout Europe. Other makers, including W. & C. Scott and W. W. Greener, aggressively marketed their guns, which were available in a broad range of qualities, in the United States and earned the admiration of shooters because of the soundness of workmanship and value. Scott and Greener guns were used to win many shooting contests throughout the world and both companies were quick to capitalize on these successes. Westley Richards was brought to the attention of American shooters largely because of production of their very successful hammerless boxlock gun. E. M. Reilly was another well known British gunmaker among 19th century shooters in America. Some manufacturers, particularly from the Birmingham area, concentrated on the lower end of the market. Of these companies, P. Webley, J. & W. Tolley, J. P. Clabrough, and C. G. Bonehill, were probably most familiar to American shooters of that era. Some companies, including Greener and Clabrough, established offices in the United States, and others appointed agents. America was a primary market for a number of British makers during the 19th century.

The affection towards British guns has waned little during the 20th century, but some things have changed. At the turn of the century, there were several dozen major makers in London, Birmingham, Edinburgh, Glasgow, and other towns and cities throughout Britain. Many makers produced several hundred double guns each year and the larger makers manufactured several thousands annually. By the 1930s, nearly all makers had abandoned the lower end of the market, and by the 1980s, few British guns in the mid-range were being produced. As we near the end of the 20th century, only a handful of makers have survived (some in name only) and their cumulative production has dropped to approximately 500 double guns a year. The market for the high end of the mid-range guns and for best guns seemingly has remained strong, but as production dropped, prices of both new and used guns escalated. Nevertheless, interest among Americans in British guns and gunmakers, especially from the period of 1870 to 1940, remains high. However, no source of information specifically about British guns in America has been available.

The need for information about British guns in America became particularly obvious to me during the past decade while I have served as historian for one of the last of the great British gunmakers, W. & C. Scott of Birmingham. Much of the history of that company had to be reconstructed from catalogs, articles, advertisements, patents, the scant factory records, and even the guns themselves, which sometimes yielded critical information. In addition to requests regarding Scott and Webley & Scott guns, people frequently would contact me hoping to obtain information about some of the less well known British makers. Because much of the history of many British makers has been lost, I could provide little more than names and dates on the company. Now, thanks to the efforts of Geoffrey Boothroyd and Worth Mathewson, American owners of British guns have a reference designed specifically for them. I have been in awe of Geoffrey Boothroyd since I first read his books and his weekly columns in *Shooting Times & Country Magazine*. He is an internationally recognized expert on gunmaking, and the depth and breadth of his knowledge of British guns and gunmakers is second to none. Worth Mathewson is an avid bird hunter and has pursued his quarry throughout the world. He has chronicled his experiences in the finest sporting magazines in the United States and Europe. With the publication of this volume, information about British guns in America has been brought together for the first time and is now preserved for future generations.

John A. Crawford, Ph.D.
Oregon State University
Corvallis, Oregon — 1990

ABOUT THIS BOOK

As with my previous two books on shotguns I have drawn heavily on articles published in the British weekly sporting magazine, *The Shooting Times and Country Magazine.*

Now in its 108th year of publication it is remarkable if only for one thing, it has survived! I first started writing for the magazine in 1958 so I now have clocked up over thirty years, during which time I have written well over one thousand articles.

Such an output, on what is a fairly limited subject, would not have been possible without the help and assistance given to me by the readers during this period.

To-day, with a postbag which averages over sixty letters a month, I have what can best be described as "Research Assistants", drawn from all walks of life and from many countries. These "corresponding readers" have kept me on my toes, provided answers to many of my questions and ensured a two way flow of information which has been one of the major reasons why the series has continued to flourish.

It was an American reader who first suggested that a book based on the articles would prove popular. In fact, he ran out of space to keep the articles in magazine form (they take up nearly 12 feet of shelf space) and got tired of tearing out the pages to keep those. So, the first Shotgun book was born, *The Shotgun, History and Development,* to be followed, a year later by *Shotguns and Gunsmiths, The Vintage Years.*

These two books nowhere near exhausted the amount of material available so, following a series of discussions with Worth Mathewson it was decided to publish a third Shotgun book, again based on the *Shooting Times* articles and since it was to be published in the U.S.A., it would also incorporate some of the material which had been published in the previous two books.

To those of my devoted readers who already have the first two Shotgun books, please bear with me, if you have bought this book. This course of action was not taken without some considerable thought and it was based on the fact that the present book is published in another country by another publisher.

Talking about publishers, I have to thank Worth Mathewson for his faith and forbearance since the venture was a new departure for both of us. I sincerely trust that you, the reader, will consider that it was well worth while.

Geoffrey Boothroyd
Glasgow

ACKNOWLEDGEMENTS

In addition to the valuable help given to me over the years by readers I have to thank a number of other people, mostly members of the gun trade, for their help and advice which have been given freely and which I acknowledge with warmest thanks.

Atkin, Grant & Lang, Ron Solari.
Frederick Beesley, Amersham, Bucks. Fred Buller.
The Birmingham Gun Barrel Proof House. The Proof Master and his Staff.
David McKay Brown, Gunmaker, Bothwell, Hamilton, Scotland.
A. A. Brown & Sons, Alvechurch, Birmingham.
Christie's, King Street, London, Mr. C. Brunker.
John Dickson & Sons, Edinburgh.
John A. Feyk, California. U.S.A.
Gunnerman Books, Auburn Hgts. Mich. U.S.A.
The Gun Trade Association, Mr. N. G. Brown.
Holland & Holland Ltd., London.
John Harris, Gun Stocker, Birmingham.
Graham Holloway, Birmingham.
Kenneth C. Hunt, Gun Engraver, Weybridge, Surrey.
Info-Arm, New York, U.S.A.
Matched Pairs Ltd., Durham.
D. A. Masters, Beare Green, Dorking, Surrey.
The late Harry Lawrence, O.B.E., James Purdey & Sons.
Sotheby & Co., London.
W. & C. Scott Ltd., Witton, Birmingham, Mr. P. G. Whatley
Alan Wey, William Evans Ltd., London.

HISTORY

The British sporting shotgun is a product not only of generations of gun-makers and inventors but also of the times during which it has been developed and used.

Advice on the best fowling piece and on the choice and care of gunpowder was given in *The Gentleman's Recreation* published in 1697. On shot, the author suggested that it should be "of moderate bigness; for if it is too great then it scatters too much; if too small it hath not the weight nor strength to do execution on large fowl".

Shooting with very costly wheelocks firing a single ball, at stationary targets was one thing, but most sportsmen found that if they loaded their guns with a number of small shot they stood a better chance of a kill.

Lead shot, then known as hail shot, was probably first made by cutting up sheet lead into cubes which were roughly polished by tumbling. By the last quarter of the 17th century shotmakers had discovered the method of pouring molten lead through a sieve and allowing the drops to fall into water.

In *The Merry Wives of Windsor*, written by Shakespeare in 1597, Master Ford is described as being out "a birding". We learn little about the gun he used, although what we do learn is that Master Ford unloaded his birding piece by discharging it up the chimney when he returned home, a somewhat wasteful practice but it probably kept down the chimney sweep's bills!

During the 16th and 17th centuries fowling was done with nets, "springes" (snares) and bird lime. When guns were used it was common practice to employ a "stalking horse" which was specially trained for the purpose.

During this period, fowling was not so much a sport or pastime but a very necessary means of augmenting a sparse winter diet. Since the birds were stalked and shot on the ground there was little incentive to improve the weapons employed and the only major change which took place was to replace the matchlock with the very expensive wheelock and then by guns employing flint and steel which were not as expensive either to make or to keep in repair.

The early flint gun, the snaphaunce, was in general large and rather clumsy and in a portrait of Sir Thomas Southwell c. 1630, he is shown in sporting attire holding a snaphaunce fowling piece similar in size to a military musket.

It is to the French that credit must go for the refinement of the true flintlock lock which resulted in a smaller and neater lock with considerably faster lock time.

This was important, since the next development was the introduction of shooting flying instead of shooting at birds on the ground. It is not easy to determine exactly when the hunter began to shoot at flying targets since it was far easier to stalk or wait in a hide for sitting birds!

I recall many years ago being taken shooting on the Isle of Skye in Scotland. My fellow gun fired at a small covey of partridge on the ground and when he saw the look on my face, I was told, in no uncertain terms, that here shooting was to put meat on the table and if I was at all concerned he would shoot them on the ground and I could shoot at those which were flying!

The first illustration of the sport of shooting flying seems to be that of Venetian sportsmen shooting from boats in a lagoon(1609)and then subsequently the subject is discussed in books published in Italy and Spain.

The first mention of the new sport in England is given in Richard Blome's book, "The Gentleman's Recreation" published in 1686 although it is interesting to note that in an earlier work (1644) by Nicholas Cox with the same title, there is no mention of shooting birds on the wing.

Opinion, in the 17th century, was that the French were far better than the English at shooting flying and the return of the exiled Royalists following the restoration of Charles II in 1660, no doubt did much for the sport in England, since the returning exiles brought with them French flint lock guns and they had become well practised in the art during their exile.

Throughout the 18th century the length of the barrels of sporting guns had been steadily reduced from 48" to less than 40". The benefit of having a gun which could provide more than one shot was also appreciated and a number of complicated repeating flint lock guns were made in England, but they were far too expensive and prone to breakdown, to be more than an object of interest and curiosity.

The easiest way to provide more than one shot was to provide the gun with more than one barrel. The French produced guns with four barrels but the most popular were guns with two barrels, either placed side-by-side or one above the other.

The over and under style was made as a "turnabout" gun with two barrels but one lock. Each barrel was provided with a flash pan and combined steel and pan cover and after the discharge of the top barrel, the whole barrel assembly was rotated through 180 degrees to permit the lower barrel to be brought into position ready to be fired. Guns of this type were made in Geneva and in France and by 1660, the well known London gunmaker, Harman Barne had produced a gun of this type with two 32 in. barrels of 32 bore which must have been not only an extremely delightful gun to own but also an effective weapon.

A fairly short lived attempt at a multi shot sporting weapon was made during the 17th century by employing the technique of superimposed loads. An example of this type of fowling piece has survived. It is of 17 bore with barrels 34" long. The maker was T. Wallis of London and the date is about 1685. The left hand lock fires the first or top charge and the right hand lock the lower, second charge. The right hand lock is fitted with a safety device to prevent the lock being fired first and the gun has a single trigger!

Guns such as these were the prerogative of the very wealthy and in Britain it took some years before even the simple double gun was accepted. Even as late as 1781, a book was published by Dr. John Aikins, "Description of Double Firearms" to be followed by the comment of R. B. Thornhill in the 1804 "Shooting Directory", that the double gun was introduced from France, as a great many other foolish things have been".

The complaints against the double gun were that "the extra weight of the second barrel, which was not often used, had to be carried and that it was often fired accidentally and when loading was done in a hurry two charges were sometimes put into one barrel."

In spite of what the pundits of the period were writing, the great British gunmakers of the day were making double flintlock shotguns in the closing decades of the 18th century which were to set the pattern upon which future development was to be based.

John Manton made a 22 bore double flintlock shotgun about 1785 which is typical of the early flint period. The front trigger is much shorter than the rear and both are protected by a large bowed guard. As yet the gun is fairly broad in the beam, but this was to be dealt with by the patent breeching which allowed the lock plates to come closer to each other and so reduce the width of the gun at this point.

By the turn of the century, the locks had been greatly improved, both in certainty of giving fire and in speed of ignition. Rain proof pans were fitted to the locks, the inside of the pan could be gold plated as a defence against corrosion and roller bearings were fitted to reduce friction.

The bore sizes tended to increase to 16 bore and the barrel length continued to be reduced to around 32". Efforts continued to be made to reduce the lock time and locks by the brothers John and Joseph Manton were marvels of ingenuity and mechanical skill. In tests carried out in 1889, R. W. S. Griffiths showed that the average time for the charge to reach the muzzle after the fall of the cock was, for the flintlock, 0.094 seconds and for a hammer breechloader, 0.005 seconds.

To the man used to a modern shotgun firing a late 18th century flint double gun is like experiencing a bad hangfire at each shot. The improvement in speed of iginition was not due to mechanical improvements but to chemistry!

It was not one of the great London gunmakers, nor indeed an ingenious French arquebusier, but a Scottish clergyman, the pastor of a remote Parish in the north of Scotland who first tamed the irascible fulminating compounds that were to banish the tyranny of flint and steel and usher in a new era, that of the percussion muzzle loader.

Legend has it, that it was due to the birds he missed when wildfowling in Aberdeenshire, because of the flash from the priming of his flintlock that made him wonder if there was not a better and easier way of igniting the charge of powder in his fowling piece.

By 1805 he had made a successful lock and he eventually set up shop in London's fashionable Piccadilly, where, with the aid of James Purdey, lately with Manton, he produced what the collector of to-day calls, "Scent Bottle" locks for both new guns and to convert existing flint guns to percussion.

Forsyth's patent of 11th April 1807 which describes "an advantageous method of dicharging firearms" was momentous, although at first the principle was not widely adopted. This was of course, due to the cost and difficulty of manufacture of the Forsyth "Roller Lock" which demanded considerable skill to make and care to maintain. This lock, nevertheless, led the way to a whole range of pellet, pill, tape and patch locks until, finally, the invention of the copper caplock showed the way forward. Indeed, that simple little copper cap, in some ways, is still with us, right in the centre of every shotgun cartridge we fire, even to-day!

By the mid 19th century the percussion double shotgun had been brought to the height of perfection and, indeed, many of the men who made these superb shotguns were of the opinion that they could not be bettered.

Other factors now contributed to the development of the British sporting shotgun and the type of sport which it served. The first was the appearance of "driven game" in the 1860's followed by the appearance of the perfected breechloader in the 1870's. The rise of a wealthy "middle class" through "industrialisation" and the steady increase in both wealth and the leisure time to enjoy it which resulted in an increase in the popularity of "Game Shooting" as an acceptable social activity. Many of the areas devoted to this new sport were remote but the rapid extension of an efficient railway system provided a rapid means of transport to those parts of the country which had been formerly inaccessible to all but the most dedicated of sportsmen.

The development of the breechloader from its birth as a French curiosity, from pin-fire to central-fire and from underlever hammer gun to the self-opening, double hammerless, single trigger ejector game gun can be traced in the pages which follow but one other factor had its effect, the competitive art of live pigeon shooting, followed by glass ball and later clay pigeon shooting. The results of matches were followed avidly and the names of not only the winning shots but also the names of their gunmakers were widely known and publicised.

The British side-by-side double shotgun of to-day was the result of the habits and social behaviour formed by nearly two centuries of a highly specialised form of sporting shooting for not only did the British export the game gun they also exported the often curious but strangely very practical etiquette of the shooting field.

When this, for whatever reason is lost, the world will be a sadder place and the British sporting game gun can then be relegated to a sporting museum!

SIDELOCKS

One of the first books on guns which I bought was *Shotguns, Their History and Development*. The author was H. B. C. Pollard and the date of publication 1923. This book is quite fascinating, since it reflects the attitude of a period not so long ago measured in years but separated from us today in so many ways that it could have been written on another planet!

However, I intend to use this book to illustrate something else. In the chapter which deals with the selection of a gun it is interesting to see the illustrations which are used. The first is of a Boss double trigger 12-bore sidelock. The second illustration is of a Churchill "best" quality 12-bore sidelock, the third Holland's sidelock 12-bore with detatchable locks and the fourth a Purdey sidelock 12-bore.

Pollard says "The 'best' gun is usually made with sidelocks instead of the box lock action of the Anson and Deeley type. Side locks make the arm more expensive and in no way add to its efficiency, but they make it rather more delicate in balance, graceful in appearance, slenderer and more tapered at the action than can be achieved with the Anson and Deeley type".

Greener, writing 13 years before, a staunch advocate of the Anson and Deeley type of lock, stated that the A & D lock gave quicker ignition and almost the sole advantage of sidelocks was that they could be easily removed. Even this advantage was not allowed, because Greener stated that ease of removal was "not a matter of importance since a well-made box-lock will work well for years without any attention".

In 1906 Henry Sharp had pointed out, that by using the Westley Richards box lock, ease of dismantling could be offered with their hand-detachable lock. Sharp condemned the sidelock on the grounds of over-complication, and in his book Modern Sporting Gunnery all the illustrations of "best" guns are of Anson & Deeley type actions.

Coming closer to our own times, Gerald Burrard, writing in 1931, comes out in favour of the sidelock because on his system of assessment the sidelock is the better "in five out of six points". Some of the aspects he considered important included safety, efficiency, strength, trigger pull, ease in cocking and quickness. Burrard, like Pollard before him, mentions the question of beauty. He goes on to say that this aspect should not be thought unimportant, and that the lines of the box-lock cannot compare with those of a really well designed sidelock.

In considering the appearance of the sidelock we must bear in mind that there are three basic types; first, the bar-action with the mainspring in front

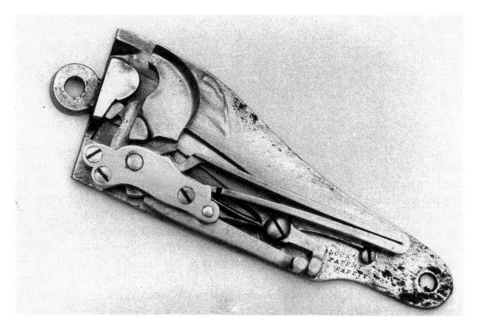

Back action sidelock

of the tumbler and lying along the bar of the action; second, the back-action, in which the mainspring is behind the tumbler. In back-action sidelocks we have two types, the first looking exactly like a normal bar-action lock except that the pins are in a different place on the lockplates. The earlier type of back-action sidelock cannot be mistaken, since the lockplates are of a completely different shape. The third type of "sidelock" is that in which a box-lock action has had dummy sideplates fitted in imitation of a sidelock. Although there have been occasions when someone has purchased a box-lock with these sideplates and thought he had a true sidelock, no reputable firm would practise such deception. Such dummy actions can be detected by the fact that the triggers are much further forward than would be the case with a sidelock and the sideplates lack the necessary pins.

Let's come up to date and see what is said in 1970 about the merits of sidelocks. We can take the opinion of the late Gough Thomas in his book Shotguns and Cartridges. Times have changed since Burrard wrote his comments but "G.T." agrees in the main, "the sidelock is a more elegant weapon than the box-lock, usually better balanced and with superior trigger pulls. Everlasting in the best grades if well treated". One could, of course, write just as convincingly about box-locks but, like it or not, the sidelock has that certain indefinable something about it. The appraisal of the relative merits of sidelock and box-lock can provoke heated arguements, but Gough Thomas, I think, is as impartial a judge as any; he puts the benefits of both systems forward and leaves you to decide.

6

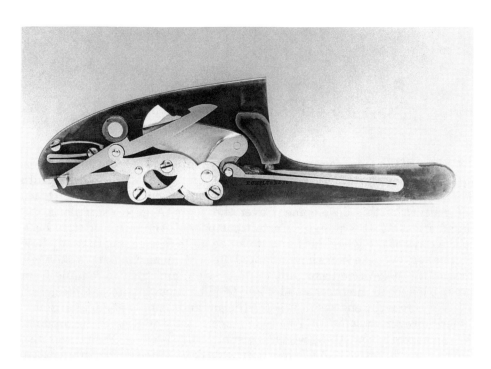

Bar action sidelock

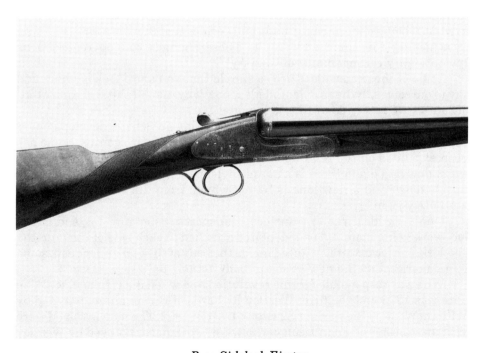

Boss Sidelock Ejector

BOXLOCKS

Many of the manufactured items we encounter in everyday life are evolutionary, they started out as one thing and then, they gradually develop into something quite different. Upon close examination you can quite often trace the pattern of this development over the years. A good example is the hammerless sidelock shotgun. Certain components can be traced right back to the days of the wheel-lock and it can be quite fascinating to study how gunmakers over the years have adapted the original mechanism to changes, first of all in ignition-from flint to percussion, and then in loading-from muzzle loader to the breechloader and from hammer gun to hammerless.

Very often the end result is both efficient and visually attractive. Sometimes however, at some intermediate stage in the evolution of the product, we can arrive at something which is visually unattractive. Often it was also functionaly defective and left much to be desired. Some of the hammerless Victorian shotguns with unsightly lumps and bumps fall into this category.

This of course is not the only way in which things we use have been created. Every now and again, someone comes along who takes a close look at what is being done or being made and decides that there is a far better way of achieving the same end result. These changes can be regarded as revolutionary rather than evolutionary!

Some of these new ideas are so simple that you and I look at them and say to ourselves, "What a splendid idea, now why didn't I think of that!" But, of course, we rarely do until it is too late!

Guns of all types and in particular, sporting guns have developed over the years as a result of a massive expenditure of inventive genius. Some has been expended on the refining of existing ideas as we have seen, however, every now and again there is a quantum leap forward, old ideas are turned upside down and a new idea is borne, which, from the very beginning, is absolutely right.

One such idea was to transform the sporting shotgun. Instead of the lockwork being mounted on sideplates attached to each side of the gun, the sidelock, the locks were mounted inside the body of the gun and indeed, some gunmakers called the new action a "body action gun".

Who was responsible for this revolution and when did it take place? The date was 1875 and the firm, Westley Richards of Birmingham, founded by William Westley Richards at 82 High Street in 1812. The men involved were William Anson and John Deeley who were "workmen employed by Westley Richards Ltd of Birmingham". At least that is what we discover if we read

The first Anson & Deeley box lock

Burrard's *Modern Shotgun*.

This is not strictly true. Sadly, we know little of William Anson, other than he was Foreman of the Westley Richards Gun-Action Department and that two years after the patent was granted he was in business on his own account at 77 Slaney Street. The firm changing its style to Anson & Co. in 1891. The firm then moved to Steelhouse Lane in 1896 where they continued to trade well into the 20th century, changing their name once again to E. G. Anson and remaining in business until the late 1930's.

The other man whose name has gone into the firearms history books was John Deeley. Born in 1825, he joined Westley Richards in 1860. By 1871 John Deeley had become the commercial manager and for the next thirty years or so the flow of patents in his name and jointly with others, covered many aspects of gun and rifle design and has left us with a rich legacy of invention.

In the eyes of many, the most important of the patents was that of 1875 taken out jointly with W. Anson, No. 1756. This was for what we to-day call the A&D action or boxlock. It was not the first hammerless shotgun, nor, indeed, was it the first self cocking shotgun, but it can lay claim to being the first truly successful hammerless shotgun, cocked by the fall of the barrels. Interestingly, the patent also allows for the gun to be cocked by an under-lever. I have never seen this type of A&D action though no doubt it was made. The patent does not say cocking is effected by the fall of the barrels as we tend

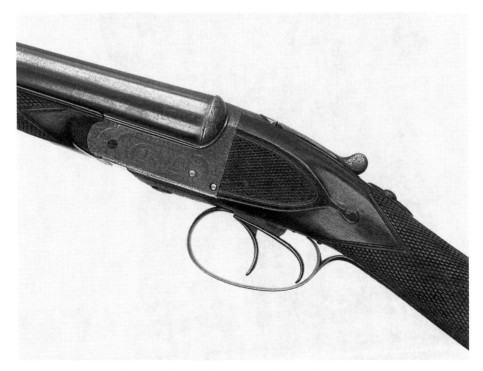

Westley Richards Anson & Deeley Number 1

to do to-day, the patentees tell us that cocking "is effected by the rising of the breech ends of the barrels for charging. " The patent also covered the locking bolt for the barrels, earlier versions of which had been patented by Westley Richards in 1862 and 1864.

The total enclosure of the mechanism, the smooth and clean lines of the action allied to the ease of barrel cocking and the convenience of top lever opening ensured the success of the Anson & Deeley action. Improvements, some valid the others spurious followed and we can now follow some of these developments and also chart the progress of the A&D action which was to become known where ever shotguns and rifles were used.

Shortly after its introduction by Westley Richards the manufacture of this type of gun was licensed to other gunmakers and there can be little doubt that the A&D action has been the most widely manufactured type of side-by-side sporting shotgun ever!

In sharp contrast to the information we have on John Deeley, largely because he remained with Westley Richards until his retirement, by which time he had risen to become one of the senior officials of the company, we know very little about Anson.

William Anson appears to have left Westley Richards and set up on his own about 1877. His last patent, one of many improvements he made to the A&D action, was taken out in 1888 but when he died is still unknown. His son, Edwin George Anson also became a gunmaker, but he is better known perhaps for his interest in air guns. E. G. Anson's first patent is dated 1886 and refers to the ejecting mechanism of "drop down" guns. Interestingly, the

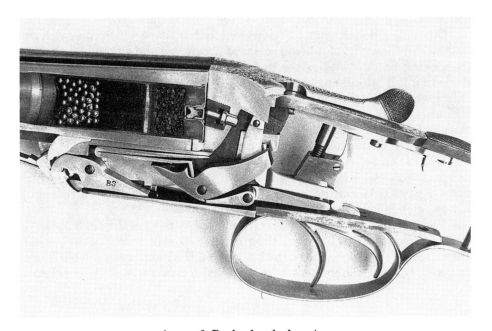

Anson & Deeley box lock action

patent drawing shows a side lock not a boxlock!

A second patent, taken out in 1887, covers a somewhat complicated cocking mechanism for A&D action guns. Further patents are taken out by E. G. Anson in 1893. Strangely, his next patent was for an interesting air pistol which was later to be made by Westley Richards as "The Highest Possible" air pistol. This was in 1907 and he uses one initial, the patent being in the name of E. Anson. In 1918 there is a flurry of invention and once again the second initial appears since he now describes himself as E. G. Anson on four patents in his name in that year, all concerned with modifications to the A&D action. The last patent I have been able to trace is dated 1921 and this deals with modifications to his air pistol, originaly patented in 1907.

E. G. Anson died, aged 73 in 1936, bringing to an end a remarkable family history of firearms invention. By this time the last firm bearing the Anson name had ceased to trade. Exactly what effect if any, the later patents had on the practical development of the A&D action is hard to discover.

Two patents are of interest. The first, obtained in 1882, is No. 4089 in William Anson's name and it deals with a matter of some importance, the provision of an intercepting sear.

Even to-day, there is a touching faith in the safety device fitted to most shotguns. What is often not appreciated is that the slide safety on many guns merely bolts the triggers, the safety does not prevent the gun from being discharged. The sear and bent can be jarred out of engagement by a blow, such as the gun being dropped or heavily "grounded". The likelihood of this happening can be increased by wood binding or swelling, rust, dirt, congealed oil and faulty construction or faulty adjustment by the local gun bodger who reduced the trigger pressures to an unsafe level!

On many sidelock guns an additional limb is fitted which can catch the hammer in the event of it being released accidently and so prevent the gun from being fired. Most boxlock guns do not have this intercepting safety device but it is interesting to see that A & D patent drawings show a blocking safety which bolts the hammers, not the triggers. For some reason, Westley Richards do not appear to have made their version of the A&D action with these safety bolts, which lie one on each side of the action body, at least they are not fitted to the very first A&D actioned gun that they made.

What is quite fascinating is that Greener did fit these or similar bolts to the A&D gun which bears the 40 Pall Mall address. In fact this gun, which I saw at the 1982 Game Fair, is earlier than the address would indicate since it was remodelled by the makers at some time after 1933.

The interesting feature of the original safety bolts of the 1875 patent is that they were automatic. When the gun was cocked by the fall of the barrels, the weight of the lever rotated the bolt so that the hammers were blocked at full cock. In fact the hammers were beyond full cock, the sears being clear of

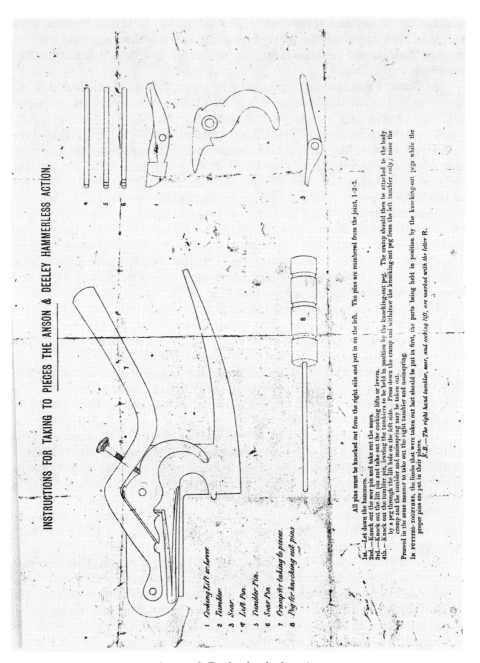

INSTRUCTIONS FOR TAKING TO PIECES THE ANSON & DEELEY HAMMERLESS ACTION.

1 Cocking Lift or Lever
2 Tumbler
3 Sear
4 Lift Pin.
5 Tumbler Pin.
6 Sear Pin
7 Cramp for taking to pieces.
8 Peg for knocking out pins

All pins must be knocked out from the right side and put in on the left. The pins are numbered from the joint, 1-2-3.

1st.—Let down the hammers.

2nd.—Knock out the sear pin and take out the sears.

3rd.—Knock out the lift pin and take out the cocking lifts or levers.

4th.—Knock out the tumbler pin, leaving the tumblers to be held in position by the knocking-out peg. The cramp should then be attached to the body by a peg through the lift hole on the left side. Press down the cramp and withdraw the knocking-out peg from the left tumbler only; raise the cramp and the tumbler and mainspring may be taken out.

Proceed in the same manner to take out the right tumbler and mainspring.

IN PUTTING TOGETHER, the limbs that were taken out last should be put in first, the parts being held in position by the knocking-out pegs while the proper pins are put in their places.

N.B.—The right hand tumbler, sear, and cocking lift, are marked with the letter R.

Anson & Deeley boxlock action

13

the bents. When the levers were pushed upwards the hammers were released and they moved slightly forward, the sears then engaged and the nose of the hammer kept the safety bolts from rotating back into the "SAFE" position.

At Game Fairs, so many people bring so much that is of interest to me that ideally I would like three weeks, rather than three days to see and enjoy all that I photograph and record. Mr. Lowrie, who brought the very interesting Greener gun had left me his address and a phone call to him produced the answers I sought. Mr. Lowrie had the gun before him as he spoke to me on the telephone and it seems very likely that the original A&D patent was slightly modified by Greener. The patent tells us that the safety bolts move to the "SAFE" position by gravity. According to Mr. Lowrie, on his Greener, the bolts are spring loaded and so do not rely on gravity. This Greener gun is, so far, the only A&D action gun I have seen with the original type of safety bolt blocking the hammers. If you know of any similar safety devices to this on Westley Richards or any other gun I would like to know about them. William Anson patented conventional trigger safety devices in 1876 and then his intercepting sear was patented in 1882.

Most people, when you mention A&D action guns will tell you that they all look alike. We have seen that the mechanism inside the gun can be different and now we can look at some of the A&D guns which differ externally.

So far we have looked at the insides of boxlock shotguns and have seen that they are not all alike. Some, such as the Greener patent actions are quite different mechanically and this difference can be seen in the distinctive outline of these Greener guns.

However, the Greener's will have to wait until later! Even the run of the mill boxlock can be altered by the maker so that the gun he sells is different from other A&D boxlocks. As I have mentioned previously, if you say "Boxlock" to many a shooting man the comment you will get back is "They're all very well, but they all look the same to me!"

To disprove this I have picked out a few boxlocks by several makers and hope to show that this type of gun has variations, some of which are both interesting and attractive.

Let us have a look at the Boswell boxlock first of all. This gun has conventional under bolts of the Purdey pattern and a conventional top lever instead of the Westley Richards type. The position of the pins through the body of the gun are quite conventional but the transition from the square of the action to the rounded cross section of the hand of the stock is achieved by a side panel with sunk chequering and a neat drop point. The body of the action is shaped so that it mates with the top of the panel on the stock and, for added decoration, the gun has very attractive carved leaf fences. A conventional but very attractive gun.

In addition to dealing with the square cross section of the rear of the action there is also the problem of the square cross section of the bar of the action having to mate with the rounded corners of the fore-end. One way the gunmaker dealt with this problem was to provide shoulders on the bar of the action which allowed the front of the body to have rounded bottom corners. Interest on the Martin boxlock is concentrated on the action body with its shoulders and neat engraving, the panels on the stock lack both sunk chequering and drop points and I, personally, don't think that they are needed.

Many and varied were the ways in which the A&D action gun could be made in a manner just that little bit different and one of the most useful dodges was to alter the shape of the back of the action from the simple straight line which we have so far seen to what the Birmingham trade called a "Fancy back". One simple way was to make the back into a slight curve as shown on the Daniel Fraser box lock. This gun has shoulders, panels, drop points and a fancy back and to my eyes the whole treatment is very effective.

So, when your shooting friend with the posh sidelock looks at your boxlock he need not look quite so superior! The boxlock is a fascinating gun with a long and interesting history and more than enough variations in design, style, and decoration to keep everyone happy, at least those who take the trouble to look a little more closely at the skills and craftsmanship that went into making the boxlock the effective gun that it is!

There is one other important development in the Anson & Deeley action

Westley Richard's Hand Detachable Lock

which has not been mentioned, except in passing. This came over twenty years after the original patent had been taken out and was No. 17,731 of 1897 in the names of Deeley, J., and Taylor, L. B.

The patent describes how guns built to the A&D pattern may be constructed so that the whole lock mechanism can be readily removed for cleaning and repair. Each lock is mounted on a plate and the assembly is then inserted into the bottom of the gun and is secured by a side pin or screw. The bottom of the gun is then covered by a sliding plate.

A later improvement was patented by Deeley and Taylor in 1907 which was intended to improve the pull off and also to aid cocking the mechanism when it was detached from the gun.

Indeed, the locks, when detached, are a delight to behold and, if I were fortunate enough to own a Westley Richards gun of this type, I think I would keep these jewelled masterpieces separate from the gun and have them mounted in a suitable display case so that I could enjoy looking at them when not in use!

The detachable lock has a number of benefits. There is the utter simplicity of the lock, four moving parts, and the ease of removal and replacement. Spare locks can be provided and carried in the unlikely event of failure. Locks can also be provided with a different weight of pull if required and, of course, with the locks removed the gun is completely safe, for it cannot be fired. We are of course, fortunate, that Westley Richards are very much still in business and that they also still build guns and double rifles with their detachable locks, although of course, they also build guns and rifles with sidelocks and of course, bolt action rifles.

To-day, as built by Westley Richards, the Anson & Deeley action still has the elegant simplicity which has endeared it to countless thousands of users since its introduction over a century ago.

I don't have a Westley Richards with detachable locks, but I do have a Westley Richards 20 bore shotgun which was made in 1884. Originally built as a double rifle it was converted afterwards to a 20 bore shotgun. The lines are classic Westley Richards and those with a keen eye will notice something unusual, there are no Purdey bolts under the barrels. The barrels are bolted solely by the doll's head extension and the single bolt in the Westley Richards patent top lever.

This gun was bought by me for £5 many years ago, had £50 spent on sleeving and an overhaul and was used to teach my son to shoot. A close look just behind the fences will reveal a tell-tale pin for the intercepting safety. The gun has seen some use and in spite of the single bolt it locks up as tight as a bank vault. However this was not good enough for Anson & Deeley, for in 1883 they obtained Patent No. 1833 for a means of interconnecting the top Westley Richards doll's head bolt and lever to a Purdey type flat bolt which engaged in bites in the barrel lumps. By this means the Westley Richards A&D action gun had, and, of course, still has, the best of both worlds!

THE LONDON TRADE

The development of the firearm as an effective military weapon in Britain was delayed by the continued importance and effectiveness of the English archer. An inventory of the Tower of London taken in 1532 included a mere thirty iron "handgonnes" compared with several thousand longbows.

The effectiveness of the archer and longbow, in the field, was countered by the length of time required for training. It was cheaper, quicker and easier to train a conscripted soldier to use a firearm and this was an important factor in the more widespread adoption of this weapon.

In addition, there was considerable opposition to the introduction of firearms, many of the old nobility had been brought up "in the age of chivalry" and they had a hatred of "the vile saltpetre".

At first, increased military use was not backed up by an increase in the manufacturing capability of the country and, in times of dire need, the Crown had to rely on importing weapons; canon from Flanders and handguns from Spain and Italy. To foster domestic manufacture foreign craftsmen were encouraged to work in London and many did so.

The early "gunmaker" was in fact an armourer engaged in the making, repair and the buying and selling of English and imported firearms. Henry VIII (1509-1547) did much to encourage the gunmaking industry, primarily to ensure that military weapons could be made at home but his interest did much to boost interest in the new industry and it also encouraged the manufacture of fine quality firearms for domestic use.

The reign of Elizabeth I (1558-1602) saw a relocation of the stores of armament and in 1562 the buildings on the north east side of the Tower of London, the old Monastery of the Minories was taken over and by the end of the century, gunmakers, both native and foreign congregated in the areas of the Minories and Tower Hill.

Here was to be found the barrel smiths, lock smiths, the gun stockers, gun engravers, indeed whole families of gunmakers were growing up in the area making this an important centre of gunmaking in London.

An attempt to organise the trade was made in a petition of 1581; this was followed, in 1589 be a Draft Proclamation for the control of the Gunmaking trade in London.

One of the main obstacles to the adoption of the proposals was that many of the gunmakers were already members of existing Trade Guilds or City Companies, such as the Blacksmiths and the Armourers.

These long established organisations quite understandably resisted any break away movements which might diminish their power and authority. They fought for their privilege in much the same manner as present day Trade Unions, and in the 17th century, battles were fought between the various factions until, in 1638, the Gunmakers Charter was granted under the Great Seal.

However, it was not until the closing years of the 17th century that the Gunmakers Company became fully independent. Their authority was enforced by ensuring that every gun bore the stamp or mark of the maker and the view and proof mark of the company. The rules of the Company were effectively upheld by the threat of withdrawing the gunmakers proof which, in effect, took away the livelihood of the errant gunmaker.

By the mid 18th century gunmaking, in and around London was divided into some twenty one different branches including barrel forging, breech forging, barrel filers, barrel polishers, barrel loop makers, lock forgers, lock filers, lock polishers, lock hardeners, trigger and nail forgers, trigger and nail filers, stock makers, furniture forger, furniture filers, tip and pipe makers, side piece and thumb piece makers, engravers, browners, stick makers, flint makers etc.

The manner in which the trade was organised provided great flexibility not only with regard to manufacturing capability but also in the quality range available.

Larger gunmakers could afford to train, keep and employ a number of craftsmen on their own premises, the smaller firms might employ a few people directly, but would rely for the majority of the work on outworkers, who were independent craftsmen.

Acknowledged to be the master craftsman of his day, Joseph Manton, born 1766, served his apprenticeship with his brother John before setting up on his own at 25 Davies Street, London in 1793. Apart from the guns made for private people, Manton was Gunmaker to the East India Company, and Gunmaker-in-Ordinary to George IV.

In 1844, Colonel Hawker, an acknowledged authority of the period, described Manton (1844) "as the greatest artist in firearms that ever the world produced".

Manton employed craftsmen directly, such as lockmakers, barrel filers, polishers, barrel borers and stockers. One of his stockers was James Purdey, who started on his own in 1814 and founded a firm still pre-eminent in gunmaking to this day.

Not employed directly by Joe Manton were silversmiths, lockmakers, barrel forgers and barrel makers (Charles Lancaster made gun barrels for Manton before he set up as a gunmaker) engravers and polishers were also employed as well as other gunmakers, who often were "gunmakers' gunmakers", they rarely sold guns under their own name, but made for other gunmakers.

It was not the practice to refuse an order because the workshop was full of work in progress, when the order could be executed by putting some of the work out "to the trade".

Regardless of who did the work, the man whose name was on the barrel and lockplate of the gun staked his reputation on the high quality of the work done, regardless of whether it had been carried out, "in or out of House".

Not only does this system provide a valuable degree of flexibility well able to meet times of "feast and famine" but also it fosters the training of skilled craftsmen and ensures that these skills are fostered and developed.

As the name LONDON on the barrels of sporting guns increasingly became a guarantee of quality others set up premises in London so that they could benefit from using the name, whilst others, lacking scruples and, indeed, any connection with the London trade engraved not only LONDON of their barrels but also the names of both legitimate and spurious London "makers".

The "modern" era of gunmaking in London can be said to have had its origins with the establishment of the manufacture of military weapons at Enfield about 1804. This was in some measure due to the difficulty of obtaining weapons from Liege and Hamburg during the Napoleonic Wars, since, of course, these sources of supply were cut off!

Further changes took place in 1849, and in 1853, the manufacture of the 1853 Pattern Musket by mass production means, using American technology was established.

The use of machinery on a wide scale such as adopted by Colt in his

James Purdey & Sons

London factory (established in 1852) was not undertaken by any of the manufacturers of sporting guns, machine tools were used more as "powered files and chisels", the skills required for fine finishing still residing in the hands of the craftsman rather than the skills being inbuilt into the jigs and fixtures employed by the "American System" of gun manufacture.

The fitting of the various components of the sporting gun, the barrels to the action and the making of the gun stock remained highly skilled jobs for specialist craftsman and has remained so to this day.

The effects of two world wars and the social changes which ensued all contributed to the economic pressures on the London Gun Trade which resulted in a reduction in the number of independent makers, either by amalgamation thus accounting for the number of "multi-barrelled names" or simply by the firm ceasing to trade.

More recently there has been a revival in the demand for the traditional London sporting shotgun and rifle in spite of the tremendous apparent increase in cost. The price now paid for a "Best" London gun appears enormous if the gun is merely regarded as a tool. However, if looked upon more properly as a piece of sculpture in wood and metal, each gun unique, the cost is not just the cost of the raw materials, expensive though these are and one might as well equate the cost of a painting by say, Picasso, with the cost of wood, canvas and paint to the price realised in the sale room!

In the pages which follow, the history of some of the great names of the London trade will be found. Among them are those whose products still survive (for a "Best" London gun, properly cared for has an almost unlimited life) although the maker's name has long since vanished from the London trades directory. Then, fortunately, there are those firms who are still making guns by traditional methods, many a century or more after they were founded.

The demand for these guns, both old and new, is a clear indication of the enduring qualities of the London gun, qualities which are appreciated and acknowledged by the discerning sportsman of to-day.

HOLLAND & HOLLAND

In 1835 Harris J Holland set up in business at 9 King Street, Holborn. The firm he founded soon established a world-wide reputation not only for fine sporting shotguns but also double and single rifles used in pursuit of big and dangerous game.

Harris Holland was not a gunmaker but he was a well-known sportsman and highly regarded as a fine shot. He excelled in what was then the highly competitive sport of live pigeon shooting and was equally well-known on the moors of northern England.

In 1860 Henry William Holland was bound apprentice gunmaker to his uncle, Harris John Holland, for seven years. The year also saw the first change of address, from King Street to New Bond Street in fashionable Mayfair.

In 1867 Henry William, having completed his apprenticeship, was taken into the firm as a partner and his uncle retired at the age of 70 in 1875. The founder lived on to the ripe old age of 90.

The firm became Holland & Holland in 1876 and in 1883 they took part in the London rifle trials. Concentration was on rifle making and the firm entered every class open to them. Their endeavours were well rewarded since they took all the prizes from rook rifle to 4-bore. Their success was well merited since, of course, they had more to lose in the way of reputation than some of the less well-known provincial entrants.

The rifles had been prepared by Henry Holland, assisted by Mr Froome who was in charge of rifle manufacture at the H & H factory. Mr Froome also shot all the rifles and when, on the death of Harris Holland in 1895, control of the company passed to Henry Holland, Mr W Froome was made a director.

A new factory was opened at Harrow Road in 1896 and in 1899 the firm became Holland & Holland Limited.

A few years before, in 1885, H & H registered the name 'Royal', which was used to describe their best-quality double rifles and shotguns, and in 1886 the firm publicly tested a gun patented by Colonel George Vincent Fosbery, VC. This was designed to fire both shot and a single projectile (either ball and bullet) without detriment to the pattern or penetration of the shot or the

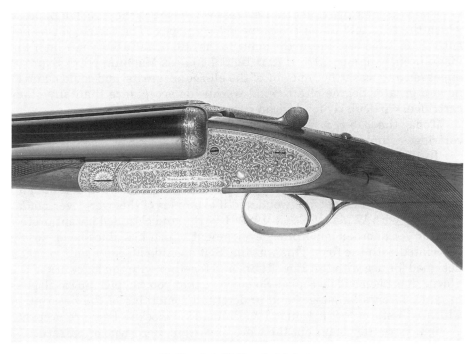

Holland & Holland sidelock

accuracy of the projectile. The gun, aptly named the 'Paradox', was made by H & H in 12-bore but also 8, 10, 16 and 20-bore.

As indicated in the patent, the Fosbery invention consisted of forming spiral grooves in the choke of the barrel. The number, form and shape of the grooves was specified and the system rapidly gained acceptance, making the so-called 'Cape' rifle, which had one rifled and one smoothbore barrel obsolete. The name Paradox was registered and, although attempts were made by other gunmakers to produce similar results none enjoyed the same degree of success.

Unlike many of its contemporaries, the firm was innovative, and the list of its patents impressive. The first I have been able to trace is in the names of Henry W. Holland and Thomas Perkes and details improvements on safety devices described in an earlier patent by Perkes of 1878. The 1879 patent was followed by another of 1882 in H W Holland's name which covered the cocking of hammerless guns.

Henry Holland then sought protection, along with James Robertson (later of Boss & Co), for a system which cocked one hammer when the gun was opened and the other on closing the gun. Patents for ejectors, try guns and single triggers followed and in 1904 came a patent which probably did more than any other to bring the name of Holland & Holland to the attention of sportsmen. This was the belted rifle cartridge case. The patent was granted to Henry Holland for a cartridge case having a ridge or belt at the rear.

The first cartridge to use the new case was based on the .400/375 Express which the firm sold under the name .375 'Velopex'. The cartridge was not entirely satisfactory, due, in the main, to the bullet, and a few years later the magnificently named '.375 H & H Belted rimless Magnum Nitro Express' appeared and was to become one of the all-round 'greats' and could claim to have a greater degree of all-round worldwide acceptance than any other cartridge, particularly for African game.

Today the .375 H & H Magnum still holds its own and over 25 different cartridges employ the belted rimless case.

In 1908 H W Holland, together with T Woodward, patented the 'Detachable Lock' which was to be a feature of many of the sidelock guns which the company were to make. Also in 1908 Holland and Woodward patented an automatic gun. I have often wondered if examples of this were ever made.

Along with W Mansfield, in 1922 H W Holland obtained patent protection for yet another important development which has since been closely associated with the firm. This was the 'Self-opening Mechanism', specially designed for use with the 'Royal' gun, and together with the lockwork of the 'Royal', has been widely copied. So much so that you can pick up catalogues in many foreign languages and understand something of the description which will state: "With Holland & Holland Sidelocks". Few are accurate though, since they leave out the more important word type or pattern!

Henry W Holland retired in 1930 and Colonel J.E.D. Holland became

Chairman of the company. His name was to be associated with William Mansfield, then factory manager, on a patent which was obtained for cartridges in 1939. The patent referred to the use of a metal liner, which, on the production 'Royal' cartridges, was of zinc. The case was paper, though the patent also described the use of a plastic case. The cartridges were made for the company by ICI Metals Division at Witton, but due to the outbreak of war manufacture ceased and was never re-started.

In the years following the war Holland & Holland were actively engaged in maintaining the high level of craftsmanship which had been traditionally the mark of the London gun trade. One of the first guns made for exhibition was the 'Chatsworth', so-called because it was first exhibited at the 1966 Game Fair at Chatsworth. The 1968 'Set of Five' in 12, 16, 20 and 28-bore and .410, all with gold inlay work, and contained in a rosewood cabinet, set the pattern for the future.

Another 'Set of Five' was finished in 1968 and a pair of guns engraved and inlaid in Japanese style were followed by a gold-inlaid 'exhibition-grade' gun completed in 1971. In 1975 a 'Royal' Model .600 Nitro Express double rifle, No 35478, was completed as "The Last .600". This rifle took over five years to make, starting with David Winks in 1970 in Holland's barrel shop and ending with the magnificent engraving of Ken Hunt. Many sportsmen regard the gun as the finest Holland & Holland double rifle ever made.

After 100 years the firm moved from New Bond Street to 13 Bruton Street and then to their present address at 33 Bruton Street.

CHARLES BOSWELL

Many letters have passed through the slot in my front door, a lot of mail has been sent to far distant places, hundreds of miles have rolled beneath my car and a lot of film has passed through my camera, all I might add, to do with Charles Boswell and the guns made by this important firm. It all started with an article in the April 24, 1975 issue of the Shooting Times when I described a 16-bore Boswell under-lever hammer gun I had owned and enjoyed for many years.

This produced one or two letters and then things took off with the receipt of a photocopy of a Charles Boswell catalogue from Roy S Smith of Ontario, Canada.

Adverts taken from the Shooting Times of 1884, a gun case label and a fine Boswell A & D action gun with sunk side panels illustrated the next article on the firm which was published on December 10, 1981.

I then started "trawling" in earnest, flinging the net over the side and using my "letters" column to keep things going. As a result of this I was able to meet Professor Charles Boswell. I had some facts to go on; the first gunmaking Charles Boswell had served his time with Mr Gooch of Hertford, Charles Boswell being a native of that county and born in 1850. From

Charles Boswell boxlock

Professor Boswell I had the opportunity to photograph the indentures of Charles and start the ball rolling to get some information about Gooch. In this latter endeavour I had stalwart assistance from Mr Howard Day who went to enormous trouble on my behalf. From Mr Day's work we find that there are two firms by the name Gooch, one in St. Albans and one in Hertford. From the data collected it became apparent that the "Mr Gooch" who was to train Charles Boswell for some seven years was Thomas Gooch who is first listed in 1834. We can almost see young Charles starting work but can only wonder what life was like for him in Mr Gooch's gunshop in Hertford. We then learn that he worked for the Royal Small Arms Factory at Enfield where he stayed for two years. By this time he was married and he took a very bold step of setting up on his own without connections or capital. His premises were in Edmonton and his main work must have been repairs and we can assume that there must have been some worrying times before the business became established.

In addition to being a gunmaker Charles Boswell was also an expert shot in the sport of live pigeon shooting. A connection was speedily built up based on his prowess as a shot and skill as a gunmaker and in 1884 he moved to more prestigious premises at No. 126 The Strand. Boswell guns went out to Australia where they speedily gained an enviable reputation and, with Harry Ackland of Woollahra as representative, the business "down under" expanded. In the late 1880s Mr Sayer, founder and secretary of the Melbourne Gun Club, was active in promoting Boswell guns. In South Africa a similar story is told. Overheads were kept down by the founder of the firm working on the bench himself and quality was maintained by careful supervision of all aspects of gunmaking.

The firm survived the First War but it was bombed out in 1940 and the direct family involvement ceased in March of 1941. The firm continued under various managements until the 1960s with an address in Connaught Street. My request for photographs and details of Boswell guns brought a splendid response. Regrettably some of the photographs cannot be used for publication and one or two determined people are doing a short course in firearms photography to raise their standards. From Robert Braden of Houston I have a fine series of photographs of his top-lever Boswell gun which show the styling of the fences and percussioning has developed from the earlier underlever Boswell in my own collection.

The 1982 Game Fair brought more contributions. A splendid single-barrel Boswell, No. 17625, was brought by Stuart Hirst. I can't tell you much about this gun since it is not shown in the only catalogue I have but it does show how a skilled gunmaker treats the styling of a single, top-lever, sidelock hammerless gun.

The three articles on Charles Boswell show how, with the help of readers, a fuller picture of the life and work of a gunmaker can be built up. It is this interchange of information, extremely difficult to obtain by any other means, which has contributed in a very significant way to the total quantity of data now available on many gunmakers, most of whom were far less well known and who would have been undocumented otherwise.

CHARLES LANCASTER

Just behind Grocers (Wholesale) and in front of Gun Carriage Makers will be found the names of Gun Barrel Makers. Heading the list in "Pigot & Co's" Directory for 1821 is the name Wm. Fullerd, who is to be found at 56 Compton Street, Clerkenwell. Next comes Chas Lancaster, Gun Barrel Maker, Coach & Horse Yard, Great Titchfield Street, London.

Whether Coach and Horse Yard still exists I cannot say but certainly many best quality sporting guns still exist which proudly bear the name Charles Lancaster, and unusual amongst gunmakers there is a quite extraordinary book "The Art of Shooting" which bears the same name. I have a first edition, 1889 and a 13th edition of 1962 and any book with a span of over 70 years is remarkable if only for that reason.

That celebrated sportsman and author Colonel Hawker refers to Lancaster in his *Young Sportsmen* and tells us that it was on his advice that Lancaster "came forward to the west end of town to produce with his own name" and that if the rest of the gun was as good as his barrels "he need not fear as to standing one of the first on the list and making a fortune". Lancaster did set up in business as a gunmaker at 151 New Bond Street in the year 1826. Charles Lancaster died in 1847 and the business continued under his two sons Charles William and Alfred; both contributed to the art of gunmaking and their names appear on many patents.

One of the more unusual patents was that taken out by Charles William in 1850 which covered the use of oval boring for rifle barrels. The specification also described the system being used for Cannon and Lancaster devoted much of his time to the development of his "elliptical" cannon. It is a wonder that Gilbert and Sullivan made no mention of him!

In 1859 Alfred set up on his own account but after the death of both Charles William in 1878 and Alfred in 1890 the businesses were again combined under the direction of Henry Alfred Alexander Thorn, who, in effect, became "Mr Lancaster". Thorn was an even more prolific inventor than the Lancasters. Today he is remembered for his multi-barrel pistols and long guns (*Shooting Times & Country Magazine*, May 16, 1970) but he also made popular his best guns with back action locks which featured the distinctive lock plate. Later this gun, which was Lancaster's Grade "A" was to be fitted with their "detachable and attachable" side-locks "at no extra charge". "East Sussex", writing in 1914 in *The Shotgun and its Uses*, doubted whether it was wise to permit the amateur to "squint at the machinery", and one is left with the impression that no GENTLEMAN would inspect the lockwork of his gun!

The year 1897 saw the introduction of the "Pygmy" cartridge, a development which anticipated the 2in cartridge of 30 years later. The Pygmies were loaded in Joyce's or Eley's Pegamoid cases and were 2 1/8in long and 1 7/8in when loaded. The standard load was 28 grs of Walsrode powder and 1oz of shot. Made in 12-bore only, the Pygmies were not a success but they did pave the way for the later light game gun, the famous Lancaster "Twelve-Twenty". Lancaster as a separate entity ceased to exist in 1932 when the firm was bought by Stephen Grant and Joseph Lang.

Today, guns bearing the name Charles Lancaster are now no longer made; however, his name may well be revived in the future.

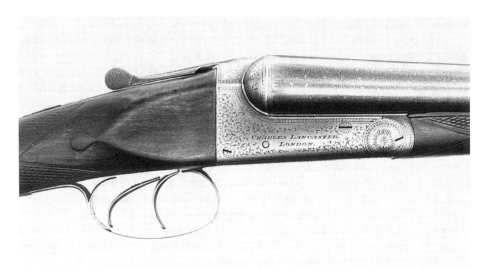

Charles Lancaster boxlock

JOSEPH LANG, LONDON

The readers will by now be well aware of my constant plea for data and information on gunmakers, no matter how trivial the information may at first appear. Let us take as an example one of the oldest and most respected names of the London trade, Joseph Lang.

We know, for example, from their published catalogues and also from their letter heading that the firm was established in 1821. From other sources we know that Joseph Lang served his time with Wilson of Vigo Lane. His reasons for leaving and setting up on his own are not known, but there is evidence to show that his business prospered since, five years later, we are able to read in the Morning Chronicle of September 13 that "Gentlemen sportsmen are respectfully invited to inspect J. Lang's extensive stock of New and Second-hand Detonating and Flint Lock Guns, by all the first rate Town Makers, at his repository, 7 Haymarket. J.L. has just had the whole of Joseph Manton's valuable stock of highly-finished Guns, in cases complete, consigned to him, which he is now selling at reduced prices".

Joseph Lang married the daughter of James Purdey, and by 1853 had moved to 22 Cockspur St. In 1875 the firm changed its style to Joseph Lang and Son and shortly afterwards the two brothers, Edward and James, established separate businesses. Edward traded as Joseph Lang at 10 Pall Mall, whilst James Lang traded from New Bond Street.

By 1898 a number of changes had taken place and the firm of Joseph Lang & Son issued a circular letter to their customers dated June 22. The style of the firm is still Joseph Lang and Son and the address is given as 10 Pall Mall. We can also see from the letter that the Pall Mall premises are to be closed as from the 28 June, 1898, and that the business is to be carried on from 102 New Bond Street. This, of course, was the address of James Lang & Co, in 1894.

However, in 1895, James Lang had become Lang & Hussey Ltd, Mr H J Hussey having been the "late assistant manager" of Holland & Holland Ltd. In addition to moving to new premises the name of the firm was to be changed to Lang & Hussey Ltd and the combined firms were to be under the personal supervision of Mr H J Hussey.

Mr H J Hussey became the managing director of the combined firm with Henry Webley as chairman, but such was the importance of the name of Joseph Lang that the style was again changed in 1901 back to Joseph Lang & Son and so it remained until the firm became Stephen Grant & Joseph Lang Ltd in 1925.

From the foregoing you can see how many of the great London makers had histories of quite astonishing complexity. The power of old, respected and important names was too great to be discarded easily and the sight of such names on top rib and lock plate had an effect which could not be lightly

Lang 10 bore under lever sidelock

ignored. The wish of Mr Hussey to see HIS name on a best London gun can full well be appreciated but pride had to succumb to business sense.

The difficulty of untangling the takeovers, mergers and just simple changes of style and address can be appreciated and the importance of saving every little scrap of paper, of noting each change of style and address should be evident. Look at what we have been able to discover from a simple circular sent out by a London gunmaker on that day in June 1898. Even today the name of Lang still carries weight, for although over a century and a half has passed the name Lang is still borne by a London gunmaker — Atkin, Grant and Lang. We also learn that this firm was established in 1821, but we know better. The firm of Joseph Lang was established in 1821, and I for one can't help but wonder what Joseph Lang would have thought about it all if he could have foreseen the future that day in 1821 when he left to set up on his own in the Haymarket.

MASU BROTHERS

The questions which I am asked by readers provide me with much interesting research and quite often the answer comes from another reader. Sometimes it is not the complete answer but I am given a clue or a theory is confirmed. The only matter upon which I am not qualified or prepared to give an answer is that of value. If I could be accurate on matters of value I wouldn't be writing about guns, I would be buying and selling them!

Let's have a look at one question put to me by Mr M. B. Wood. He wanted to know something about a gun he had recently purchased. I was given the name, G. Masu, 10 Wigmore Street, London and was told that the gun was a double 12-bore with damascus barrels, back action hammer locks and a rotary under-lever. Mr Wood also told me that the fore-end was attached to the action and was not removable. He also offered to provide a photograph and fortunately the quality was good.

Masu Bros. of London

The first thing that strikes one is that the name is unusual. Apart from the "attached" fore-end and perhaps the treatment of the fence surrounding the strikers, the gun appears to be quite normal for one made during the second-half of the 19th century. The hammers are rather fine and the table of the action bar is also interesting. The impression I got was continental. A search through my own records brought to light a little more information. Gustave Masu was listed as being at 3a Wigmore Street, in 1864. The firm became Masu Brothers from 1865 to 1869 and then appeared to have reverted to Gustavus Masu at 10 Wigmore Street from 1870 to 1882. Finally, the style of Masu Bros. is again used from 1883 to 1892 when the firm appears to have gone out of business.

In order to check the continental aspect of the history and background of this firm I then examined my records of European gunmakers and came across a Masu, Liege, 1845. A rather more careful check on the members of the Liege gunmaking fratenity did not confirm the existence of Masu so further information was not forthcoming from this quarter.

At this point I decided to sit back and await events. Events did take place in the form of another letter enquiring about a Masu gun. This letter came from Roger I. Jones who had a 16-bore pin-fire gun, and on the top rib was the legend Masu Freres a Lieges & 3a Wigmore Street, London. The barrels bore Liege proof marks so we have another brick in our building, an important brick since it clearly establishes the link between Liege and London.

Recently, another letter told me about a Masu Brothers, 3a Wigmore Street, London gun. This letter was from Mr John Ward and his gun is numbered 2994. This is a double 12-bore with rotary under-lever and is perhaps similar to the illustration of Mr Wood's gun which is numbered 4674.

From what we now have I think that Mr Jones's pin-fire will be the oldest, bearing as it does the Liege and London address. Then comes Mr Ward's gun, No. 2994 with what I take to be the first Masu Bros. address, 1865 to 1869 and finally Mr Wood's gun with No. 4674 and the final Masu with the "G" initial, Gustavus. This supposition is based on one bit of guesswork, namely the firm throughout its history kept to the consecutive series of serial numbers and didn't change the number sequence when the style of the firm was changed.

The fundamental question raised by these three enquirers is the extent to which the Liege industry was active in Britain. Their interest in the supply of barrels is well known but of their other activities the 19th century Belgian gunmakers were remarkably coy, perhaps with good reason?

J D DOUGALL

J D Dougall was one of those men whose lives continue to arouse interest in the minds of those who are familiar with the development of the British breechloader. It is, I suppose, a slight blow to the pride of the British shooting man to have to accept that the early work on breechloaders came to us from France and it is to the gunmakers of the country which lies across La Manche that we owe one of the major steps in gunmaking—putting the charge of shot and powder in the rear end of the barrel instead of stuffing it down the muzzle.

The early breechloaders fired cartridges which Dougall insisted be called *douille* which is the French word for socket. It was Dougall's contention that since the device which contained the powder, propellant and means of ignition was in fact a temporary breeching at the moment of discharge, to call this a cartridge was a misnomer.

The cartridge was already well known as being a container to hold powder and ball for muzzle-loading rifles, while Eley's wire cartridge for holding shot was equally well known to the muzzle-loading sportsman.

None of these devices contained the means of ignition as well as powder and projectile, and none formed part of the gun at the time of discharge.

Dougall was equally adamant that the word "socket" should not be used since in his opinion the word had an already widely established general use. In his book "The Art of Shooting", Dougall painstakingly referred to what we would now call a pin-fire cartridge as a douilles and even instructed his readers that their order for pin-fire cartridges should read "Please send me 1000 douilles".

He also suggested that the sportsman should give the word the English pronunciation, and it has intrigued me ever since I read Dougall's book as to whether any English sportsman ever used the word douilles. Certainly the literature is silent on the subject, except for Dougall himself.

Dougall came from Glasgow and later established himself in London, also becoming a Director of a smokeless powder company.

To the Englishman, Dougall's middle name, Dalziel, is apt to cause as much of a problem as his douilles when it comes to pronunciation. The Scot would call him DL, the whole of the middle of his name being unpronounced.

Dougall was a keen advocate of the breechloading system and he mentioned that when in Liege in 1861 he saw upwards of 40 different

Dougall side lever

31

breechloaders "in one room". He went on to say that all had a radical defect — want of locking powder. This defect was overcome in Dougall's own design, the rightly famous "Lockfast" in which the hinged barrel of the French Lefaucheux was combined with a rearward movement of the barrels due to the use of an eccentric hinge pin.

Guns and rifles on the Lockfast principle were probably made for at least a period of 20 to 25 years, and during this period a variety of designs appeared. The earliest has a side lever which lifts upwards and this is, of course, a pin-fire. The locking system also changed and the majority of the Dougall Lockfast guns have levers which are pushed downwards.

BOSS & CO

Were I asked to determine which was the greatest period in British gun-making, I think I would say it was between 1875 and 1925, 50 years in all. I would have some difficulty in stating which were the top 10 gunmakers of that period because I would have to define what was meant by "top". Invention, innovation, consistent high quality, cost, output, popularity — all have to be taken into account. If we take the first three criteria as being as good a way as any to define a "top" maker then the name of Boss must be one of the chosen. We are perhaps fortunate in that this is one firm that is still in business with their premises at 13 Dover Street in the West End of London, a street which has seen so many famous names in British gunmaking over the past two centuries.

To find the beginnings of Boss we don't have to go back that far. Their letter-heading states, "Established 1812", and it is when we come to verify this date that some of the problems that plague the researcher come to light.

The first Boss was Thomas. He worked with Joseph Manton, leaving "the king of the gunmakers" when Manton moved from Davies Street to Hanover Square, in 1819. Boss parted company to join James Purdey, who in 1826 had taken over the premises in Oxford Street formerly occupied by Manton.

Thomas Boss then left Purdey to start up on his own at 3 Grosvenor Street in 1830. This is when we encounter the first discrepancy, the difference between the date on the letter-heading of the company, Est 1812, and the fact that the first address from which a business was conducted dates from 1830. Possibly the answer is that Thomas Boss as an independent craftsman worked on his own from 1812 but did not establish himself as a gunmaker until 1830.

By 1835 he had moved to No 1 Lower Grosvenor Street and three years later he was at No 76 St James's Street, moving to No 73 in 1842. On the death of Thomas Boss, his widow took Stephen Grant into partnership in about 1860. Grant then set up on his own in 1866 at 67a St James's and a nephew of Thomas Boss carried on the firm until John Robertson was brought into the business in 1891. The direction of the company under the

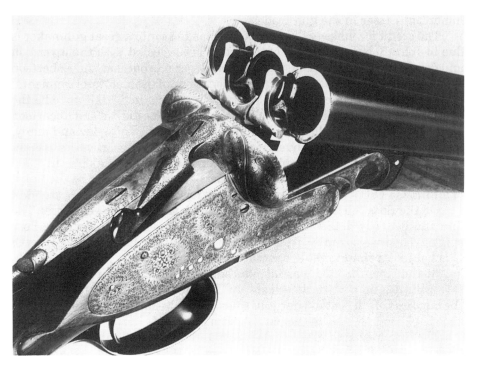

Boss three barrel sidelock

nephew might account for a brief change in style to E. F. P. Boss & Co dating from the early 1880s. The style reverts to Boss & Co shortly afterwards.

Stephen Grant was responsible for one of the patents taken out when he was with Boss which covers a rotary under-lever action with the barrels hinged at the end of the fore-end instead of the end of the bar. Grant had worked with Lancaster before joining Boss and he went on to become one of the foremost gunmakers in London.

The firm of Boss appears to have concentrated on high quality rather than invention and innovation. This was to change significantly with the appearance of new blood in the firm, John Robertson. Robertson, who became a partner in 1891, hailed from Haddington, just south of Edinburgh where the family had an established gunmaking business. John left the family firm to work for Whitworth in Manchester, then moved to Westley Richards in Birmingham before working for Purdey in London. Robertson began making for a number of London gunmakers before his association with Boss and in fact had taken out a number of patents, some in association with H. J. Holland for cocking mechanisms and ejectors before his first patent for a single trigger mechanism which dates from 1893, some two years after his partnership at Boss.

Some 14 more patents were taken out before his final patents in 1909 on O/U guns which can rightly be said to have been the culmination of an important career in the gun trade.

The credit for making the firm of Thomas Boss into a great gunmaker is due to John Robertson. Much of the credit is connected with the invention and development of a satisfactory single-trigger mechanism and Robertson spent some considerable time on perfection of one of the last "improvements" to what was to become the standard British game gun. This was to be the standard by which all other guns of this type were to be judged and Robertson along with Beesley, Holland & Holland, Scott, Anson & Deeley and many, many others produced the inventions which allied to superlative craftsmanship placed Britain at the pinnacle of the world's gunmakers. In 1909 Robertson patented the Boss O/U gun, considered by many to be the finest of all British O/U's. This is arguable : there is now but one other contender!

On the Boss the lumps are placed on either side of the lower barrel. The fore-end is easily detachable and bar action sidelocks are used. The Boss single trigger was usually fitted. Still in very limited production the Boss O/U is not just a shotgun, it is a work of art.

At the time the O/U was introduced Boss moved their premises to 13 Dover Street and with the death of John Robertson his three sons carried on the business. Jack was in charge of sales, Sam, the factory and Bob was the shooting instructor at the Regent Shooting Ground.

The firm moved to Albermarle Street and then to delightful premises in Cork Street before moving to Dover Street in 1982. I should rather like to complete an inventory of Boss guns which have survived. This was done for Holland & Holland and William Powell and was quite successful. There should be a three-barrel Boss gun somewhere — do you have it?

WILLIAM EVANS

If you were to compare the number of gunmakers listed in the London Directories at the turn of the century with those listed today I am certain that your first comment would be "Where have they all gone?" and your second "Look who has survived!"

Not all that many have survived two world wars and a radical alteration in the British way of life — from just under 100 in 1900 down to just over 20 over 80 years later. In the first list many of the names were true gunmakers, but the address given was merely the London trade outlet; an example here would be W & C Scott & Son who had showrooms in Shaftesbury Avenue, but the guns were made in Birmingham. Other firms had a London address but no manufacturing facilities at all in the United Kingdom — such as L. LePersonne & Co, who, at the turn of the century, were the London agents for the famous Liege firm of Auguste Francotte et Cie.

Other firms — whose names were to be found on the top ribs of best London guns — were independent in 1900. Such firms as Atkin, Beesley, Churchill, Grant and Lang, found that in order to survive they had to pool their resources and trade under a communal name before they too succumbed to the economic problems created by two world wars and a vanished Empire.

Some firms did survive, two outstandingly so — Purdey and Holland & Holland. Others lasted longer than the rest only to vanish, and then, like Cogswell & Harrison, to rise again, showing signs of a firm future.

Other gunmakers, with a special niche in gunmaking history, are also still with us, firms like Boss, and John Rigby, with a long tradition and a special name for sporting rifles.

One name I haven't mentioned so far, a name which is on both lists, is that of William Evans. In 1900 they were to be found at 63 Pall Mall and in the 1980s, not all that far away, at 67a St James's Street, a fine corner location just a stone's throw from Christie's in King Street.

Evans is one of the makers who has, so far, escaped being immortalised in this series. One of the reasons is that we know little about William Evans. We know that he worked for Purdey and then spent 12 years with Holland & Holland. He first set up on his own at 95a Buckingham Palace Road in 1883, moving to Holden Terrace in Pimlico two years later. He was at 4 Pall Mall in 1888, the address changing to No 63 in 1896, and this is where we find him in 1900.

In the closing years of the 19th century Evans had an impressive range of guns to offer: his best London-finished boxlock sold for £47 with ejectors, with either Damascus or best Siemens steel barrels and, for the same price, Evans offered his bar sidelock, again with a variety of options, for example, Sir Joseph Whitworth's "Fluid Compressed Steel" barrels cost an additional £3.

Evans also had a very wide range of hammer guns in all qualities including wildfowling guns bored for the Kynoch thin brass cases. An interesting double was his hammergun with the Purdey 'thumb hole' action and many of his guns were signed "William Evans, From Purdey's".

The unauthorised use of the Purdey name created somewhat of a

William Evans "Best" sidelock

problem. The Purdey of the day was of the opinion that if a man was good enough to start on his own, he should do so under his own name. This was quite a reasonable attitude to adopt but for the fact that the founder of Purdey's had, on his earliest labels, used a similar phrase himself: "James Purdey, From J. Manton's"! Purdey's took legal advice regarding the use of their name and Councel's opinion was that nothing could be done about it. A case of the biter bit!

There were those who were against the practice and those who, like Frederick Beesley, felt that the mention of a former connection with one of the great London was entirely justified. Certainly, it helps the researcher of today!

By the 1920s Evans was firmly established and offered his guns with the option of his patent single trigger; this was a joint patent taken out in 1905 by Evans and Corrie.

The firm had extensive shooting grounds and held warrants as gunmakers to HRH The Duke of Connaught and HRH Prince Arthur of Connaught. They also held very large stocks of second-hand guns and offered facilities at their shooting grounds for trial so that alterations "can then be made to any stock at a trifling cost". Most reassuring!

The second world war made even greater inroads into the London trade but, once again, William Evans survived although they had to move from their Pall Mall shop to their present premises in St James's Street.

Here the firm sells a wide range of clothing and accessories, their own brands of cartridges — the 'Marlboro', 'St James's' and the 'Pall Mall' — and, of course, they still offer the Evans best sidelock and the Evans best boxlock. These guns are built to the best traditions of the London trade and have that air of quality about them which, to those who know and love best guns, is unmistakable. In addition Evans also offer traditional bolt action sporting rifles built on the Mauser '98 action. Prices are about £12,000 for the sidelock, £5,000 for the boxlock and in the order of £2,500 for the rifles.

It is now, of course, over a century since William Evans set up on his own. It is a remarkable tribute to those who have worked for the firm which bears his name that it has survived to this day in St James's. Here, in what I call a real gunshop, those who love fine guns can find a courteous welcome where the traditions of the past are still very evident.

COGSWELL & HARRISON

Cogswell & Harrison were established in 1770 and they sold a range of shotguns under the names "Victor", "Huntic", "Konor" and "Blagdon".

The shop at 168 Piccadilly was opened in 1917 and at the same time the Strand shop was closed. To find the date of the opening of the New Bond Street shop I have to refer to my records of London gunmakers and find that the date was 1879.

Cogswell & Harrison back action sidelock

By this time Edgar Harrison had been with the firm for five years and from 1880 onwards he had taken out a number of patents, both on his own account and with others, such as Southgate, Beesley and Jeffery, for cocking mechanisms, vernier sights, safety devices and ejector mechanisms.

Edgar Harrison was responsible for the establishment of Cogswell's factory in Gillingham Street where the application of machine tools to the manufacture of sporting guns was taken rather further than the more conservative members of the gun trade deemed advisable.

According to my records the style of Cogswell & Harrison was first used in 1863 but other authorities have it slightly earlier, 1860. Certainly Benjamin Cogswell started in business at the Strand address about 1845, acquiring a business first established by a relative in 1770. This was the firm of Essex of whom I have been able to discover little although examples of his work appear to have survived.

There can be little doubt that many of Cogswell & Harrison's guns will also have survived. The "Victor" of the 1880s with back-action lockwork and the cheaper "Desideratum", probably made in their Harrow factory, and their "Avant Tout" A & D gun, are no doubt still in use.

Tucked away in some forgotten corner will, no doubt, be specimens of the pre-First World War cartridges sold by C & H, the "Victor" and the "Blagdon". Also on some bookshelf may rest a copy of "Shooting with Game and Gun Room Notes" by "Blagdon". My copy, dated 1900, was given to me by Frank Holroyd and is a very good example of the prestige type publication issued by many of the London makers. One of the most interesting advertisements in this book is for The Shooting Times which, in 1900, sold for 2d per week.

In the 1980's the firm suffered the first of several "reorganisations". The future is now uncertain.

ARMY AND NAVY C. S. L.

A surprising number of quality double shotguns have survived and are still in use which bear the name 'Army and Navy C. S. L.' or 'Army and Navy Stores Limited' on the barrels and lockplates.

The story begins in 1871 when a group of army and navy officers decided that they were paying too much for their wine! If the wine could be bought at wholesale prices a saving could be made in much the same manner as the Civil Service had done when the clerks at the Post Office had clubbed together to buy a chest of tea.

The Army and Navy Co-operative Society Limited was formed and membership originally restricted to serving officers and NCOs, their wives, families and friends and to officials of the various service organisations. The premises acquired by the A & N were in Victoria Street, Westminster, and the store soon took on the atmosphere of a club, with reading rooms, waiting rooms and facilities for meals. In 1901 branches were opened in Bombay, Delhi, Calcutta and Karachi.

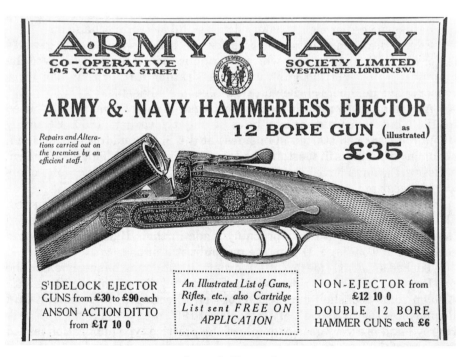

Army & Navy ad

The Society aimed to provide quality goods for domestic use and general consumption, amongst which were shotguns, rifles, pistols, ammunition and related accessories. We are told that the factories of the Society made shirts, watches, saddlery and golf clubs. We are also told that they made guns but extensive research has failed to find proof of this ; the guns in the extensive catalogue were made by a number of gunmakers in Britain, Germany and, of course, America.

Factory mass-produced shotguns like the Winchester and Browning Auto and pump-guns were sold under the manufacturer's name, double and single barrel shotguns were sold under the Army and Navy C. S. L. name and details of these guns were carefully kept by the Gun Department of the Society. Cartridges were also sold under the Society's name with brand names such as 'The Victoria', 'The Nitro' and, of course, 'The Reliable'.

In 1907 the best sidelock was 45 guineas with five lower quality grades bringing the price down to £19. Plain quality sidelocks were sold for as little as £13 with A & D guns ranging between £12 and, at the lower end, £7.

By 1938, the price of the first quality sidelock had risen to £90 with the fourth quality gun at £35. The Army and Navy 'Anson' gun was £25 and double hammerguns were as low as £6 15s.

The Society offered full facilities for gun fitting and testing and even coaching could be provided in the years between the wars by the resident 'expert', Mr P. D. Jack. If you bought a gun costing more than £15 then the shooting school charges, 25 cartridges and 12 clay birds were free!

The shotguns bearing the Society's name came from a number of sources in Britain, in total about 18. Many were made by famous names such as Webley & Scott, who made both sidelocks and A & D action guns. Other names were Hollis, Osborne Allport, London Armoury Company and BSA.

Exactly what resources the Society had in their 'armoury' is not known. Three people worked in this part of the establishment in 1878 and their duties were probably confined to repairs, adjustments and examination of guns before dispatch.

Mention has been made of the stores established in India. Guns were sent out to India from the London headquarters but a member could have it fitted in London and then sent out with the rest of his baggage and effects.

There was even an Army and Navy store on board ship and, of course all travel arrangements could be made through the Society.

The Society's workshops did make the 'Shikari Gun Case', and cleaning rods and other accessories but appear to have relied on the London and Birmingham gun trade for shotguns and double rifles.

Many thousands of guns have passed through the Gun Department in a century of gun sales, dispatched to the sportsmen of a vanished Empire. The Empire has gone but the guns survive to give valiant service in greatly altered times.

CHURCHILL LTD.

Churchill, though well known as a London gunmaker, was not a firm with a long tradition going back to Joe Manton, in fact the founder E. J. Churchill served his time, not with the London trade, but at the old established business of William Jeffery & Son of Dorchester, a business founded in Plymouth by the first William Jeffery (Born 1815) in 1849.

Young Churchill then sought fame and fortune in the big city, working first of all for Mr. F. T. Baker in Fleet Street before he set up on his own at 8, Agar Street, Strand in 1891.

He was joined by his son, H. E. J. Churchill who died tragically at the early age of twenty. The fortunes of the firm were founded on the success which Churchill guns achieved in competitive shooting at trap pigeon. Churchill had a shooting ground at Eltham in Kent, where his customers could receive tuition and also be provided with ample practise.

Churchill was joined by his nephew Robert (born 1886) and after the death of the founder in 1910 the running of the business was taken over by Robert.

Robert had inherited a business which was on the verge of bankruptcy. He was, however, able to persuade one of his uncle's friends to put up enough money to purchase the business on the understanding that he, Robert, would be kept on as Manager, at the princely salary of £4 per week, plus commission!

Although not a practical gunmaker Robert Churchill had some firm ideas about sporting guns and he decided to cater more for the game shooter rather than the pigeon shooter.

In the post W. W. I era Robert Churchill experimented with a lightweight short barrelled game gun which eventually evolved into his 25" barrelled Churchill 'XXV' Game Gun.

His uncle had been a staunch protagonist of fast light weight loads and attributed much of his success to his specially loaded cartridges. The appearance of smokeless powders, which did not require lengthy barrels for complete combustion, meant that the concept of a short barrelled lightweight game gun could be advocated by Robert, and this he did with some considerable success.

The firm moved to Leicester Square in 1925 and in 1934 the firm moved again, this time to Orange Street. Meanwhile the Churchill Gun Club Shooting Grounds had been opened at Crayford in Kent where clients could be fitted for their guns and given tuition.

The guns and services offered by the company were very widely publicised and added publicity was provided by Robert Churchill's book, "How to Shoot".

Unlike many London gunmakers the firm survived the second war and offered a range of guns, "The Premiere", a "Best" sidelock, with easy opening action, the "Imperial", also a sidelock, and a range of boxlock guns, the

Churchill sidelock

"Hercules", the "Regal" and the "Crown". The entire range could be had with 25" barrels, or longer, if so wished, and with the exception of the "Crown" model, all could be had in 12, 16 and 20 bore.

The firm also offered a range of sporting rifles, based on the Mauser action, available in a wide variety of calibres.

To-day, Robert Churchill is probably best known as the author of *Game Shooting* which was published in 1955 and which contained an exposition of his original methods of teaching shooting.

This book set me off on a search which has lasted nigh on half a century, for inside the front flap of the jacket there is a photograph of an unusual Over and Under shotgun, the Churchill "Zenith" and I have, over the years, devoted considerable time and effort to researching the history of this unique gun.

The Zenith was not the only O/U gun which Churchill made although it is perhaps the most unusual. Others, more conventional, were built and a very unusual O/U patented by Robert Churchill and A. L. Chevallier in 1926, vied with the Zenith in the number of its unusual features. These two O/U guns are the rarest of all the Churchill guns, very few having been made.

Robert Churchill died in 1958 and the business moved to Bury Street, St. James, where further amalgamations resulted in the formation of the firm of Churchill, Atkin, Grant & Lang, which itself, ceased to trade in 1980.

However, all is not lost, the traditions of the past are now in the capable hands of Don Masters of E. J. Churchill Ltd., Cannon works, Ockley Rd., Beare Green, Dorking, Surrey.

SILVER & CO

The fame of many gunmakers, both London and Provincial, spread far and wide; some were renowned for their shotguns, others for rifles. Some specialised in target rifles, some in big-game rifles while others made wildfowling guns and punt guns. Then there were those firms whose fame rested upon one invention. With the passing of time it was forgotten that they were ever gunmakers; their name being solely associated with the special "patent" item.

If we have a look at A. G. Parker & Co's catalogue (this firm became Parker-Hale Ltd in 1936) we will find an illustration of an anti-recoil pad, Silver's Pattern. For many years when you talked about a recoil pad for either a high velocity rifle or a heavy shotgun the term was practically synonymous with the name Silver. Even today the current Parker-Hale catalogue refers to the Silver recoil-pad and it is interesting to realise that the original patent for this recoil pad, which has been so widely copied, is dated 1874. The original design was rather complicated and it wasn't until 1886 that the simplified version made from rubber-fenced vulcanite was introduced.

S. W. Silver & Co's premises were at 67 Cornhill, London but little is known of the founder of the firm or of its subsequent history. An early advertisement advises that an illustrated catalogue is available of every article of equipment for "Sportsmen, Colonists, Settlers, Explorers and Travellers, on application to".

This conjures up a splendid vision of a never-ending stream of intrepid Empire Builders wending their way to Silver of Cornhill. What must have been the thoughts of the shop assistants as these bronzed heroes of the great outdoors came to have Silver's recoil pads fitted or to buy a patent "Transvaal Rifle & Gun". I don't know what the shop was like, for Cornhill was not the "fashionable" gun centre — this was much further west — but Cornhill did have at least one other gunmaker in 1855, namely Edward Bond and near at hand was the Minories, the historic centre of London gunmaking.

I haven't seen a Silver gun and, of course, since we have dealt with Golden guns it would be approriate that the series contains at least one article on a Silver gun!

Most of Silver's gun patents were devoted to safety devices of one form or another. There were safeties in the tang of the trigger guard; another plan had the safety lever in the top strap where it would be depressed by the ball of the thumb when the gun was fired and yet another automatic safety was incorporated in the butt plate so that the gun was "safe" until placed against the shoulder ready to fire.

Few of these devices appear to have withstood the test of time. Several that I have seen in recent years have been rendered inoperative by taping them with adhesive tape or copper wire.

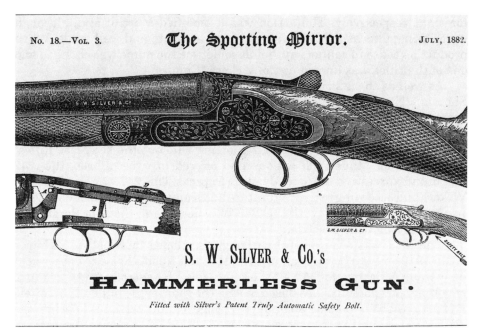

S. W. SILVER & CO.'s

HAMMERLESS GUN.

Fitted with Silver's Patent Truly Automatic Safety Bolt.

S. W. Silver & Co. ad

Rarely encountered in this country today is Silver's "Transvaal Rifle and Gun". This was a Martini-action to which could be fitted interchangeable barrels, either smooth-bored or rifled and, in addition, each barrel was supplied with the necessary bullet moulds and equipment for reloading.

It is very possible that some of the Silver & Co shotguns survive and perhaps remain in useful service, but whether any with safety devices of Silver's design are still used is less likely.

Although the name Silver may be forgotten to all but a few with surviving guns by this maker (it is too much to hope that the "Illustrated Catalogue" might have survived) the name of Silver will be remembered for some years to come because of the invention of the recoil pad. Today rather splendid pads can be purchased with "white line spacers" and other eye-catching additions, but Silver was first!

VICKERS LTD

My first contact with the firm of Vickers came through the purchase of a .22 rimfire target rifle which was used for indoor small-bore rifle shooting. It was bought secondhand in Steelhouse Lane, Birmingham and served me well during my membership of several rifle clubs. I re-stocked it and still have it. Vickers made two target rifles, the Grade 1 and the Grade 2 which, in 1929 cost £7. 10s and £6. 15s with a Vickers rearsight and a Parker-Hale foresight respectively. The action was a modified Martini and, although never as popular as the BSA range, it was accurate and well made. When production ceased I cannot say, but at sometime the name was changed and one of the rifles was known as the Vickers "Empire".

As well as the .22 rifles (which as an advert in the May 28 issue of the Shooting Times for 1927 assures the reader could be had for target and sporting shooting) a range of central-fire rifles and shotguns was also offered.

I have not encountered the .22 sporting rifle but the "Express Rifles" were based on Mauser 98 actions and offered in two calibres, the .242 Magnum Express and the .318 Magnum Express. The .242 was developed by Vickers and according to their literature had a muzzle velocity of 3,000 ft/sec. It can best be compared with the .243 Winchester and the .244 Remington and it has long been obsolete.

The .318 was a successful cartridge developed by Westley Richards about 1910 for their bolt-action rifles and became a popular cartridge for non-dangerous African game. About the same time BSA introduced their range of bolt-action sporting rifles based, not on the Mauser '98 but on the Enfield P14 action. They, too, had a special cartridge of quite advanced design, the .26 rimless Nitro-Express which, although listed as a "rimless" cartridge, was actually a belted rimless case similar to the H & H designs.

Neither the BSA nor the Vickers Express rifles enjoyed commercial success. Production must have been relatively small and today production figures are unobtainable.

Vickers Ltd, later to be Vickers Armstrong Ltd, were armament manu-facturers and their venture into sporting firearms was unusual. BSA, on the other hand, had been formed by a consortium of Birmingham gunmakers in an attempt to ward off the threat posed by the establishment of the Royal Small Arms Factory at Enfield.

Vickers did have an interest which BSA did not enjoy — the automatic pistol. As Vickers Sons & Maxim Ltd, they were UK agents for Deutsche Waffen-und Munitionsfabriken of Berlin and instrumental in arranging trials for what we know today as the Luger pistol. These trials took place before the British Small Arms Committee in 1900 and it is a quirk of fate that the basic action of the Borchardt-Luger owed much to the earlier toggle link mechanism of the Maxim machine gun, made by Vickers.

Further efforts were made by Vickers on behalf of DWM, without success and then WW1 put an effective stop to negotiations. The story did not finish, however, since one of the notable "mysteries" is the story of the "Vickers Luger" purchased by the Netherlands Indies Army shortly after the end of WWI. Even today it is not known if Vickers merely acted for DWM in the transaction, assembled DWM Luger components in the UK, or actually manufactured Luger pistols on machinery supplied by DWM.

One of the most interesting aspects of this story concerns the Mauser '98 actions used for the Vickers Express rifles. Were these also from DWM? The bitterness and resentment which followed the First World War would ensure that any relationship between Vickers and DWM would be shrouded in secrecy. The effectiveness of this shroud coupled with the passing of the years makes it now impossible to discover the true story.

International conspiracy cannot be the cause of the mystery which still surrounds Vicker's manufacture of shotguns. The best known was the single-barrel, semi-hammerless ejector gun sold under the name "Vanguard". We are told that the Vanguard is made from British materials, by British workmanship throughout and that the barrel is forged from Vickers steel. The Vanguard guns bore London proof marks which was understandable, if they had been made at the Crayford Works, but Vickers also offered the rather rare Vickers "Imperial" double sidelock. This employed a back-action coil spring sidelock similar to that patented by Baker but what is of greater interest was their "best" sidelock. This appears, from the illustrations, to have been a "best" London gun with Chilton locks, and, although the barrels are made from Vickers nickel steel, this is possibly the sole contribution by Vickers to the actual manufacture of this gun.

I have never seen either the "Imperial" or the "Best Quality" Vickers side-by-side double guns although one has just "surfaced" in Australia! We go back again to the years just after WWI, to November 1919. In March of that year the Australian Government offered a prize of £10,000 for the first

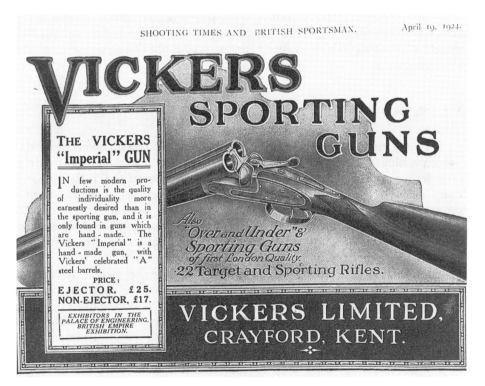

Vickers Ltd. ad

flight made by Australians from Britain to Australia in a British aircraft. Vickers Ltd had just the aircraft, the Vimy.

Too late to make an impact on the war, the Vimy became immortal as the first aircraft to make a direct Atlantic crossing. This was in June 1919, so it is not surprising that Vickers entered the Vimy for the Australian flight. Flown by Captain Ross Smith of the Australian Flying Corps and navigated by his brother Lt Keith Smith with Sgts Bennett and Shiers as mechanics, the Vimy left Hounslow at 8am on November 12, 1919 reaching Darwin at 4.10pm, December 10 after flying 11,130 miles. The Vimy, G-EAOU, was presented to the Australian Government by Vickers and survives to this day along with the Vimy of Alcock and Brown which is preserved in London.

So far we are going on fact; now we move to heresay. The story goes that Captain Ross Smith was presented with a shotgun by Vickers Ltd after his successful flight. What better shotgun than a Crayford-built Vickers "Best" sidelock? The Vimy was built at Crayford Works but G-EAOU had been built by Vickers at Weybridge. Did Vickers build the "Best" shotguns at Crayford or have them made for them elsewhere; if so, where?

The Aviation Dept of Vickers went on to even greater things — the Spitfire and the Viscount — but what happened to the sporting gun department, if indeed there ever was one? Vickers today do not have the answers but there may be someone who does remember or who has the relevant literature. If so, I would be most interested to learn more about the guns and rifles made by Vickers or sold by them, and any facts about the presentation shotgun now in Australia would delight the owner and satisfy my curiosity.

WATSON BROS.

Perhaps my greatest interest in firearms lies in the unravelling of the many problems which confront the researcher into early breechloading hammerless guns — the guns of the closing decades of the 19th century. Many, because of a conventional external appearance, are overlooked until something goes wrong and a strange and interesting mechanism is exposed for examination. With guns other than those which appear to be sidelocks the difference in the mechanism from, for example, the standard Anson & Deeley, can quite often be guessed.

Such was the case when I was handed the 12-bore non-ejector by Watson Bros, 4 Pall Mall, London, not long ago. The date of the gun was not too difficult to discover, this style and address apparently having been used for quite a short period, from about 1885 to 1894, which would appear to place manufacture between those two dates; near enough for all practical purposes.

I was fortunate to be able to examine this gun since the external appearance was sufficiently different to make me curious about the type of

Watson Bros. boxlock

cocking mechanism and lockwork employed.

Apart from the name Watson Bros on each side of the action bar, and the full name and address on the top rib, the sole remaining clue were the words "Carlton Patent Hammerless" on the small "box" beneath the bar and in front of the trigger guard. Proof marks were those of 1875 which were themselves altered in 1877. Simple arithmetic then narrows down the date of manufacture to the years 1885, '86 and '87.

With the gun in front of me and the opportunity to take it apart and inspect the "works" instead of having to work from photographs as I often have to do, the next problem was to discover who was responsible for the design of the cocking mechanism and the lockwork.

A search showed that this was none of the Watsons, but research elsewhere for quite a different purpose provided the linking clue. In my research on Watson I had discovered that the firm had been founded by Thomas William Watson and after that trading under this name for a period the firm had then been known as Watson Bros, reverting to Thomas W. Watson again. This information had been obtained as a result of very much earlier work on the firm of Atkin, Grant & Lang. Watson had been taken over by Grant & Lang in 1935, some three years before Charles Lancaster had been acquired and shortly after F. Beesley. So, Watson's were in very good company at 7 Bury Street, St James's.

How exalted the company was I had yet to discover! I had thought that the important connections were in the closing years of the life of the firm, but this was not so. Further research revealed the fact that Watson was the son-in-law of a very famous Birmingham gunmaker named William Tranter. To most people the name Tranter is linked with revolvers, and although Tranter had a marked influence on the development of the British revolver, this was by no means his only interest in what was to become, in his lifetime, the gun industry.

The name Tranter was to link all the loose bits of information together because I remembered having seen a drawing of a shotgun action patented by him which had a rather odd, old-fashioned box underneath the action bar. A search of the records showed this to be so; the action used by Watson was that patented by his father-in-law in 1882 and, with the aid of the patent and being able fully to dismantle the gun, details of the rather unusual type of action were disclosed.

The Tranter action never became popular. It was complicated and slightly unwieldly and the external box did detract from the appearance. It offered no advantage over the earlier Anson & Deeley (patented in 1875) and few appear to have been made; fewer still have survived. Unfortunately, the barrels are no longer in proof and their condition is such that I would not like to risk using even black-powder cartridges, so how the gun would perform under field conditions remains a mystery.

JOHN WILKES

As you turn off to the right from the splendour of Regent Street down Beak Street into Soho you move into a different world, almost a different time, for the area bounded by the four circuses, Oxford, Picadilly, Cambridge and the less well known St. Giles, is full of interest, full of history. As you move deeper into Soho you can sample gastronomic delights, the best fish and chips in London in Old Compton Street, glad rags in Carnaby Street, the pub in Poland Street where this poor scrivener used to meet Tim Sedgewick, one-time editor of the Shooting Times and then on to the "delights" of the modern "pornographic palaces" of today.

Every nationality has been represented here in Soho at one time or another; Greek Street reminds us of the Greeks who fled to this country, the French Huguenots brought with them their skills and Soho has always been an area replete with skills from tailoring to gumaking.

A Venetian artist who called himself Canaletto moved into No 41 Beak Street and stayed for four years, Karl Marx lived in Soho at 26 Dean Street and along with all the other trades that were to be found in the streets, lanes, squares, yards and even mews of Soho were the members of the gun trade. Thomas Perkes was to be found in Duck Lane, a patentee of shotgun actions. Over a century ago, Thos Parkin made gun barrels in Soho, James James made gun cases and William Norcott sold gunmakers' tools. Charles Fisher, John Hoskins, and S & C Smith were all gunmakers in Soho whilst just

John Wilkes, London

beyond the boundaries in Regent Street, Oxford Street and St James's were to be found "the gunmakers of quality".

Alas, many of the gunmakers of quality are no longer to be found in their prestigious premises, but in Beak St, Soho, a gunmaker is still to be found — John Wilkes at No 79.

It would be nice to be able to say that the firm had been in Soho since 1830. This we cannot do for at the beginning of the 19th century the Wilkes were in Birmingham — where, exactly, we don't know. We do know that in the 1860's the business was prospering largely due to the Civil War in America.

With the surrender of the last Confederate Army at Shreveport, Louisiana on May 26, 1865, the war ended. A year later a family upheaval nearly wrecked the Wilkes' gun business. The John Wilkes of the period did not arrive for work and an investigation brought to light the fact that John had taken all the money from the bank, mortgaged the business to the hilt and absconded to America. The younger Wilkes brother, Tom, went to America to search for John and for a time worked at the Colt Armoury and with Singer's to gather enough capital to search for John and to replenish the family coffers. It is part of the family history that Tom did in fact locate a John

Wilkes, Gunmaker, in a small town near St Louis but by the time he arrived the bird had flown and Tom returned to England. A business was established in Soho at 1 Lower James Street, Wilkes & Harris, and the year was 1894. Mr Harris was not a gunmaker; he looked after the books and when the Wilkes decided that they could do this just as well themselves, the firm became John Wilkes in 1895. This is the name it has borne ever since. In St James's was the famous firm of James D Dougall, formerly of Glasgow, with whom the Wilkes had both family and business relationships. The John Wilkes who died in 1968 aged 84 remembered sleeping on a pile of heather in Dougall's shop at the time of Queen Victoria's Diamond Jubilee. Whether this is correct or not depends very much on the dates for the Jubilee was in 1897 and Dougall had died on the train of a heart attack in January 1896! Wilkes could not take over the Dougall business and the firm remained in Lower James Street. It is important at this stage to realise that James Street is in Soho, Golden Square, to be exact and must not be confused with St James's. Golden Square has another claim to fame for here it was in 1849 that John Snow, the first specialist anaesthetist in the world and one of the earliest epidemiologists, investigated a severe outbreak of cholera. The houses in Golden Square were not supplied with water from pipes but drew the water from surface wells. One former resident of Golden Square was the widow of William Eley who had left the square to live elsewhere. She died of cholera. Although living outside the area it was later proved that she had been in the practice of sending a servant to draw water from "the sweet well" she had been used to — this caused her death.

The John Wilkes of today told me the location of the well which is now suitably marked and I understand that this is a place of pilgrimage for students from all over the world.

The pump for the well was in Broad Street, Golden Square and the Wilkes moved here in 1925 after a brief sojourn in Gerrard Street. The outbreak of cholera had been stopped, incidentally, when John Snow on being asked by the Guardians of the Parish, "What should they do?" had replied, "Take the handle off the Broad Street pump!" In 1950 the Wilkes moved from Broad Street to their present address in Beak Street where in spite of ever-rising costs they remain to this day.

The Birmingham end of the business closed in 1933 and all the gun work is now done on the Beak Street premises. The years between the wars saw quite an output of guns from Beak Street: sidelocks, boxlocks, rifles — both double and a bolt action of a particularly pleasing design. Shotgun cartridges were also sold under their own brand name, "Doughty" and a pun on the name of the younger brother in the family "Tom-Tom". After the last war, during which all sorts of highly specialised firearmery had been produced, guns and rifles were still being made not only on special order and for the "shop" but also for some of the "bigger" names who no longer had the facilities they formerly enjoyed.

Today John and Tom Wilkes still work away at the bench, taking time off now and again to discuss some problem with a customer, who can be a French aristocrat, a rich American or the local plumber who brought his gun in to have a new top-lever screw made, and which was made by John as he talked to me about the past and the present.

What the future holds is difficult to say. People no longer "live over the shop" and traveling costs and "time" have increased, as has the cost of living in what one might call the 18th century London. Trying to carry on a business, with the overheads and restrictions imposed by a 20th-century bureaucracy is increasingly difficult. John and Tom Wilkes still manage to produce a London-style "best" sidelock shotgun to order, a quality gun with a long tradition to back it. Wilkes is unique in London and, as a family business with five generations behind it, not a little unusual in Britain as a whole — long may they continue to do business.

JOHN BLANCH & SON

The history of the long established firm of John Blanch and Son of London is lengthy and somewhat complex. The first John Blanch was born in 1784 and he was then apprenticed to Jackson Mortimer and it must have been during his apprenticeship that he met and later married Ann, the daughter of his master.

Mortimer went into partnership with his son-in-law as Mortimer & Blanch in 1811, but this partnership appears to have been dissolved in the following year.

Prior to this Blanch worked for John Manton and he then set up on his own, aged 29, at 39 Fish Street Hill in 1813. In 1826 the firm moved to 29 Gracechurch Street.

John's eldest son, John, moved to Hull where he established a business prior to moving to Australia. He was killed by an explosion in his shop in Melbourne in 1839.

The second son, Henry Mortimer (named after his grandfather) also emigrated to Australia and it was the third son, William, who was apprenticed to his father and then joined the firm in 1848 as John Blanch & Sons.

William H. Blanch, a grandson of the founder, was apprenticed to his Uncle William and he then subsequently founded the firm of W. H. Blanch of Liverpool. William H., was a prolific inventor, particularly in the field of rifle sights and accessories. He is responsible for the first vernier scale rifle sight to be used in this country which dates from 1862.

As with many gunmakers of the Victorian age, Blanch went into the business of publishing. The book, "A Century of Guns" was written by Herbert John Blanch, the son of William and was first published in 1909. The frontispiece of the book shows Fish Street Hill, London as it was in 1793, just before Jackson Mortimer started in business there. The book also has the Statute of Henry VIII which required "every lord, knight, esquire and

Blanch & Son back action sidelock

gentleman and the inhabitants of every city, borough and market town to have and to keep in every of their houses such hand guns of the length of one whole yard whereby they may the better aid and assist in the defence of this realm, when need shall require." Henry VIII obviously had more confidence in his subjects than does Elizabeth II!

Blanch were one of the first of the London makers to offer the French Lefaucheux pin-fire breech loader. I have not been able to locate any patents relating to shotguns in the names of the family but the firm appears to have been well in the fore front of advances and popular with its customers since they remained in the Gracechurch Street premises from 1826 until the first war when they moved to 20 Cullum Street, EC. 3. In the thirties they moved to Mitre Street, Aldgate, ceasing to trade in 1942.

In the century and a quarter of the firm's active life they made a very wide range of guns, from percussion muzzle loaders to sidelock hammerless ejectors. If I were asked to comment on the guns made by Blanch I would, I think, mention what appears to me to be a preference for back action guns, whether hammer or hammerless and a surprisingly high proportion of their guns sported unusual engraving during a period when "rose and scroll" with the odd animal was the norm.

THOMAS BLAND & SONS

The number of gunmakers who are still in business to-day and who can trace their ancestry back to the days of the muzzle loader are now very few and rather far between! One such firm is Thomas Bland & Sons (Gunmakers)

Ltd., of 21-22, New Row, St. Martins Lane, London, W.C. 2N 4LA.

Although they have been in business in London now for over a century the firm started life in Birmingham. According to their history, they were founded in 1840, but the earliest record of them as gunmakers is in 1862. A James and an Edwin Bland were in business as gunmakers as early as 1827 and Edwin was the brother of Thomas who founded the firm which was to bear his name.

Thomas Bland prospered for his original premises at 41 Whittall St., expanded, so that, by 1867, they occupied a block of buildings at 41, 42, 43 Whittall Street, next to the King's Arms Public House at the corner of Steelhouse Lane.

In 1872, the firm expanded even further, Thomas Bland Jnr., the son of the founder, opened a branch of the firm in London at 106 Strand and in 1886 they also acquired additional premises at 430 Strand, the original London premises were then closed.

The following year saw the death of the founder, the business being continued by his son Thomas Bland Jr. In the period up to the first World War, Bland's made not only shotguns but also a wide range of rifles for big game, Thomas took out patents for rifle sights and with Cashmore of Birmingham a patent for a special four barrel pistol was obtained which was manufactured by the company.

The 1880's saw an interest in three barrel guns developing and Bland produced one of their own and they were also responsible for manufacturing the "Field" patent gun. Three makers built Field guns, Greener of Birmingham, Green of Cheltenham and Thomas Bland. Of the three, Bland was the only firm who persevered with the design and produced the "Field" gun in all

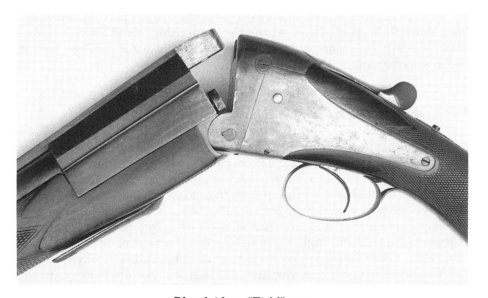

Bland 4 bore "Field" gun

bores up to a massive 4 bore.

In the 1880's the firm opened premises in Liverpool at 62 South Castle Street and at this time they advertised their "Keeper's Gun" at 6 Guineas and a "Wildfowler's Gun", a central-fire breechloader in 4 bore with nickel plated furniture, Silver's recoil pad and a weight of 17 lbs., for the sum of 21 Guineas!

The firm offered nickel plated full-choked "Cripple Stoppers" at 8 guineas and made a speciality of breech loading punt guns and harpoon guns.

In 1900 the firm had to move the London premises to 2 William IV Street and four years later T. Clifford Bland the only son of Thomas Bland Jr., became the third generation to join the firm after leaving Harrow.

It was T. Clifford Bland who concentrated on the wildfowling side of the business, so much so, that the name of Bland became synonymous with wildfowling guns.

The changed circumstances following the first war eventually saw the Birmingham end of the business closed and in 1919 the firm moved from No. 2 to No's. 4-5 William IV Street.

Throughout the inter war years Bland continued to offer wildfowling guns which included the "Magnum" ejector, a 3" 12 bore and an extremely attractive 3" 12 bore A&D actioned gun with side panels which sold as the "Greylag".

In 1943, T. Clifford Bland died and the business was continued under the direction of Mr. W. Caseley. A particular favourite amongst wildfowlers was the Bland "Brent" which was introduced in 1948 by Mr. Caseley.

A non-ejector, like the "Greylag", the "Brent" was chambered for the 3" 12 bore cartridge and with pistol grip it weighed in at 7 1/2 lbs.

In 1973 the firm moved once again, this time to their present address in New Row, St. Martin's Lane. At the time of writing Bland have ceased to trade and only the future will tell if with over a century of tradition behind them, the company might be again actively in business.

FREDERICK BEESLEY

A friend of mine, and noted fellow author, John Brindle of Canada, asked me some years ago to write about Frederick Beesley. From the other side of the world, Port Elizabeth in South Africa, John Shinn in a rather more pointed, more recent letter also told me to produce something on Frederick Beesley, who was, according to both John's, "without doubt the most superb gunsmith, gunmaker and inventor of all time". This is qualified by the statement "in the best English gun field". This is quite a claim and we have to do quite a bit of work to justify such an uncompromising eulogy.

The first thing is to see whether or not these views are held by anyone else, and what credibility they have. We could take as an authority, Sir

Gerald Burrard, author of *The Modern Shotgun*. He states that "Mr F Beesley was one of the most fertile inventors the gun trade has known." So, let us first of all look at the inventions of Beesley, bearing in mind that we can only assess those which have been published. It is not unlikely that this man could have invented other mechanisms not subsequently attributed to him — and this must be borne in mind. We go back to 1880 for the first patent ascribed to F Beesley. This deals with self-cocking hammerless guns and is perhaps one of, if not the most important patent of the 21 he took out. The patent of 1880 deals with a number of systems for cocking the internal hammers of a "hammerless" shotgun when the gun is opened. At least six variations on the basic theme are included in the patent, but fundamentally Beesley had invented what was to become one of the most famous double shotgun actions of all time, the mechanism that we to-day know as the Purdey action.

In any assessment of a shotgun lock there are a number of factors to be considered. These factors would include ease of cocking, speed, efficiency and safety. Additional points might be ease of manufacture and cost. The last two are not of vital importance when we are considering a "best" gun of whatever country of origin. On the basic points the Purdey action scores highly. It has been slightly altered and modified during the years it has been employed by Purdey, but fundamentally the design is now nearly 100 years old and a tribute to the inventor, Beesley, and to the craftsmen, who over the decades have translated his ideas into what still remains the most consistently sought after sporting shotgun in the world.

The story of Frederick Beesley starts with his apprenticeship at the age of 15 to the old established firm of Moore & Grey in Old Bond Street, in the

Beesley "Best" sidelock

heart of London's gun quarter. Here he would have been working with craftsmen who had worked with the Mantons, the two men, who, probably more than anyone else, were to establish the standards that raised the London trade to such enviable heights. He moved from one maker to another before he found himself at James Purdey. It was here that he must have worked on the lock mechanism that was to become the famous Purdey action. Beesley set up on his own at 22 Queen Street, Edgeware Road, London in 1879. It was from this address that he wrote to James Purdey on the 18th of December 1879, offering his invention of a hammerless gun, "which I believe to be equal to, if not superior to anything of its kind yet produced". Brave words indeed. Words which were, however, to be fully justified even after the passing of more than a century!

The value of the Beesley action, which incorporated the means of compressing the mainsprings when the gun was closed, was quickly realised by Purdey. One of the additional benefits of Beesley's invention was that the mainsprings were always "at rest" when the barrels were dismantled from the gun and the gun in its case. Looking back at the agreement signed between Beesley and Purdey it is of interest to see that Purdey agreed to pay "Five shillings for every gun made by the said James Purdey until the number made shall have amounted to two hundred, whereupon such Royalty shall cease". The last payment was made on the 16th November 1880 and Purdey then had full control of the patent and protection for fourteen years.

Not all of Beesley's ideas were so long lived. I doubt if some ever got on to the work bench. Three years after his "Purdey" lock, Beesley patented a mechanism for the recoil cocking of hammerless guns. I have yet to see an example of this. In the same year further patents were taken out with Woodward for self-cocking guns and in 1884 Beesley collaborated with E. Harrison (of Cogswell & Harrison) to patent a safety device. In 1886 Beesley moved on to the slightly different world of the A & D type action, where he patented cocking devices for boxlock guns. In 1889 came the first of many ejector systems and in 1895 the first of five single-trigger mechanisms. After initial difficulties the business prospered and Beesley moved, first of all, to 85 Edgeware Road in 1879 and then to 3 St. James's Street in 1893 and to No. 2 in 1900. They remained at this address until the outbreak of W. W. II when the firm became part of Atkin, Grant & Lang.

We have, however, to return to the year 1913 which saw a period of considerable activity on the part of the firm, no less than five patents having been obtained for over-and-under guns. The last patent I have been able to find of Beesley's is yet another for an over -and-under taken out in 1914. I had to wait some time before I was able to see and handle a Beesley O/U shotgun. This happened at the 1980 Game Fair where a lady, appropriately named Diana brought along a cased pair of Beesley O/U shotguns for me to see. I was entranced and later was allowed to have the guns at home for examination and photography. The guns were Beesley's "Shotover" and they dated from the early 1920's. Comment on Beesley's O/U gun by contemporaries included such statements as, "It is a marvel of ingenuity".

With the ingenuity came the penalty of complexity and, as is common with thoroughbreds, the guns were of a temperamental nature. Few appear to have been made but those I have seen were quite magnificent. The Beesley could not have been made by machinery, it could not have been mass produced and the problems of striker blows, extractor/ejector mechanisms, solved with such ingenuity by Beesley have, to-day, easier solutions well adapted to factory production. The Beesley "Shotover" was, I suppose, a casualty of the First World War, since the customers for whom it was intended had left for the battlefields of Flanders, and few returned.

STEPHEN GRANT

Without doubt one of the most famous names in the London gun trade is that of Stephen Grant. His background lacks just one thing, he never worked for James Purdey, unlike so many other famous London gunmakers of the late Victorian and Edwardian period!

However, after he had completed his apprenticeship with William Kavanagh of Dublin, he came to London where he worked for Charles Lancaster, subsequently moving to Boss & Co., where he became the Managing Partner. In 1867 Grant set up on his own at 67a James's Street, in the heart of the London gun quarter and his gun case labels from this period bear the legend, "Late Managing Partner in the Firm of Boss & Co." Later labels in the post 1889 period have added "& Sons" and these later labels now proudly bear Appointments to H.M. The Queen, H.I.M. The Emperor of Russia, The King of Spain and the Prince of Wales. The relationship with Boss is no longer mentioned!

The aftermath of the first World War saw a move to 7 Bury Street, St. James's which was followed in 1925 by an amalgamation with the old established firm of Joseph Lang. Then, in the "hungry thirties" Grant & Lang were joined by Hussey, Atkin, Lancaster, Beesley, Hellis and Watson Bros., until by 1960 the firm was trading as Atkin, Grant & Lang.

It was the practice of the firm to continue to build "Best" guns under the names of the constituent companies so that the name of Grant was to be found on best side lock hammerless ejector guns, many of them fitted with sidelever opening for which Grant had become renowned. In my opinion Grant had built the best looking breech loading hammer guns made distinctive with the side lever curving gracefully around the external right hand hammer. Lang built Over and Under guns, best quality box locks and sidelocks and Watson Bros., specialised in small bore guns. The fact that the names of many of these famous firms were retained and guns were built in the style and manner associated with these famous names was due, in no small measure to the business philosophy of the man who welded together these gunmakers into a viable whole, the late Mr. W. R. H. Robson.

Further changes had to take place after W.W. II and in 1971 the firm became Churchill, Atkin, Grant & Lang, moving in 1976 to 61 Pall Mall. In 1980 the firm ceased to trade and Atkin, Grant & Lang were acquired by new proprietors. Alive to the need to adapt to rapidly changing conditions, the London gun trade showed itself to be remarkably resilient and as many of the craftsmen had already moved out of the centre of London it was decided that the vast expense of a prestigious West End address could no longer be justified and the operations centre of the company was moved out into Hertfordshire, north of London, not far from Welwyn Garden City. The registered office is in Lincoln's Inn Fields which is the address the present Trade Label bears and it is also the address on the top rib of this Grant gun. The traditions and high standards of the past are jealously guarded and even a cursory glance at the illustrations of this Grant gun cannot help but convey something of the extremely high quality of the workmanship built into every part of this gun.

The photographs, no matter how good, cannot replace having the gun in your very own hands. First of all you have to undo the canvas case, amply reinforced with leather which protects the leather gun case itself. Here, the slim hide motor case not only looks good, but it also smells good as well! Even the lock has the sound of quality when you release the catch, then as you open the lid, the gun itself is revealed, above it the trade label, and in the case, lined with the finest quality red baize you will discover, a pair of snap caps, an oil bottle, cleaning rods and in a leather case, a brush, jag and mop to fit the rods. In a matching case is a full set of regulated springs, finished to the

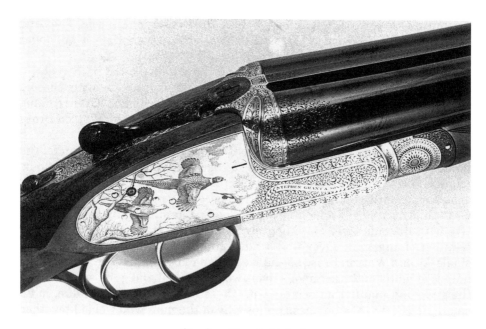

Stephen Grant sidelock

highest standards against the day when perhaps a spring breaks, a very unlikely event indeed.

The gun, No. 24016 is a double twenty bore sidelock with 28" barrels chambered for the 2" 20 bore cartridge. As you can see, the locks, action etc., are in silver finish which allows the superb engraving to be seen and appreciated to best advantage. The engraving is by one of the foremost British engravers, A. M. Brown and is a true delight! The stock has fine colour and figure with a superb satin finish most pleasing to the touch. The chequering, even under the most critical examination cannot be faulted. The locks are conventional and have the added protection of intercepting sears. The ejector work is Southgate's, Grant's having used this system since 1905. The work on the fences is splendid and traditionalists will be delighted to see that they are Grant's "Fluted Fences" and that the bar has double beads.

The cost of such magnificence is high, £22,000 (plus VAT) and delivery would be about two to three years. The customer has a choice of engraving, barrel length, double or single triggers, easy opening, self opening and the quality of the work is beyond reproach. The gun can stand against any of its predecessors and it is a credit to the name Stephen Grant and to the London Gun Trade of to-day.

CHARLES HELLIS & SONS

The gun illustrated captured my attention when I saw it at the Churchill, Atkin, Grant & Lang "open day" in Birmingham. I had not seen this type of treatment on an Anson & Deeley type boxlock gun before. I thought that I had at one time or another encountered most of the ways that the timeless A & D action could be styled. Styled is, I think, the only word that could be used in this context since I am still slightly shy of using the American "crafted".

If we think about it the basic A & D is a box-like action, and the simple but effective limbs of the action are best so accommodated. Just to jog the odd memory this action dates back to 1875. Today, it is still being built, in all sorts of variants and in many countries other than the one of its birth; these nowadays are neither replicas nor reproductions but repetitions of a soundly-designed and truly great shotgun action. Within the confines of the mechanism and excluding the numerous "improved" A & D type actions which have appeared over the years it might at first be thought that there is very little that can be done to make one A & D actioned gun different from another.

Let us have a look at what can be altered; and, of course, what cannot — the barrels, two in number and side-by-side, top lever operation, and a pretty well defined position for the triggers and guard relative to the action body. So, what is left? Well, first of all there is the type of fence. The fences fitted to the Hellis gun are, in fact, amongst the commonest employed. They are known as Webley pattern fences and they are encountered on guns of high quality like the Hellis, as well as of the lowest quality. They are quite simple

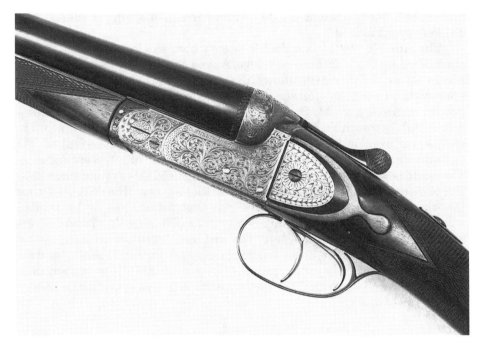

Charles Hellis boxlock

and straightforward, and this pattern of fence was also to be found on sidelocks especially when not jointed up to the action fence. (An alternative type of fence was known as the "ball fence", with a quite distinct ball shape, and when this was a "flattened Ball" one could describe it as a "Purdey pattern" fence.)

Next we come to the action body itself. This could be quite square in shape with flat sides and a quite abrupt shoulder behind the fences. Any change would be to round the body as much as possible without causing what we might call "internal problems" but in such a case it was almost essential that the shape of the hand of the stock be also changed to suit the rounded action. In the Hellis gun the action sides are quite flat and it could well have been finished with a side panel and drop point. An alternative would be for the side panel to be sunk and decorated. This was quite common practice on best A & D guns in the years following the turn of the century. What is unusual about the Hellis is the fact that the sunk panels have inlet metal plates. Such plates are sometimes encountered. They do not have anything to do with the mechanism but are there as decoration. In the Hellis these sunken metal sideplates are slightly inset into the back of the action. The sideplates are also provided with a quite distinct border and a well defined drop point. The panels are well engraved and the whole presents quite a challenging appearance which is unique in my experience. One way of treating the back of the action body is to have what was known in the

Birmingham trade as a "fancy back", the back of the action body having scroll work which, of course, requires careful fitting of the stock. The Hellis gun takes its unusual appearance from the metal side plates and is, I think you will agree, one way of making an A & D gun that is different from the competition.

When I first wrote about the Hellis shotgun I had seen at the "Open Day" in Birmingham in 1979 I knew little about the firm and lacked a catalogue which would have provided much needed details of the range of guns the firm made. However, I knew that they had been founded in 1894 at 21 Shrewsbury Road, London. In literature published by the company they date their foundation back to 1884 but this is not borne out by the London directories! The firm moved to 119 Edgeware Road in 1897. The founder died in 1905 and the eldest son, who continued the business died in 1932. In 1936 they moved to 121 Edgeware Road. The business was continued by the two following generations until it was acquired by Henry Atkin in 1956. The firm was also well known for its cartridges and it had an important business in second-hand guns.

The Hellis gun which started me off on the research into the history of its maker is a very good example of the best work of the smaller independent London maker and from a catalogue sent to me by a reader, following the publication of my article on the gun, we now know that it was described by the maker as their "Windsor". In the years between the two wars Hellis sold this model at £78 and their "Best" gun, a sidelock which they called the "Mark Over" was more expensive at £113. At the top of the range was the Hellis "Premier" sidelock but this does not appear to have been available in the years just after the last war.

A photograph of the Edgeware Road shop has survived and it looks exactly the sort of shop where you and I could have very happily spent many an afternoon looking through the stock! The proprietor is standing in the doorway, complete with his white apron and from the shop front we learn that he is "A Practical Gunsmith" and a "Cartridge Loading Expert." We can see that he is a keen business man since the shop windows display the following legends, "Second Hand Guns Bought For Cash or Taken in Exchange" and "Guns Lent on Hire With the Option of Purchase". If it were not for the evidence we have of the excellence of the Hellis guns one might be tempted to think that he was merely a dealer, but we know better, Hellis guns were of high quality and have withstood the relentless test of time!

JEFFERY — GUNMAKERS

An ideal place to start the history of any important firm of gunmakers is with the indentures, the sealed agreement which bound the gunmaker, when an apprentice, to his master. To find such papers after the passage of a century or more is unusual and in the case of William Jackman Jeffery we know little more than the year of his birth, 1857. One other thing we know is that there is always some confusion between the various firms by the name of Jeffery who were active in the 19th century and also between W J Jeffery and the well known firm of Jefferies of Norwich, later of Birmingham.

Gunmakers named Jeffery had businesses in Poole, Plymouth, Lyming-

W. J. Jeffery ad

ton, Dorchester and Farnham, all around the mid 19th century. One cannot help but wonder whether William J Jeffery, later to found his own business in London, had any connection with these 'country' makers. What we do know is that by the time he was 28, William had taken out a patent, No 124335 for a device to allow for the internal inspection of gun barrels, several examples of which have survived. His address at this time is given as 42, Great Castle Street, London. The only gunmakers in Great Castle Street in the second half of the 19th century were John Pryse at No 9 and W & C Scott at No 10. In 1885 No 42 was occupied by Joseph Hawkins who was a Corn Dealer. Perhaps Mrs Hawkins took in lodgers and this is where young William stayed during his early years in the big city?

A second patent was taken out jointly with E Harrison in 1886. This was for a vernier and wind gauge sight adjuster. We know where William was living and the joint patent provides a clue as to where he might have been working. E Harrison was the Harrison of the firm of Cogswell & Harrison and since William is described as a gun salesman in the patent, it is not unreasonable to assume that he was working for C & H as a salesman! A second patent in the same year was taken out for a sight protector and it wasn't until 1897 that William obtained a further patent for a sight adjuster; and this time his address is given as 60 Queen Victoria Street. We know that by 1888 W J Jeffery was in business at this address; there is mention that the business was founded at an earlier date, although this is not confirmed by the London Directories.

In 1890 the firm became Jeffery & Davies. In the following year the style was altered to W J Jeffery & Company and further premises were acquired at 13 King Street. In 1910 the firm had showrooms at 13 King Street, St James's and at 60 Queen Victoria Street, which, we are informed, was one minute's walk from the Bank of England! In addition the firm offered gun fitting at the South London Shooting Grounds and they had won prizes for sporting rifles at the Bisley Meetings. At the turn of the century they occupied workshops at No 1, Rose & Crown Yard, St James's.

The range of guns and rifles offered at what many would say was the Golden Age of Shooting was quite remarkable. Their 'Best' London sidelock was £55 and their 1905 Model sidelock was £30. The 'Best' A & D gun could be had for £20 and for an extra £2 the gun could be fitted with Baker's single-trigger mechanism. The No 4 A & D gun in 12 bore only was £5-10, black powder proof (Nitro proof cost a few shillings extra), and the firm offered a further range of A & D guns which could be had with either 2 3/4" or 3" chambers for pigeon and wildfowl. Similar guns were offered as hammer guns with top lever action and the lowest priced hammer gun was the Model No 5, a plain gun with Greener cross bolt at £4. Single barrel hammer guns were available as were American 'machine made' single hammer guns.

For large game the company had a range of Ball & Shot 'Cape' guns, the right barrel chambered for either 12 or 16 bore shot cartridges and the left for the .577/.450 Martini. There is little doubt that the firm was best known for its extremely comprehensive range of double rifles, the most impressive of which was the truly magnificent Jeffery double .600 bore. The rifle and cartridge was introduced by Jeffery in 1903 as a smokeless powder alternative to the massive 4 and 8 bore black powder rifles. The first of the .600 bores was actually built in 1901 and it was regulated for a charge of 120 grains of cordite and a 900 grain bullet; this monster weighed in at 12lb. Jeffery claimed that these rifles had a muzzle energy of 8,700 ft lb against the 7,000 ft lb of a 4 bore burning 14 drams of black powder. Jeffery advised the use of their under lever, push forward snap action ejector double rifle with 24" barrels. In 1910, made in best quality with doll's head extension, the .600 double rifle cost £65. A range of Mauser, Mannlicher and Mannlicher-Schonauer sporting bolt action rifles was also available in various grades as was a range of single shot rifles built on the Farquharson type falling block action. These very desirable rifles could be had in all calibres from .22 rimfire in the 1906 Model up to .600 in the 1904 Model.

Interest was maintained in sights by the company and in 1900 they obtained a patent for a vertical post graticule for telescopic sights instead of the then fashionable 'cross hairs'. The last patent was for an aperture back sight attached to the breech bolt of the Mauser action and the Jeffery 'Patent Sight Peep' could be fitted to the Model 1908 Mauser rifle for 21 shillings. The founder, William Jackman Jeffery, died in March 1909 and the direction of the company's affairs was taken over by his brother Charles.

The effect on the company of the First World War can be seen by the closure of the King Street premises and those at Rose & Crown Yard. In 1920, Charles Jeffery died and the direction of the company was entrusted to his nephew, Pierce Jeffery. Seven years later the company moved from Queen Victoria Street to 9 Golden Square, Regent Street, near Piccadilly Circus. By this time the price of the best sidelock had risen to £100 and an interesting 'Best' A & D ejector gun, the Model No 5 was now £40. The range of guns and rifles on offer had not diminished, and the .600 Cordite Express was still being built on the under lever, push forward action. The range of cartridges associated with the name of Jeffery includes the following: .255 Rook, .280, .333 Flanged Nitro Express, .333 Rimless, .400 Jeffery, the .404 Jeffery, .450 No 2 Nitro and the .475 No 2 Nitro and, of course, the .600.

The effects of the Second World War reduced the business available for the company and their 1949 catalogue reflected the change in fortunes, not only of the company but also of the country. On offer were three A & D actioned guns, Models No 1, No 2 and No 3. The top of the range was the No 1 at £105 and the firm made some .404 magazine rifles on the P.14 Enfield action at £75. In 1955 a move was made to No 5b Pall Mall and their catalogue of that year now included a sidelock as well as the three A & D action guns. Bolt action magazine rifles were still being built on the P.14 action and were now available in a wider range of calibres, 275, .30-'06 and .404 Magnum. The effects of inflation were now noticeable in that the catalogue no longer contained prices; these were now listed on a separate sheet. The price of the

Best sidelock, available to order only, had risen to £250 and the No 1 A & D ejector was £102. The .404 bolt action magazine rifle was offered at £90.

The firm of Jeffery was saved from possible extinction by the purchase of the company by Holland & Holland in 1960. Jeffery continued to be listed in the directories under their own name but they now shared the same address as Holland & Holland. One cannot help but wonder what the future may hold. A single shot falling block rifle bearing the Jeffery name may again feature in some future catalogue or perhaps a boxlock with the distinctive Jeffery 'Fancy Back'. The shade of William Jackman Jeffery would rather like that.

In Holland & Holland's archives are two old scrapbooks pertaining to Jeffery's business in the early part of this century. One contains cuttings of the many advertisements placed by Jeffery's predominantly in The Field and Shooting Times, but also in such long-deceased publications as the Indian Army List, Colonial Office List, Fighting Forces and the West African Review. They advertise Jeffrey's own sporting guns, rifles and cartridges, and occasionally a range of second-hand guns in stock at the time. The latter includes other makers as well as Jeffrey, and it is interesting to note that a second-hand Holland 12-bore hammerless ejector could be had for as little as £35 in 1931.

The second volume, marked "Testimonials and Photographs of Game Secured with Jeffrey Rifles", contains as may be expected letters from satisfied customers, with gruesome proof of the writers' prowess. Dating mainly from the late 1920s and early 1930s, the letters bear witness to the company's truly international clientele, although of course the majority were colonial administrators and tea and rubber planters of British nationality. They come from countries which a school boy or girl, fifty years later, would hardly recognise: Nyasaland, Tanganyika Territory, Northern and Southern Rhodesia, Kenya Colony, the Belgian Congo, Portuguese East Africa; Siam, Indo-China, The Dutch East Indies, Malay State and Ceylon. Jeffrey's had customers too in India, Canada, the USA, Brazil, South Africa and Australia. The faded photographs, of slaughtered tigers, lions and elephants, bears and bison, sometimes with proud riflemen in pith helmet and African or Indian bearer, can't be reproduced here. However, they certainly are a testimonial to the efficacy of the Jeffrey range of rifles!

JOSEPH NEEDHAM

The ejector, along with the single trigger are probably the most complex parts of the modern sporting shotgun. They are the most difficult to describe how they work and are the most difficult to put right when they go wrong.

I have for this reason never dealt with the subject of ejectors until now and intend to leave the subject of single triggers for quite a while longer!

The reason why I have not written about ejectors is that I have been waiting for an example of the earliest type of ejector to be made available to me.

This happened at the 1988 Game Fair, the "Mud Bath" at Floors Castle in Scotland where torrential rain on clay soil nearly brought disaster as those who were there will remember. An important happening, for me at least, was the visit of Chris Wynne with a hammerless Greener ejector gun. Game Fairs are not the place to take guns apart and at Floors one could not only have lost the screws but the entire gun as well!

Chris very kindly arranged for me to have the gun on loan and gave permission for me to take it apart and also take some photographs.

The Greener gun No. 46816 was the No. 3 gun and it was fitted with the Greener "Rational" stock. What was of interest was that this gun was an ejector and that the mechanism was based on a Joseph Needham patent. The problem was, which one? The gun was not like any of the Needham patent ejectors of which I had seen illustrations. It did share an under lever operating mechanism but the Greener was a side lock whereas the other Needham ejectors had trigger plate actions. This is not perhaps a true description of the action, I think I would like to call the lockwork a trigger box mechanism. It shares with the Gibbs & Pitt that peculiar "Victorian" look, it looks as though it was designed by a Great Western Railway engineer rather than a gunmaker!

Exactly where this Greener fits into the scheme of things I have yet to discover. It shares with the Needham the under lever which cocks the mechanism and it also has the Needham ejector.

A "true" Needham ejector gun is shown in my book, *Shotguns and Gunsmiths* page 30, this was taken from *The Sporting Mirror* of 1882. A more rounded version of the Needham then appeared. During this time a number of patents were taken out by Needham, one of which, that of 1874, No. 1205 not only protected the first barrel cocked hammerless action (earlier hammerless guns had been cocked by lever, like the Murcott) but the same patent also protected what was the first of the selective ejector mechanisms.

The Needham family were quite prolific and some years ago I had the pleasure of meeting a descendant who had spent a lot of time tracing the "family tree". He was very interested in the gun making activities of many of the members of the family and somewhat sad when I told him how much a double Needham needle fire shotgun would cost!

The Needham "Needle Gun" is remarkable for several reasons. It was the first hammerless sporting shotgun to enjoy any measure of popular acceptance and it was the only sporting shotgun which employed a special cartridge in competition to the central-fire paper tubed cartridge which was to become universally accepted. It had a further distinction in that, contrary to, for example, French practice, it was one of the few British shotguns which had non-pivoting barrels. To add to this list of "Firsts" it was also one of only two double barrelled British breech loading shotguns, the other being the Bacon. Although this Needham shotgun, made under license by the famous

Needham hammer gun

firm of John Rigby of Dublin, was in fact a blind alley, those who used it during the second half of the 19th century spoke very highly of its virtues. It was possible, (and I have done it!) to make the cartridges yourself and since the cartridges were largely self-consuming, one did not need to eject the fired case although the patent records refer to a Provisions Specification in the name of Joseph Needham for an extractor to remove the remnants of the case. The Rigby made Needham needle guns were of the highest quality and it is very possibly that the success they enjoyed for a brief period was, in no small measure, due to the excellence of manufacture.

The inventor of the barrel cocking and ejector gun patented in 1874 was Joseph Needham of the firm of Joseph & William Needham of Piccadilly, London. The family started in Birmingham as gunmakers, then moved to London and by 1843 are established at 26 Piccadilly as William Needham and by 1851 as William & Joseph Needham. The style becomes Joseph Needham & Co in 1854 and the firm was acquired by Greener in 1874 although it continued to trade as Joseph V. Needham from Damascus Works, Loveday Street under the Needham name.

The Needham ejector gun has an importance which, in the past, was probably overlooked. With the benefit of hindsight we can now see that this gun was not only a barrel cocking hammerless design utilising the longest lever available to cock the mechanism, the barrels, but, in the search for perfection in the sporting shotgun, Needham invented a working ejector mechanism which threw the fired case clear of the gun when it was opened but left the unfired cartridge in the gun, although slightly withdrawn to permit its removal by hand if necessary. The mechanism is somewhat complicated and the gun requires some manipulation to remove and re-install the barrels but it was on this foundation that the later simplified ejector guns were built and which brought the British sporting shotgun to its peak of enviable perfection!

JAMES PURDEY & SONS

The first Purdey of whom there is any record worked in the Minories, the centre of the London gun trade since the reign of Elizabeth I. His son worked for several gunmakers before joining, in about 1803, Joe Manton as a gunstocker. Purdey then left Manton to work for Forsyth, the inventor of the percussion principle, who started a company to make guns with Forsyth patent locks in 1808. Purdey was employed by the Forsyth Patent Gun Company of 10 Piccadilly, as a stocker and lock-filer. In 1814 James Purdey set up in business for himself and in 1826 he took over the premises of his former master, Joe Manton, and set about making guns which were to enhance the reputation of London as a centre of gunmaking, a reputation already established by Manton.

Even the early Purdey percussion guns show a distinct style of their own which was in no small way to determine the fashion for sporting guns and which still exerts a very strong influence.

The founder died in 1863 and his son carried on the business until 1909. The "house style" was restrained and totally respectable. It is indeed rare to find a flamboyant Purdey, but in this sober magnificence you will not find the smallest flaw in even the smallest screw. Superlative workmanship was not enough; to reach and maintain these heights technical innovation was also required. This was achieved by the introduction of the famous Purdey bolt which has securely fastened the barrels of countless shotguns to the action and is still the most widely used system for side-by-side shotguns to this day.

Purdey had built flint guns, percussion guns, pin and centre-fire hammer guns and in 1880 there appeared the Purdey with the famous Beesley self-opening action. Frederick Beesley is a somewhat neglected figure, but his invention, patented in 1880 was to secure the position of the firm of Purdey even more firmly. The Purdey action is now over a century old, a

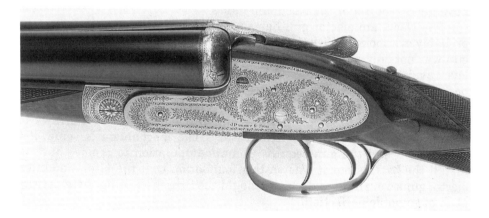

James Purdey & Sons sidelock

remarkable achievement by any standards, particularly when it is enhanced by the fact that catalogues which show guns made in other countries refer again and again to the "Purdey system". This is not all, for Purdey established the traditional style and finish which has become the pattern for the side-by-side double sporting sidelock shotgun.

There are, of course, all sorts of odd stories which could be told, but one odd minor point is the use of the term "forepart" by the House of Purdey, instead of fore-end.

The firm moved to the premises which they at present occupy in South Audley Street in 1881. One hundred years later I spent a truly delightful day in the company of the late Harry Lawrence, O.B.E., who, as the son of the factory manager, Ernest Lawrence had started his apprenticeship in the factory in 1914, eventually rising to the position of a director of the company.

It was with Harry Lawrence that I was given a privileged peep behind the scenes, rather like being allowed into the workroom of a "bespoke" tailor where some of the secrets of his craft are revealed. There can be seen the expensive suit covered in chalk marks and with the lining hanging out!

It all started when I wrote about the British over-and-under shotgun. I had stated in the first article in a series on O/U shotguns (Shooting Times Feb. 5-11, 1981) that Woodward was bought by Purdey in 1949 and that Purdey ceased to make their own O/U and made the Woodward instead. This statement was criticised by one man with whom I would not cross swords, Harry Lawrence, who, without intending any disrespect to the directors of this famous company, is to me, at least, "Mr Purdey".

I was told that the true facts of the situation were that in 1947 Mr Woodward approached Mr Tom Purdey and offered to sell him his business. No offer could be made on the trading results which were then available and Mr Woodward asked Tom Purdey, then the senior member of the family, whether he would build the Woodward O/U gun in the future. This was agreed with the proviso that the Woodward side-by-side would NOT be built by Purdeys. The tooling and templates were collected from the premises of Woodward in March 1948 and the first pair of O/U Woodward guns made by Purdey were 16-bore, subsequently the design of the original Woodward was modified quite considerably.

In defence of what I wrote, I quote a Purdey catalogue in which it is stated that "Purdey have acquired the world-famous business of James Woodward, makers of the Woodward O/U gun which has proved so successful that it may be considered the finest O/U gun that has ever been built by craftsmen in this country or where-ever best guns are built by hand!" The comment continues by stating that "Mr Purdey had decided to build his over-and-under guns in the future on the Woodward principle in Purdey's factory in London by Purdey craftsmen".

That there is a considerable amount of the Woodward gun in the Purdey O/U of today cannot be denied but the building of a gun by traditional means is such that each one is individual; it is unlike those made before and those that will be made in the future. Today it is difficult to compare a hand-made gun with anything else, the nearest thing would be a sculpture in wood and metal. It is not an assembly of machine-made interchangeable components. For one thing, there are no engineering drawings, just the tooling and some metal templates and a lot of skill.

I was met at Purdey's by Harry Lawrence and then introduced by him to Richard Beaumont, Chairman of Directors and to Nigel Beaumont who had brought a Purdey O/U "in the white" from the factory. This means that the gun lacked stock and fore-end, "slave" screws were in use and the gun was neither finished nor engraved. The only marks were those impressed by the Proof House.

Before we have a look at the Purdey "in the white", let us consider a little bit of past history on the Purdey O/U. We have to go back to 1924 when Mr Ernest Lawrence Sr., then works manager at the old factory, was approached by Atholl Purdey to build an O/U gun. Harry Lawrence was then in the factory and the making of the Purdey O/U which drew on the ideas of E. C. Green was entrusted to him with the instructions that this gun must be the "strongest O/U made".

This gun, the first O/U Purdey, had six grips, and not many were made. It was strong, but with this strength came the penalty of weight and in the years before the War, when the direction of the company was in the hands of Mr Tom Purdey, instructions were issued to lighten the gun by eliminating two of the six grips and the top extension. This, the second Purdey O/U, can be regarded as the "four-grip" Purdey and it was made in small numbers until 1939 when Purdey's unique talents were put to the far more serious work of winning a war.

After the War the offer by Woodward was accepted as I have mentioned and three later types of Purdey O/U can be said to have evolved: The Woodward gun made by Purdey, the Purdey-Woodward and today's Purdey O/U built by Purdey in their own factory. More of the last gun is now made by Purdey than ever before. Due to changes in the gun trade Purdey now make their own locks, and the O/U can be offered in .410, 28, 20, 16 and 12-bore.

Now it is time to examine the Purdey O/U "in the white". Let us take first the action body with the left-hand lock removed. We can see the inside of the right hand lock, the tumbler, the bridle, back action mainspring and the sear spring. Above on the tang of the action is the safety. To understand the very considerable work which has to be done to make an O/U gun of this sort we next take a look inside the bar of the action. The superimposed firing pins can be seen, also the two locking bolts. You can also see the camming surfaces on the sides of the wall of the action and the recesses on the top of the wall and inside which interlock with the intricate work which is very evident at the breech end of the barrel. Here the extractors have been removed, but the bites for the bolts can be seen and the undercut mating surfaces for the interlock between breech and action body.

The fore-end iron is attached to the barrel (but not the fore-end) and the "wings" on each side of the barrel can be seen. This feature prevents the ingress of water into the areas of the ejector mechanism (not fitted) and also helps to prevent damage to the wood of the fore-end. A solid rib is fitted to these barrels since ventilated ribs can be dented. They will be provided if requested.

In addition the barrels can be made "ribless", i.e. with the side ribs removed. If you have to know the price, you can't afford one!

If you can afford one then the current waiting list is two and a half to three years. If you look upon the Purdey O/U merely as a GUN it is too expensive and not for you anyway; it can be justified on the basis of an INVESTMENT. It should be regarded for what it is, and for what a gun of this type has always been, a work of art. Art and craft allied to utility and beauty make each finished gun something unique. To attempt to place an economic cost on skilled craftsmanship is extremely difficult and to many the end result is difficult to justify. You may not be able to own a Best gun, but I am thankful that I live in a society where the ultimate in perfection is still realizable, since in the last analysis it forms the basis for comparison.

Now I would like to make a plea for any information of the whereabouts of existing Purdey over-and-under guns with details of their construction. This is for a projected book on the British O/U shotgun on which I have been working for several years. Few O/U shotguns were made by the British guntrade since none were suitable for mass production. There are few available in this country and if those of you with a Purdey O/U abroad (or indeed any British made O/U) can let me have details and photographs for my records I would be greatly obliged. If we do not now record such information as is available I greatly fear that it could well be lost. All information, without exception, will be kept in strict confidence.

The firm of Purdey do occupy a unique place in the history of the sporting shotgun and their appointment as gunmakers to H.M. Queen Elizabeth II, to H.R.H. The Duke of Edinburgh and H.R.H. The Prince of Wales, is I feel a more than adequate testimony to the excellence of the guns which bear the name of Purdey and to those traditions of British gunmaking which they have done so much to enhance and maintain.

JOHN RIGBY

A very fine photograph of a Rigby underlever hammer gun taken by Mr R Chesmore of Harrogate has been lying in my "In" tray for some time looking at me with what can only be described as a measure of reproach. The photograph is exceptionally good, since not only does it show the Rigby gun to advantage but because of the angle from which it is taken the photograph is lent a certain impact. Also seen in the original is the style of lettering used by Rigby which became almost a trade mark with the firm. Talking of trade marks Rigby was one of the few firms with one — addorsed Rs or, put more plainly, "Rs" back-to-back!

If we turn for a moment from the gun to the firm whose name it bears the first thing which strikes us is the date of foundation, 1735, long before even percussion guns were thought of.

Surprisingly, the firm flourished in Dublin until it was sold in 1892 to the firm of Truelock and Harris. As an aside, I have often thought what a truly splendid name for a gunmaker "Truelock" is. One just couldn't go wrong with a name like that!

As one might expect, the Dublin end of the firm was renowned for the excellence of its duelling pistols and some of the finest examples of this type of weapon bear the name Rigby. Equally distinctive were the damascus barrels used by the firm on pistols, guns and rifles. These were more deeply etched so that the harder metal was brought into relief and to the knowledgeable such barrels needed no name on the top rib — they were Rigby barrels.

There was another quite distinctive feature of the Rigby, the percussion locks fitted to the Rigby muzzle loaders, the additional notch or third bent to let the cock be raised slightly above the percussion cap to allow the weapon to be safely carried and yet ensure that the cap could not be dislodged from the nipple.

John Rigby & Co., opened their London shop at 72 St. James's Street, in 1866 under the management of John Rigby. In 1860 John Rigby devised a method of forming cartridge cases from coiled sheet brass. Rigby Match Rifles were used with great effect in the great rifle competitions in the second half of the 19th century, not only by the "gentry" but also by members of the firm!

The London end of the business had, from 1866, a most prestigious address at St James's Street W1, where they remained until 1955. In the early years at the London address John Rigby senior spent most of his time as Superintendent of the Royal Small Arms Factory at Enfield, Middlesex. During this period the London business was managed by his son Ernest John Rigby who had gained valuable experience in the Birmingham Small Arms factory, and in addition, had followed in his father's footsteps by winning a number of prizes at competitive shooting at the Bisley meeting.

The Rigbys were well known to a small select group as builders of extremely fine target rifles and also for the manufacture of high quality sporting shotguns. It is for their work in connection with the manufacture of sporting rifles, both double and magazine, that the firm is perhaps best known. For example, they introduced the first .450 calibre cordite rifle and this was followed by the Rigby .470 and the famous Rigby .416 for the big game magazine rifles.

Rigby made rifles of .577 calibre firing 100 grains of cordite behind a 750 grain bullet. Even with a rifle weighing 14 lb this is quite a combination for anyone to handle, and in the 1930s Rigby offered their .470 in a best quality sidelock for £147. May I make it quite clear that the price was £147 even in 1930!

John Rigby sidelock

The Rigby shotgun of Mr Hane's is earlier than 1930 and probably dates from pre 1900. The barrels are fine damascus but they do not display the Rigby "finish" mentioned earlier. Bolting is by an underlever which is pushed down and forwards, while there is a small "pedal" on the right which clears the guard and assists in opening. This gun is an example of a "vintage" weapon saved from the scrap heap by careful restoration and, although I haven't seen the gun myself, the photographs show that care and thought have been given to the problem of restoration. Mr D A Mills of Harrogate did the work and I hope that the present owner Mr T Hare appreciates that not only does he have a gun with an historic name but one which he can be proud to own.

Increasingly, careful restoration is saving guns from destruction (for in years gone by they would have been placed on the anvil in the workshop and clouted with a hammer) and allowing those with a discriminating taste to own a gun of quality.

JAMES WOODWARD AND SONS

Two people are responsible for the inclusion of Woodward in this book. The first is a reader, who does not wish to be named, who mentioned in a letter to me that he has collected all the articles which have appeared in the series in the *Shooting Times* and he has sorted them into special sequences —breechloading shotguns, ammunition, tools, personalities, revolvers and so on. After I had read his letter I thought that an additional series — within the whole as it were — could well be one which dealt with special guns, or super guns, as we might call them.

In the present shotgun series, inclusion has been due to some aspect of historical significance, for example the importance of the design of the gun to the mainstream of sporting shotgun development or a radical re-think of a well established design.

What was then needed was to find a suitable gun to get the series going. It was here that another reader, Mr Brian Storey, suggested that I might consider the Woodward over-and-under gun as worthy of the honour of starting such a series. He went on to suggest that a truly magnificent specimen — a 20-bore — had recently come up for auction at Christie's. This was one of a pair.

A letter to Christie's produced details of the pair of guns — numbers 6718/9 — made by James Woodward & Sons in 1924.

A word about the makers. The founder of the firm, James Woodward was born in 1815 and worked in Pimlico until he joined Charles Moore in St James's Street in 1844. The firm of Charles Moore had distinguished antecedents since Charles Moore had founded his business at 2, Regent Circus as long ago as 1821. He was renowned for the making of superb duelling pistols of the highest quality and from 1835 to 1838 he also had a shop in the Place Vendome in Paris.

In 1844 the firm became Moore & Woodward at 64 St. James's Street and then the style again changed, this time to James Woodward & Sons, in 1872.

Woodward became known for finely finished guns of elegance and style and nowhere is this seen to better advantage than in the over-and-under gun which they introduced in 1913.

In view of later events (see James Purdey) it is of interest to discover that Purdey's Factory Manager, from 1914 to 1946, Ernest Charles Lawrence originally applied for a job with Purdey in 1898. Ernest had served his time with Edwin C. Hodges of Islington, a famous gun action maker to the London trade and a man with a number of patents to his credit. Hodges went into business with Henry Atkin and so Lawrence, now out of his apprenticeship went to work for James Woodward. Here Lawrence worked as an actioner but was then put to work on the Woodward single trigger mechanism. Whether or not he worked on the Woodward O/U gun during its development is unknown to me but it seems likely. Ernest Charles left Woodward and

James Woodward patents used on this Purdey over / under gun

went to work for Purdey, where no doubt, his knowledge of the O/U was passed on to his son Harry who was responsible for much of the later work on the Purdey O/U guns.

The Woodward O/U, along with the Boss over-and-under is, in my opinion, the most graceful of all the guns with this barrel configuration. The slim lines of the action are obtained by having the barrel lumps bifurcated and placed one each side of the lower barrel. The bites or locking slots are just below the centre line of the two barrels.

The slim lines of the action are further enhanced by the fact that the front locking lugs are also bifurcated and fit into dovetails on the inside walls of the U-shaped action bar. There are a number of other interesting points about this action, one of which is the hold-open feature. The locks are bar action sidelocks and the ejector system is a modification of the Southgate.

Apart from their technical merit and elegance of line these guns have qualities which become apparent only on close examination. There is a "feel" about the best London gun and a "rightness" which one rarely encounters elsewhere.

Such qualities today cost a great deal of money. This particular pair of guns made, as already mentioned, in 1924, had in December 1975 a total purchase price of £16,170, which then represented a new record for a pair of modern sporting guns. There are many who would argue about the qualities of these guns, but, in my opinion one cannot argue, as they are there if you have the knowledge and appreciation to discover and realise their worth. It is however, a matter of opinion whether such qualities are worth the sums of money now paid but, by definition, they must be, for that is the price which guns of this quality can fetch on today's markets.

HENRY ATKIN

Guns bearing the name of Henry Atkin, have, for over a century, been highly regarded by those who appreciate quality gunmaking.

The history of the company is impeccable, the first Henry Atkin was one of James Purdey's original workmen, and, as was the practice, his son, Henry, served his apprenticeship under father's stern eye. We can guess that the eye was indeed a stern one, since the skills and knowledge which the son acquired are not gained without a good measure of discipline!

When he had finished his time, young Henry went to work for the firm of Moore and Grey, then, after twelve years, he set up on his own in Oxenden Street, where he prospered, moving to more prestigious premises, in Jermyn Street, in 1890.

During this time Henry Atkin gained a well deserved reputation for finely balanced and well finished game and pigeon guns. Atkin guns were used by the men shooting at the Gun Club and at Hurlingham under extremely competitive conditions. Atkin's skill in boring and regulating guns ensured him of continued patronage and by 1900 his price for a pair of guns was £120.

In 1904, the firm became Henry Atkin Ltd, and in 1907, the founder died. The business continued under the guidance of Mr. Arthur Hodges and it was just before the first German War that Atkin built their self opening gun, the "Spring Open" pattern. A search through the patents will not bring to light any patent for this action in the name of Atkin nor indeed Hodges. The reason? The action was based on the Beesley "self-opening" action, patented by Frederick Beesley in 1880.

The patent was granted in January and in July an agreement had been drawn up between Purdey's and Beesley (for whom Beesley had also worked before setting up on his own). This agreement assigned the patent to Purdey for a period of fourteen years.

At Atkin's, a close look was given to Mr. Beesley's action and it was decided to make certain alterations to the cocking pads and alter the ejector mechanism. One of the main complaints against the "self-opener" was that this type of gun was indeed very easy to open, but could be difficult to close!

The modifications made by Atkin Ltd did much to eliminate this problem and by 1907 the first "Purdey" action gun, (so described in the records) had been finished and the "Spring Open" pattern Atkin gun began to attract the cognoscente, amongst whom was a man later to become the Gun Editor of *The Shooting Times*, G. T. Garwood, "Gough Thomas".

On the 22nd of January, 1947 "G.T." wrote to Dennison, a Director of Henry Atkin and asked him to — "Please proceed to build me .... on the strict understanding .. that you guarantee that in respect of materials, workmanship, finish and shooting qualities. the gun will conform to your highest pre-war standards . . . ."

On receiving an affirmative reply work started on Atkin gun No. 3510 in 1947 and it was completed in 1948. "G.T." accepted the gun and confirmed that ". . I am particularly pleased with the smoothness of opening . . and the uniformity of the effort required to close it . . . . there are no hard spots, which is more than one can say of some self opening ejectors."

I visited Henry Atkin Ltd during a business trip to London in 1954, when they had moved to 27, St. James's Street, and I still have the catalogue which was given to me by Mr. Hodges!

The price of the "Spring Open" sidelock ejector, available in 12, 16 and 20 bore had risen to £285.

Then, in 1960, the first of many changes dictated by shifts in both the economic and social structure took place. Customers of Henry Atkin were advised by letter that on the 1st of April 1960 Stephen Grant and Joseph Lang Ltd. will amalgamate with Henry Atkin Ltd, the new company to be known as Atkin, Grant & Lang Ltd, which will operate from 7, Bury St., St. James's.

Mr. W. R. H. Robson and Mr. Arthur Hodges were joint managing directors with Miss. M. E. Brown as a director and company secretary. Mr.

W. R. H. Robson, a successful businessman, had already gathered together the firms of Harrison & Hussey, Watson Bros., Lancaster and Beesley saving these names from a post war oblivion!

It became the policy to continue building the type of guns which had been the "trademark" of the constituent companies so that the Grant name was to be found on the "Best" sidelocks, some of which had the famous Grant "side lever"; the name of Lang was on boxlocks and an Over/Under and the name of Lancaster was still to be found on the "Twelve Twenty" and that of Watson on high grade small bore guns for ladies and boys.

The name of Atkin continued on the "Spring Opener". However, in 1971 the firm became Churchill, Atkin, Grant & Lang with a move from Grant & Lang's premises in Bury Street, St. James's to, in 1976, 61 Pall Mall.

In 1980 the firm ceased to trade and part of the company, the former Atkin, Grant and Lang, was purchased by new proprietors, under whose direction the company is now once again building guns bearing the names of Henry Atkin, Stephen Grant and Joseph Lang.

When recently I was given the opportunity of seeing and handling the latest Atkin gun I was delighted. Built on the Beesley self opening action with the Atkin modifications, Atkin gun No. 24007 was engraved by Keith Thomas and finished to the highest standards of the London trade.

Photographs cannot give more than an indication of the quality of the gun, the standard of finish of the stock, the absence of any over-run on the chequering, the general feel and balance coupled with the overall appearance which states, unequivocally, "Quality".

Cased, with all accessories, which include a full set of finished and regulated springs, this gun is a credit to those who had a hand in its creation and, I am certain, would delight Henry Atkin himself, were he here to pass judgement.

Henry Atkin gun, recent make

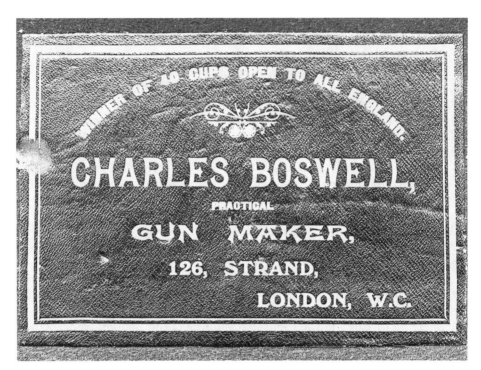

Charles Boswell label

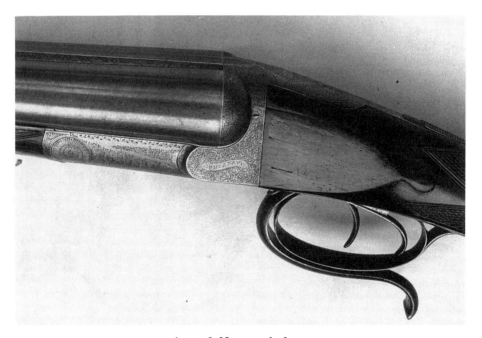

Army & Navy underlever

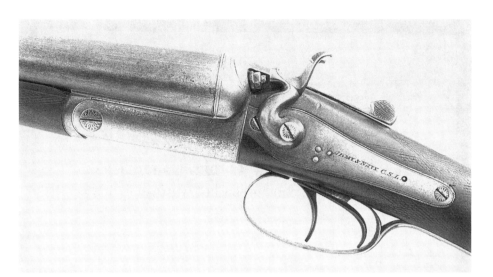

Army & Navy hammer gun

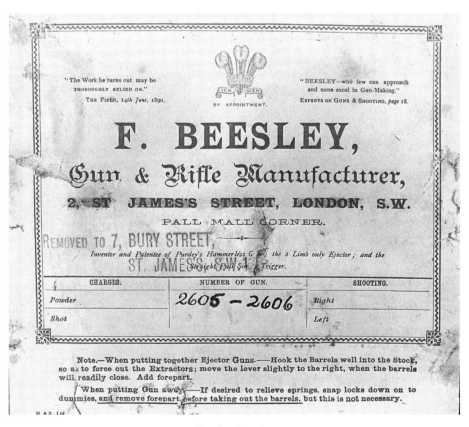

Beesley invoice

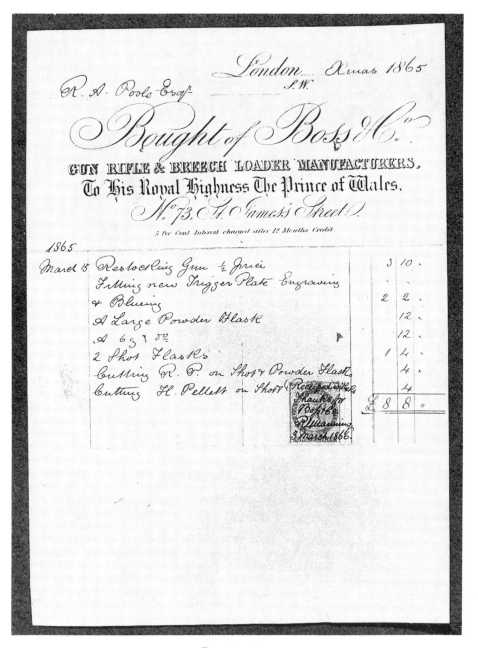

Boss invoice

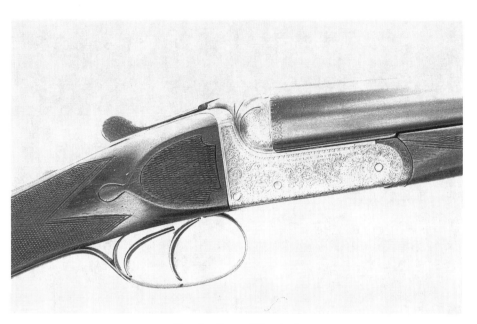

Charles Boswell boxlock

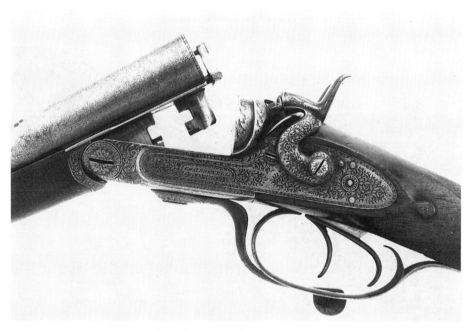

Charles Boswell hammer gun

John Blanch & Son hammer gun

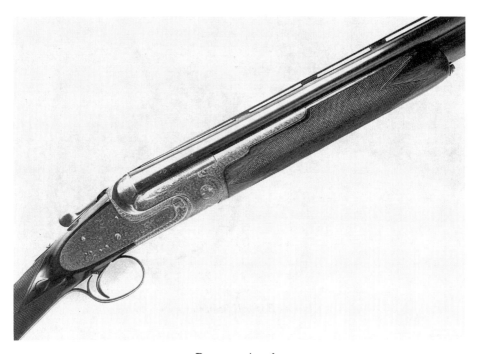

Boss over/under

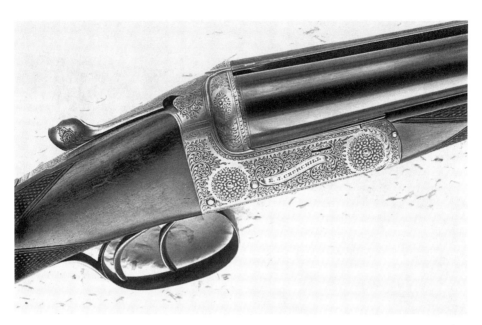

Churchill boxlock

Churchill sidelock

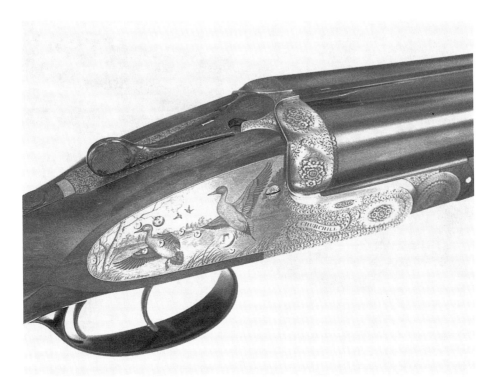

Churchill sidelock

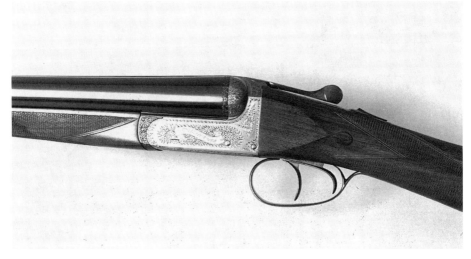

Evans boxlock

William Evans, London

Grant side lever

STEPHEN GRANT & SONS'

Best Quality Side-Lock Hammerless Ejector Gun

Top Lever

Since Stephen Grant started business over eighty years ago, his name on a gun has always been a sign of the highest quality. It is our constant endeavour not only to keep to this ideal but by improvements in design to present to sportsmen those refinements which are also reliable and useful.

The most important recent development is the production of an easy-opening action which also has the great advantage of being easy to close both before and after firing. The sales of this gun are clear evidence of its well-deserved popularity.

4

Stephen Grant sidelock

Charles Hellis, London

Holland & Holland "Royal"

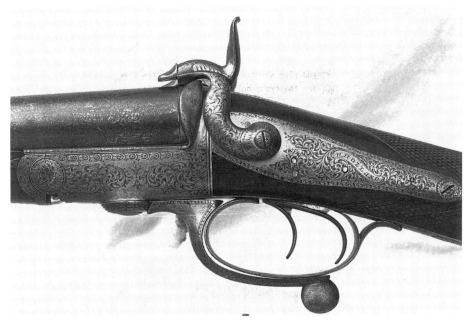

Henry Holland pin-fire

HOLLAND'S
NEW PATENT 'A.B.' ROYAL EJECTOR GUN.

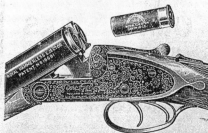

This is the **ONLY** ejector which consists of but two pieces and has no connecting rod between the lock and ejecting mechanism.

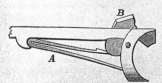

(BEST QUALITY ONLY.)

'We do not see how it is possible to further reduce the number of parts, or simplify the form of mechanism.'
       See *Field* Notice, March 3, 1894.
'One of the best—and certainly one of the safest—Hammerless Actions I am acquainted with is Mr. Holland's, of 98 New Bond Street, who, by the way, can build and fit a gun as well as any maker can, and second to none.' —Sir R. PAYNE-GALLWEY, Bart., 'Letters to Young Shooters,' *Field*, April 19, 1890.
  Field, Feb. 3, 1893.—'I can honestly say that my shooting average improved very considerably. The fit of the stocks is perfect.'—*Purple Heather*.

Capt. R. S. writes:—'I am very pleased with the guns; and there was no hitch of any sort during the season.'
E. C. writes:—'I have been very pleased with the guns; they shoot beautifully, and are the pleasantest guns to handle and shoot with I have ever tried or used.'
C. G. E. writes:—'I am perfectly satisfied in every way with the Ejector Gun you have built for me; I have used it constantly, and done some heavy firing with it. The ejector and locks work without a fault, and its killing powers are wonderful. It has all the qualities you claim for your guns.'

Factory:—527 to 535 Harrow Road, W.
'This is the most perfect and complete gun factory we have yet seen in London.'—*Field*, May 27, 1893.

HOLLAND & HOLLAND, Ltd., Winners of all the 'Field' Rifle Trials, **98 New Bond St., London.**

Holland & Holland "Royal" ad

Holland & Holland back action sidelock

Holland & Holland double 4 bore. Weight 19 pounds.
Price in 1988, around $350,000!

Charles Hellis sidelock

The "MARK OVER" Gun

A Moderately Priced Gun built on "best" lines

SIDELOCK HAMMERLESS EJECTOR GUN of specially selected material and workmanship.

Locks and Action fully engraved in heavy scroll design.

Selected fully seasoned figured Walnut Stocks with Silver initial ovals.

When ordered in Pairs, every detail is studied to give a perfect match in balance and handling.

Standard length of Barrels 26 inches. Any other length to order.

BORING :—*Right Barrel*. Modified Improved Cylinder.
        Left Barrel. Full Choke.

    Customers' special requirements to order.

    If ordered in Pairs, numbered 1 and 2 in Gold.

Charles Hellis "Mark Over" sidelock

Charles Lancaster back action sidelock

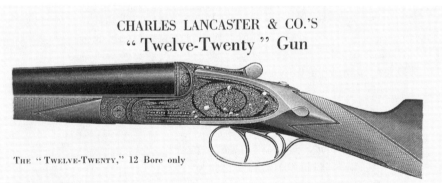

CHARLES LANCASTER & CO.'S
"Twelve-Twenty" Gun

THE "TWELVE-TWENTY," 12 Bore only

To meet the demand for light guns which is now so general we were prompted in 1924 to undertake the difficult task of manufacturing a light-weight model. The difficulty was, of course, to eliminate the discomfort hitherto caused by light guns and to retain the freedom from recoil experienced with heavier ones.

The result of our persistent experiments was the "TWELVE-TWENTY", which is of the best materials and workmanship throughout. It incorporates the easy-opening action and each component part has been designed specially in view of the fact that the gun weighs no more than a 20 bore, yet at the same time no sacrifice of strength has been made. Many of our customers are using these guns in India with the full charge of powder and $1\frac{1}{16}$ oz. of shot, but others find the popular 1 oz. load suits them better. The shooting is tested at 40 yards and with both these loads the effective killing distance is the same as that of an ordinary full-weight gun. We have had many expressions of satisfaction at the killing power of the "TWELVE-TWENTY" at more than usual sporting distances.

Continued practical research into the relationship between Man and Gun has enabled a number of improvements to be made since the "TWELVE-TWENTY" was introduced and it is now certainly the greatest achievement in gun-craft the present generation has witnessed.

6

Lancaster "Twelve-Twenty", lightweight 12 bore

HIGHEST AWARDS
BRUSSELS, VIENNA & TURIN.

LANG
BEST GUNS

SINGLE OR DOUBLE TRIGGER.

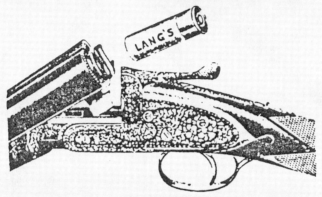

Unsurpassed for general handiness, balance, simplicity of mechanism, soundness of construction, ease of manipulation, and regular well distributed patterns.

EJECTOR.

"Field": "Displays great ingenuity, and possesses decided claims towards utility. The only criticism, in fact, which can be put forward is that the invention ought to have been made before."

SINGLE TRIGGER.
(Over 600 in use.)

Contains the same number of limbs as an ordinary Double trigger, therefore the liability to simultaneous discharge or inoperation of second barrel is entirely eliminated.

"Field": "Put through a very severe test, worked perfectly throughout."

ILLUSTRATED CATALOGUE POST FREE.

JOSEPH LANG & SON LTD.,
102, New Bond Street, W.

Established 1821.

Telegrams "Backsight, London." Telephone, 2051 Gerrard.
(Late of Cockspur-street and Pall Mall.)

Joseph Lang, London

93

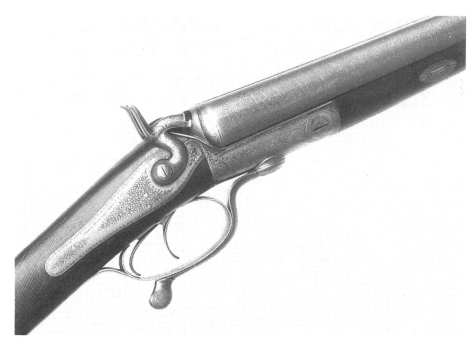

One of the last Manton guns

Purdey bottom lever sidelock

Purdey's late Harry Lawrence

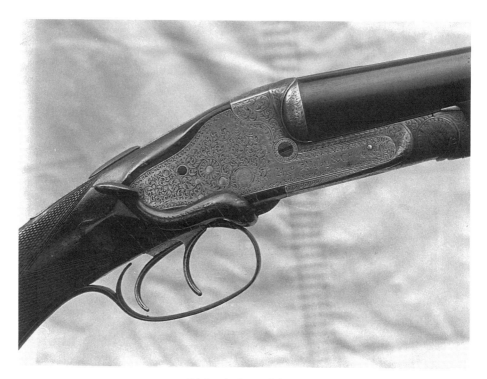

Rigby & Co. sidelock

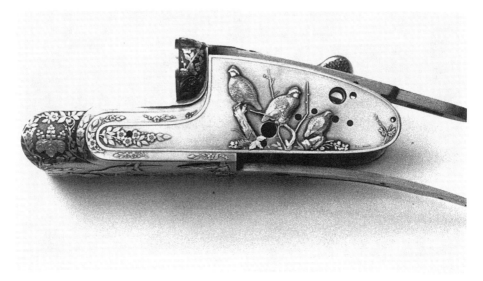

Ken Hunt's engraving

John Wilkes, London

Working the action

THE BIRMINGHAM GUN TRADE

The skills of those workers in iron who lived and worked in Birmingham and the surrounding district were well suited to the manufacture of firearms. Credit for creating a stable market for their wares must go to Sir Richard Newdigate, the Member of Parliament for Warwickshire who, in 1689, organised a group of Birmingham gunmakers to supply muskets to the Board of Ordnance.

Throughout the 17th and 18th centuries, the Birmingham gun trade prospered due to the demand for cheap trade and slave guns, mainly intended for the African market.

The series of wars in which Britain was involved during the 18th century, guaranteed a demand for military weapons. The Birmingham trade not only supplied complete arms, but also gun locks and barrels, to the London contractors to the Board of Ordnance.

Increased activity on the part of the Birmingham gunmakers did not go unnoticed by the gunmakers in London. With their, by now, well organised Worshipful Company of Gunmakers, they did all they could to hinder the activities of their Birmingham competitors.

The Birmingham trade enjoyed many advantages, the proximity of raw material and fuel, a labour force well trained in the specialist skills of the metal working industry and improved communications all contributed the the growth of the gunmaking industry in Birmingham which was to continue until the introduction of machinery for the manufacture of military arms during the 1860's.

The manufacture of sporting guns for the home and export markets was to grow in the closing decades of the 18th century and to increase in pace during the 19th. Both the London and Provincial gun trades found it increasingly attractive to purchase components and then, finished guns, from Birmingham.

As early as 1805 confirmation of the manner in which the trade was organised can be seen in the comments to be found in Morfitt's "Sketch of Birmingham".

"Be it known unto all men—that guns with the best stub and twisted barrels, eclipsing the formerly famous barrels of Spain, the best skeleton locks, the best patented breeches, gold touch holes etc., are made in Birmingham for one half, nay, one-third the price which they bring in the metropolis; and yet a person unacquainted with the secret would suppose that Birmingham never produced a single fowling piece, for our manufacturers have the policy to use the superscription of London".

In 1813, jealous of the value of the name of "London" on a gun, the gunmakers of that city brought before the House of Commons a bill that would require every gunmaker to place his real name and address on the gun. Such was the pressure brought to bear by the Birmingham trade that they were able to quash the bill!

One significant advantage enjoyed by London was the London Proof House. A Government proof house had been established in Bagot Street, Birmingham, in 1797 but commercial barrels, unless proofed by the Birmingham gunmakers themselves, had to be sent to London.

The Birmingham gunmaker could submit his barrels to the private proof houses established by the gunmakers Samuel Galton in Weaman Street and that of Ketland. The private mark of Ketland enjoyed such a high reputation that it was later developed into the official Birmingham proof mark which remained in use until 1904.

By 1800, the strength and productive capacity of the Birmingham trade had risen to the extent that Birmingham was able to supply more than twice the quantity of firearms for the Government service than did the London trade and the Government factories. In addition it must also be remembered that Birmingham supplied many of the locks and barrels for the London gun-

Bath Street, Birmingham

100

makers.

It was due to the valuable contribution made by Birmingham gunmakers that, in spite of the opposition of the London trade, they were able to obtain an Act of Parliament which allowed them to "...erect and establish a proper Proof House, with all things necessary for the Proving of Barrels of Firearms."

The foundation stone of the Birmingham Proof House was laid in 1813 and by March, 1816 the Proof House was in operation in Banbury Street, Birmingham, in the building which houses their present day operations.

The early years of the 19th century saw the establishment of many of the Birmingham gunmakers whose names are well known to us to-day. However, the most significant venture was the formation of the Birmingham Small Arms Company in 1861 by a number of shareholders, amongst whom are numbered some fourteen established gunmakers. The object of the new company was "to make guns and machinery" and within ten years the manufacture of military rifles by the traditional hand methods had almost ceased.

At the BSA factory at Small Heath commercial considerations had to be taken into account and because of the fluctuating nature of the business from both the British and foreign governments the company was forced to widen its interests to include the manufacture of cycles and cycle components.

The change to the use of machinery and a largely static work force in a factory had reduced that flexibility which had for so long been a feature of the traditional gun trade.

However, even under factory conditions some of the old traditions still survived and for a number of years the independent gunworker rented his bench space and gas light from the owners of the factory.

The manufacture of sporting guns by machinery was attempted by a number of Birmingham makers and although some success was acheived in the manufacture of damascus barrels of very high quality with the aid of machinery, in general, the use of the machine tool was restricted to the simple machining work, the final careful fitting remained in the skilled hands of the traditional gunworker.

A. A. BROWN & SONS

The term gunmaker is one which tends to be rather loosely used these days. Despite a wealth of gilt "Gunmaker" signs above shop doors, the number of firms who can truly state "we are gunmakers," is really quite small. Of those firms boasting this title Browns can claim to make more of the guns that bear their name than most and, if pushed, could probably make all of the gun in-house.

To see the transformation from rusty massive chunks of metal and baulks of timber to the grace and sheer perfection of a "best" English gun is quite an experience in itself and, to me, a very satisfactory one, since I have pride in British gunmaking and gunmakers.

The firm is in modern premises in the delightful village of Alvechurch, south of Birmingham. Unlike the traditional gunmaking establishment the machine shop is spacious and well lit and only on venturing farther into the works is it evident that this is a gunmaker's for there is the traditional bench, inches deep in files, lit by a fine, long, north-facing window above. Here is a true amalgam of old and new traditions, the best of both worlds brought together.

When the first Brown in this family started to make guns is unknown but John Joseph Brown, born in 1853, was one of 11 sons, of whom five were master gunmakers. John eventually started work with P. Webley & Sons where he met his future wife, Maria Chapman. Three sons and three daughters resulted from this marriage. Albert Arthur, one of the sons entered the gun trade with the firm of F. E. & H. Rogers who were action makers and quickly gained a reputation for high quality work. In 1911 Albert married Minnie Davis and they had a daughter and two sons, Albert Henry and Sidney Charles. The sons entered the gun trade and together the family formed the firm of A. A. Brown & Sons with premises in the heart of the Birmingham gun quarter in Whittal Street.

No sooner were they established than World War Two broke out and, with the premises damaged by bombing, they had to move out to the suburbs of Birmingham, to Shirley. After the war the firm moved back to the gunmaking quarter, not exactly to where they had been but to Sand Street, a well known little street that joined two more famous gunmaking streets of Weaman Street and Whittal Street. Here they settled down and prospered. Albert Henry joined the Board of Guardians of the Birmingham Proof House and was a member many years, five of them as Chairman.

During this period the firm designed and made about 2000 of the "Abas Major" air pistol before settling to their real business of gunmaking. Additional machinery installed enabled them to make guns complete from forgings and bar steel. Changes in the trade would have defeated less determined and less skilled people. For generations the gun trade consisted of highly skilled firms which relied on the gunmaker to bring all of their skills together. Gradually the small firms went out of business and many individual craftsmen retired and with them skills and knowledge. As changes accelerated firms had several choices. The easiest way was to be vendors of guns made by others. Mostly only the larger businesses survived as money was attracted into other Midlands industries. A. A. Brown & Sons took a harder course; they learned and acquired the skills no longer available to them through the trade.

In 1957, the founder of the firm, Albert Arthur, retired and three years later, with the development of the Birmingham ring road, the firm had to move yet again. The Sand Street premises were demolished and the little firm moved out of the gunmakers' quarter once again, this time to Bournbrook,

Best A. A. Brown sidelock

Birmingham. With small firms disappearing all around all that remained of the old gunmaking quarter was the remains of Bath Street, Price Street and part of Loveday Street.

In 1961 Robin Brown joined the firm to learn the trade and at this time Les Jones, one of the foremost gun engravers in the country, joined them. Making "best" sidelocks only, the firm concentrated on quality, making not only for themselves but also for the London and Provincial trade. Their products bore the trade mark "ABAS" and during the sixties the firm increasingly built guns for private customers.

In 1974 the move was made to Alvechurch where they concentrated on two guns, the "Supreme" sidelock ejector and the "Supreme Deluxe" which has chopper lump barrels, a self opening mechanism, disc-set strikers and individual specifications.

Today, along with the two brothers, Albert Henry and Sidney Charles, there is yet another generation, Robin Charles Brown, who is well able to carry on the traditions of the past. The important work of barrel boring and general machining is in the very capable hands of Samuel Harold Scandrett and, as well as Les Jones, already mentioned, Walter Howe, engraves for the firm.

With the exception of the forgings for the body and fore-end, and some of the barrel work, everything, except the engraving, is done on the premises.

This now includes lock making, stocking, stock finishing and the multitude of skilled operations on which the faultless functioning of a best gun depends.

There comes the time when a firm declares "let us make an example of our best work," a masterpiece. In Brown's case this has taken the form of a commemorative exhibition piece, a 28-bore "Supreme" to celebrate the Queen's Silver Jubilee. I have seen this gun several times now; the first was at the Game Fair, and it still delights me.

Not only was my visit to Brown's a trip into the past but also a lesson in gunmaking and public relations, and, not least of all, a reassurance that the arts and crafts of gunmaking are thriving in this country.

WILLIAM CASHMORE

For some time now I have been very interested in the export business conducted by the Birmingham gun trade in the years just before the First World War. A number of readers in Canada, Australia, New Zealand and America know about my interest in this subject, as do members of today's gun trade in Birmingham.

A few years ago I received a photocopy of a catalogue which bore the name William Cashmore and the address Steelhouse Lane, Birmingham. This came to me from Larry Barnes of Gunnerman Books in America and it dated from the mid 1890s. I also received a catalogue which described the Cashmore Patent Nitro Action, this dating from sometime after 1897. I had only encountered the gun previously as a line drawing in the British Patents. The catalogue really brought it to life showing that this unusual action had been widely sold. Cashmore guns in general were highly regarded and the company's literature was full of quite glowing references and testimonials including some from Dr Carver and Miss Annie Oakley.

Cashmore was renowned for its trap guns, chambered for 2 3/4in and 3in cases. These were used for live pigeon shooting and for clays. Cashmore offered a double-rise pigeon trap, complete, for just over £2; clays in the closing years of the 19th century cost 25p per 100.

Matters rested at this stage for several months, but enough material had been gathered to arouse my interest — but there was still not quite enough to sustain an article. Then, a letter with enclosures was received from Fred Shearer, a gunsmith in Malvern, Australia.

The enclosure was copy of another Cashmore catalogue which again illustrated the Cashmore Nitro shotgun and also gave a very complete list of successes which Cashmore guns had achieved in Monte Carlo, Australia and America and at The Gunmaker's Trophy competition in Birmingham.

Mr Shearer told me in his letter that the Cashmore Nitro gun was highly regarded by older shooters in Australia and it seems likely that a very high proportion of these special guns were exported and that more have survived abroad than we have here in the U.K!

Even at this stage of our enquiries, more of interest is yet to be discovered, since my original research had shown that William Cashmore had not thought up the original idea. The credit for this goes to Mr Samuel Mills of 83 Prince Albert Street, Small Heath, Birmingham, who describes himself as a "Gun Action Maker". The date of his patent is 1894 and his covers improvements in fastening breechloading actions to the barrels.

I have not been able to trace mention of Samuel Mills, so it is unlikely that he was in business on his own account. He altered the conventional action based on the Purdey bolt and Scott spindle by using one lump only (the rear lump is replaced by welding, brazing, or otherwise forming two pieces of metal on the outer sides of the barrel or pair of barrels). These 'outer lumps' act as flanges or steadies and are, in addition, locked by two pawls or bolts which engage in recesses formed in the outer lumps.

It seems likely from one remaining example that Cashmore made guns under the Mills 1894 patent and it is also possible that Mills, in fact, worked for Cashmore. However, the next development was a patent taken out in the following year by William Cashmore of 130 Steelhouse Lane, Birmingham, described as a "Gun & Pistol Manufacturer". Cashmore refers to Mills' patent and goes on to tell us that he has improved on the original idea by adding two lumps or projections on each side of the action body which match or abut against the outside lumps on the barrels. Cashmore goes on to say that his additions "greatly assist the front joint pin in resisting the longitudinal pressure of the explosion" and, in effect, the action is stronger and better able to withstand wear and strain on the joint pin.

It is also of interest to see how the styling of the action body, particularly the fence, changed from the original design of Mills to Cashmore's improvement. In fact, in production, the fences were again changed and became what I have tended to call 'pin-fire fences'.

Neither of the illustrations in the photocopies I have of the guns as built, are suitable for reproduction and at this stage in my researches I still had not been able to obtain photographs of an actual Cashmore Nitro shotgun.

It is at a time like this that I have come to rely on what is a world wide "family" of readers. Once my problem became known, I was quite certain that someone would come up with the answer and a set of prints or, even better, I would learn of the location of a Cashmore gun near enough to allow me to go and see and photograph it!

My faith in my readers was justified. A letter from Richard Schreiber who lives in New York State, U.S.A., enclosed a page from Orvis News, published by the U.S. Orvis Company, which advertised for sale at $4,500 a "William Cashmore 12 gauge boxlock (most unusual action design with side hooks and convoluted carving) action totally covered in fine scroll, 30 inch barrels, may be one of a kind?" Full marks to Richard Schreiber for identifying the Cashmore 'Nitro' from this description!

Richard told me that he would arrange to visit the Manchester, Vermont retail store of Orvis and that he would ask to see the 'Nitro ' gun and seek

Cashmore Nitro action

permission to take photographs.

I awaited the next letter with some impatience and when it arrived it contained small black and white prints of the 'Nitro' gun and negatives. The journey to Manchester, Vermont had taken Richard some seven hours. At the Orvis Gun Department he met Dave Slohm, who was most co-operative and allowed a full examination of the gun, which fortunately (for me) had not been sold. With the aid of Norman Brown, a keen local photographer, whom Richard met while trying to locate a photographer in a local camera shop, photographs of the gun were taken and Richard returned home.

Under the barrel there is the legend "For 3 1/4in Case", and this answers the earlier query I had regarding the "extra charge of Nitro Powder" mentioned in the catalogues. The standard load for a 3 1/4in case was 1 oz of shot.

The conventional Cashmore 'Imperial' could be had with 2 3/4in or 3in chambering but there is no mention of the chamber length of the 'Nitro' in the catalogues, just mention of "heavy charges".

More than a year went by before I received more input on the Cashmore Nitro shotgun. I had been given information and photographs by readers in America and Australia. Now, as has often happened in the past, the next part of the story was literally under my nose.

I still had not actually handled a Cashmore Nitro and then a local collector, who lives not twenty miles away got in touch to ask if I was still interested in the Cashmore Nitro, if so he had one!

Arrangements were made for me to see and photograph the gun. When

I had my hands on it I found that it had two pairs of barrels, one pair for 2 3/4in and the other for 3in cartridges. Of greater importance was that this was yet another variant. The original Mills patent had two external lumps each with one bite and an internal lump with one bite. The Cashmore gun now lying on my photographic bench had a lump which hooked on the hinge pin and one bite on the single central lump, just like the patent drawing and it lacked the external projections mentioned by William Cashmore in his patent.

This was not all. This Nitro had been in its travels! The history of the gun was most interesting, for it had been bought by a previous owner in Australia. He had been opal mining at Lightning Ridge, which I see from my Australian road map, is in New South Wales. The gun was bought for self protection and with 3in shells this it would most certainly have provided!

Having seen what we might call the Mills-Cashmore or Model of 1894 and the later 1895 Cashmore with Cashmore additions, I now seek any other versions which might have survived. It's too much to hope that such a gun, if it exists at all, will be local, but if not, I hope that the owner also owns a good quality camera and can provide me with some sharp photographs, one cannot help but ask, are there more Cashmore Nitro's in Australia?

C.G. BONEHILL

Some years ago when I was attempting to obtain details of Birmingham gunmakers I started my task of compiling a list of names and addresses. Amongst these names and addresses was C.G. Bonehill, Belmont Row, Birmingham. Belmont Row, although not too far from the Birmingham Proof House, is not in the gunmaking quarter and I was not able to follow up my enquiry with a personal visit. However, from friends in the trade, I was told that Bonehill's had been a first class factory and that Christopher Bonehill was a pioneer of the interchangeable system.

Mr Bonehill and his factory were then put into the rather cobwebby recesses of my mind and the data obtained filed. Then, early in 1973, through the good services of Colin Haygarth, I was shown a Bonehill gun. This was a 12-bore with 28in barrels which had been re-stocked. The address was given as the Belmont Firearms and Gun Barrel Works, Belmont Row and it was also marked "Interchangeable".

All was quiet again until I received a letter from Mr W J Willis. Mr Willis very kindly sent me a trade label for E M Reilly and Company which had been taken from an old gun case. His letter told me that he had a catalogue of guns made by C.G. Bonehill and that he had known the last of the Bonehill family. His offer to lend me the catalogue was accepted with alacrity! Catalogues are of vital importance to any study of 19th century sporting guns and too few of them have survived.

It is believed that this catalogue dates from about 1904 and in the 212 pages much of what the sportsman was buying at the turn of the century is listed. The catalogue tells us that the firm was founded in 1851 and that by 1870 it was able to undertake the supply of military rifles for the French government. In order to take advantage of the number of orders which the firm was receiving, Bonehill took over the factory of the National Arms and Ammunition Company in Belmont Row.

The factory was re-equipped with new and up-to-date machinery and the techniques which had been employed in the manufacture of military rifles was adapted to the manufacture of sporting guns with particular emphasis on the American market.

Unfortunately the catalogue does not refer to the "Interchangeable" gun, and it is likely that this was an earlier production. It is of interest to record that Bonehill was responsible for the Britannia Air Rifle. This was one of the earliest British-made air rifles and certainly one of the most powerful since it could literally blow a .177 pellet to pieces. Bonehill also made "Britannia" air rifle pellets and these were highly regarded by the Midlands air gunners — in those days air rifle shooting was a very popular sport in the Birmingham district.

But back to shotguns. Bonehill made the "Belmont" range of A & D actioned shotguns and a very pleasant range of sidelock guns, all of which could be had with removable sidelocks and optional single triggers, the latter for £10 extra. Top lever hammer guns were also offered and the hammerless range was available as a pigeon or trap gun chambered for 2 3/4 or 3in cartridges.

Bonehill case label

The range included ball and shotguns having rifled choked muzzles, and combination rifle and shotguns were made. These were to be had with the right barrel chambered for 12-bore shot and the left rifled and chambered for the .5771, .450 Martini or the No. 2 Musket cartridge. Double Express rifles in all calibres from .600 Nitro Express down to the .303 were made and also — probably what was the logical outcome of Bonehill's experiments with interchangeable manufacture — his range of "Standard" guns which repeated the range already described, but at less cost. All these guns employed A & D actions and were finished in five grades from quite plain to full engraving; pigeon guns had side clips. Extra fine work could be had including inlaying with gold "suitable for the most exacting requirements of Oriental taste". A Stag's head, with horns, cost 14 shillings per head.

Single-barrel guns were also sold, in addition to single and double-barrel muzzle-loading shotguns for the "Central and South American Markets". The catalogue also illustrates a wide range of rifles from the Martini to the Mannlicher. It is a splendid catalogue and Mr Bonehill must have been very proud of his firm and of its products.

THE BSA SHOTGUN

As the cost of hand-finishing (I don't like the term hand-crafted) continues its seemingly never ending upward spiral more and more people wishing to use a double shotgun turn to what used to be called "the machine made gun". I am often asked "Why did the British gun trade never produce such a gun?" The answer to this question is long, complicated and involved but if I am restricted to three words my answer would be "Yes, it did!" The name of the gun was BSA.

Little has been written about the BSA double shotgun. Hugh Pollard in his book *Shotguns*, 1923, merely stated that "a plain BSA hammerless shotgun — an admirable weapon — can be bought for as low as £11. 11s." The advert at the beginning of that book tells us a little more. From it we learn that BSA had, over the past 60 years, developed the manufacture of rifles and guns on repetitive machinery to a remarkable degree of accuracy. We are assured that the parts gauge to within one thousandth of an inch and that the materials used are specially selected by skilled metallurgists. We are further told that the net result is great strength, perfect balance and "feel" and because of the use of machines instead of expensive hand labour, phenomenally low prices.

The question one must inevitably ask is "What went wrong?" The price was, in 1923, just over £11.50 for a non-ejector and just over £14.50 for the ejector. A "Special" ejector gun was £25 and, until recently, I have never seen the BSA Special. I still have not actually handled one but Mr Ogden of Cheshire has this quality of BSA and he very kindly sent me a photograph. On the top rib is the statement "Made by BSA Guns Ltd, England" and there

BSA boxlock

is a rather nice fence, quite unusual in fact, and some scroll engraving and game. The top rib also bears the well-known "Piled Arms" trademark of the Company.

By 1934 the prices had altered only slightly. The standard gun was then £13. 13s. and the Special Model or "Ejector Model Deluxe" as it was now called, had been reduced in price and was £19. 19s. This compares, incidentally, with the Webley & Scott No. 300 non-ejector at £21.

For a contemporary opinion of the BSA we can turn to Burrard who said that "BSA have abandoned the top extension (did they ever use it?) but their guns are certainly strong. They are up to full weight and I am sure that the metal used in the action bodies is of better quality than many cheap guns..." This, of course, is where the BSA metallurgists come in. BSA also used "Chopper Lump" barrels as was the practice on "best" guns. However, BSA went a little further and instead of brazing the barrels together employed a dovetail secured by two pins through the lumps. Burrard agreed that this method was strong and effective if made by machine but he criticised the added width required for the dovetail which resulted in what he called a "clumsy gun".

BSA made three different types of side-by-side 12-bore, the Standard, the Standard with ejector and the Special or Model de Luxe, again with ejector. All were for the 2 1/2 inch cartridge and they also offered their 12-bore wildfowling gun for 2 3/4 or 3in 12-bore cartridges.

Just to give some indication of comparative values the F.N. Browning five-shot automatic in standard finish was selling for £9 in 1934 and the Browning over and under in standard finish was £25.

The BSA is a gun that has been grossly neglected by authors in the past and its merits largely overlooked. When it was first made is unknown to me as indeed is the date when manufacture ceased. I would say its production ceased around 1939 although the Parker-Hale catalogue for 1941 still carried details of the BSA.

JOSEPH BOURNE & SON

The history of the Birmingham gun trade has for long fascinated me. Many of the Birmingham photographs I took in the recent past are now part of history because the people and places they record have vanished. Whole areas of the old Gun Quarter have gone, streets have disappeared and buildings have been demolished to make way for new buildings and a road system that defies the law of physics! Two streets, the names of which are synonymous with the gun trade are Bath Street and Loveday Street. About one third of the original Bath Street remains and most of Loveday Street.

James Bourne & Son, a firm typical of the gun trade, was once to be found at the corner of Bath Street and Loveday Street. The name of Bourne was connected with the very earliest gunmaking activities in Birmingham. A William Bourne appears on a Government contract dated 1693 for the supply of "musquettes" at the rate of 200 a month. The beginnings of the firm are not so well documented, however. They say they were founded in 1840 though the city directories do not list the firm until 1849 when they were to be found at 5 Whittall Street. There appears to have been some connection with Thomas Redfern, a firm also to be found at 5 Whittall Street, but the nature of their connection is now difficult to discover. In 1867 the style of the firm changed to "& Son" and by 1885 they had moved to 9 St Mary's Row, still in the warren of streets and workshops between Steelhouse Lane and the Canal and with "St Mary's Chappell" giving its name to the area.

Here was a small, highly concentrated self-contained area, with chapel and school and almost the entire range of trades needed for gunmaking. In 1903 the firm of James Bott & Son, Tiger Works, Gun Makers to His Late Majesty The King of Portugal, was acquired and the directories for 1900 show this firm to be at 100 and 101 Bath Street. The 1910 directories show Bourne established at the same address.

In 1907 Joseph Bourne acquired gunmakers Walter Edwards and then, in 1908, they made a further acquisition — the large and important business of Robert Hughes & Son. This firm first appears in 1855 and in 1868 they adopted the name "Universal Fire Arms Works". A trade label of this period shows a very wide selection of revolvers and pistols and they advise that they "manufacture every description of breech and muzzle loading military and sporting rifle". Hughes sold a wide range of smooth-bore sporting guns converted from Enfield muzzle-loading military rifles and they also offered a range of muzzle-loading double percussion shotguns for the export markets.

By 1912 Joseph Bourne occupied premises at 100 and 101 Bath Street and they also extended down Loveday Street to numbers 89, 90 and 91 and 92. An illustration of the works at this period shows a handsome, three-storey building, the front of which gives us a clue about what we can expect in the 20th century. In addition to guns, Bourne are by now obviously interested in cycles.

As well as selling and manufacturing arms, Bourne also had extensive facilities for repairs. Their main business was, however, with the export market and with South Africa in particular. An early advertisement, possibly for display in a retailer's showroom, illustrates a double percussion shotgun and the potential customer is assured that Bourne guns "are Warranted Safe". A great comfort, no doubt! By 1912 the firm offered a double back-action, top-lever hammer gun with 30in barrels for £3.15s. That's £3.75! The gun had rebounding locks and was nitro-proofed.

Oddly enough, the same gun, with the Jones underlever, known as the "Old Model" cost more, at £4. Top of the market in hammer guns were the top lever, bar-action treble-grip models, the most expensive of which was £30. As a concession to foreign buyers, sizes were given in centimetres and inches — and this was 1912! Hammerless guns on offer were the A & D action 1912 Model Ejector at £16 and a sidelock with Greener-type cross bolt at £15. Top of the range was an A & D single-trigger gun at £75. Also on offer was a range of pigeon guns, chambered for either the 2 3/4in or 3in cartridge, and a fine selection of double and single-barrel duck and wildfowl guns in 10, 8 and 4-bores. To provide some indication of comparative prices Bourne sold the five-shot Browning Automatic Shotgun for £13. 10s (£13.50). Converted Mauser and Chassepot rifles bored for 12-bore were £1 and neat conversions of the military Martini-Henry in .577/.450 could be had for about £4. A range of Lee Metford, Lee Enfield and Mauser and Mannlicher rifles was on offer from about £10 - £15, and good-quality double rifles in all bores up to .600 cost from between £20 to £40.

Both automatic and revolving pistols from the famous makers such as F.N., Colt, Smith & Wesson are illustrated along with "The Bulldog" revolver at a mere 50p! Air-guns, walking-stick guns and air canes share the end of the catalogue with low-priced Continental shotguns "a selection of which are kept, without guarantee, for the convenience of customers". Joseph Bourne also sold cycles and motor cycles. I have not been able to discover if they actually manufactured them, but the motorcycle was a belt-drive side-valve sold under the name "Elmdon".

So far as the guns and rifles made by Bourne are concerned it is likely that there are more guns by this maker in South Africa than in this country. Undisturbed by the developers and planners the premises at the corner of Bath Street and Loveday Street are still there, although the factory houses a shopfitting centre. Last listed as gun and rifle makers in the late 1950s Joseph Bourne continued in business until quite recently and the building at 101 Bath Street serves as a reminder of the diversity and far-flung interests of the Birmingham gun trade of the 19th century.

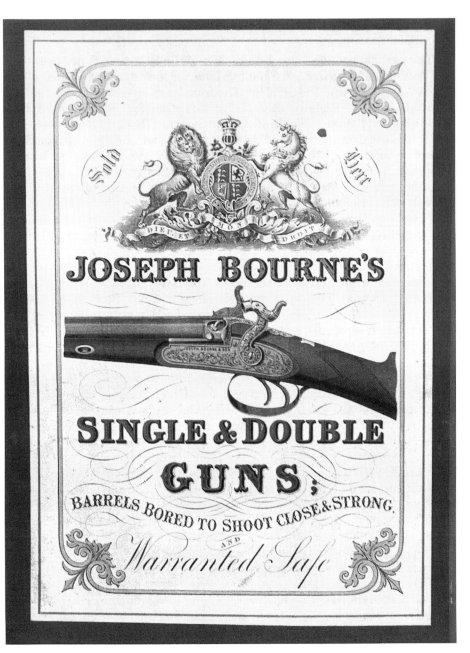

Joseph Bourne ad

WILLIAM FORD

The earliest original copy I have seen of the *Shooting Times* bears the title *Wildfowler's Illustrated, Shooting Times, Sports and Kennel News*. The date is April 1884 and the price 2d. The front page has advertisements and it is these that aroused my interest. Top left is one for "William Ford, Gun barrel borer and Maker, (New and Special System of Boring)" and we are told that this is the firm which bored the barrels of the winning guns at the Field trials.The address of the firm is given as 4A Weaman Row, St Mary's, Birmingham and perhaps the most significant fact about this advertisement is that in spite of changes of address, if you look at the back of recent issues you will still find one for William Ford!

I say "significant", I could have used "interesting" or even "remarkable" and probably the last word would spring to mind when you consider the following facts.

On the first page of that issue of over a century ago, there are five gunmakers and one ammunition maker. The other gunmakers are Charles Lancaster, J & W Tolley, Thomas Turner, Charles Boswell and W W Greener. Of the total of six advertising only Ford is still in business! The ammunition manufacturer is Kynoch & Co and although Lion Works, Witton, Birmingham is still there, the ammunition it sells is now under an old rivals name; Eley.

If we then move on some 50 years or so to 1930 we find in the issue for August 16 a William Ford advertisement offering their special "Goose & Duck Gun". This gun was made on "Dr Heath's Chamberless system" to shoot brass cases and 2 oz of shot. Ford now describe themselves as "Practical Gun Maker, Gun Fitter and Barrel Borer". Their address is now 15 St Mary's Row, Birmingham and the works is described as the "Eclipse Gun Works". We also learn that the firm has shooting schools at Birmingham and Manchester. By 1930 the magazine has changed its style to the "Shooting Times & British Sportsman" and for the 32 pages it now boasts, the reader is charged 6d.

Let us now move on through the Second World War to 1948, nearly 20 years on. The paper has increased in price to 9d., the style remains the same but the effect on austerity can be plainly seen in the size of the paper which is now down to eight pages! One thing remains the same; William Ford still advertise guns, repairs, reboring, new barrels and new stocks fitted. The address has changed again, however, the firm now being at Price Street but so that their former customers will not be puzzled by this change of address they are informed "late of 15 St Mary's Row".

Ford had in fact moved about quite a lot and some of the moves are not recorded. The earliest address is the 4A Weaman Row one in 1884 and very probably this address is not recorded earlier in the classified directories since the firm describe themselves not as gunmakers but as barrel borers. The year 1885 sees them at 23 Loveday Street, moving to 15 St Mary's Row in 1889. Gun making appears to have commenced in 1888 on a "named" basis.

William Ford trade label

In 1948 the firm had moved to Price Street, where they stayed until 1953 when they moved back to St Mary's Row, except this time it was No. 10 not No. 15.

The last William Ford died in 1946 and the move to St Mary's Row was probably dictated by an amalgamation with James Carr & Sons, who were then in business at 10/11 St Mary's Row. In 1954 the firm became a limited company and in 1965 the virtual destruction of the old gun quarter saw the move of Ford's out to Potter's Hill, Aston. In spite of moving well out of the way of the "developers", Ford's were again obliged to move to their present address at 352 Mosely Road, Birmingham where hopefully they will not be "re-developed" again.

I did not have the pleasure of visiting Ford's at their 15 St Mary's Row address. This would have been in the great days of the Birmingham gun trade and Fords made a very wide range of sporting guns many of which must have survived. Their best sidelocks, with Brazier or Chilton locks, could be had with double or single triggers and at the turn of the century such a gun cost 50 guineas. A wide range of engraving was available and at the same cost you could have a best quality A & D ejector with sunk side panels and with intercepting sears.

An extensive range of A & D guns was available with prices down to 12 guineas and the Ford "Pigeon or Trap Gun" cost 35 guineas with cross bolt, side clips and intercepting safety sears. Ford's also offered a fine hammer gun for pigeon or wildfowling together with single-barrel guns and rook and rabbit rifles. Of particular interest was the availability of double hammerless cordite rifles in all bores up to .600. The range included a 1 1/4in. bore screw breech punt gun and a hammerless "Ball Shot Gun". To give some idea of the prices compared to today a Browning 5 shot automatic cost £9.

Today Shooting Times and Country Magazine averages about 52 pages, has a full colour cover and is very different from the magazine of 30 or more years ago. However, over the years one thing has remained unchanging - William Ford still advertise "overhauls, fitting and storage, new barrels and new stocks". Quite a remarkable achievement. I only wish that I could put the clock back and visit their Eclipse Gun Works and order myself a double .600 hammerless express rifle and at the same time see the St Mary's Row of half a century ago. You will note that I am not greedy; I did say half a century ago, it could, as you now know be a century ago!

W. GREENER

Very few gunmakers receive the ultimate accolade, the use of their name to describe a type of gun or part of a gun. One thinks of the Purdey "bolt" system, "Anson & Deeley", Holland & Holland "Side-Locks", Greener "Cross bolt" and Greener "safety". Greener, who was he? Why should a French catalogue still describe a shotgun of German manufacture as having a system of locking "fermeture Greener" and why should a German catalogue state "mit Greenerverschluss"?

We have to go back quite a long way to discover the beginning. The story can be said to start in the year 1806 when W Greener was born in the village of Felling near Newcastle-on-Tyne. Now, two thirds the way through the 20th century Felling is in Newcastle-on-Tyne, between Hebburn and Gateshead. The young Greener was apprenticed to Burnand and unfortunately I still know little about this maker other than by 1848 the style was Richard Burnand and the address Pilgram Street.

Greener did not stay long with Burnand, moving to London where he worked for the famous John Manton. William Greener had an extremely high opinion of both the Manton brothers, he extolled the benefits of the "top rib" and was later to write: "Joseph Manton is entitled to the gratitude, not only of the present generation of the gun-making fraternity, but of all succeeding ones; for this reason — he not only gave a character to English guns....he raised the English artisan with himself and left them the acme of mechanics".

One has only to look at a William Greener gun to appreciate that the time spent in London had not been wasted. By 1829 William was back in Newcastle where he set up in a small way as a gunmaker. As with many "country" and also London gunmakers Greener had to travel to Birmingham, the home of gunmaking, both to get work done and for material. The time spent in travel was begrudged and in 1844 Greener decided to establish himself in the Birmingham area where he was able to engrave on the top rib of his muzzle-loading percussion guns "W Greener, maker (By Appointment) to HRH Prince Albert."

Not content with gunmaking he invented and used one of the earliest types of electric light, improved the miners' safety lamp and invented a self-righting lifeboat.

One of the reasons why William Greener is still remembered is because of his writings, otherwise it is very possible that he would have been overshadowed by his son W.W.Greener. His first book "The Gun" was published in 1834, his second "The Science of Gunnery" in 1842 to be followed by "Gunnery in 1858" in that year.

Perhaps his greatest contribution was the invention of the first "expansive" rifle bullet. It was rejected by the British Government who later paid £20,000 to a Frenchman, Minie, for a bullet designed on similar principles. Greener petitioned that he had a prior claim and was granted £1,000 in 1857, "for the first public suggestion of the principle of the 'expansive' bullet". To the last, William Greener was firmly convinced of the superiority of the muzzle-loader.

In his "Gunnery in 1858" Greener states "Notwithstanding all the skill and ingenuity brought to bear upon it, it is, we think, sufficient to prove that

W. Greener hammer gun

breechloading guns cannot be made sufficiently durable to yield any reasonable return for the extra expense and trouble attending their fabrication". Greener died in 1869 still firmly convinced of the superiority of the muzzle-loader, so it was left to his son W.W.Greener to exploit the benefits of breechloaders and his patent, the first in his name, was for a pin-fire with half-cocking facility and pin-fire extractors.

W. W. GREENER

William Wellington Greener was the second of four sons born to William Greener, his birth, in 1834 at Newcastle, coinciding with the publication of his father's first book "The Gun". The book was dedicated to the Duke of Wellington and his admiration for the Noble Duke was also shown by christening his son Wellington.

As a boy "WW" was occupied with his father's business, then in Newcastle, he delivered pistols, powder and equipment, on board whaling-ships and East Indiamen which were being fitted out on the Tyne. With the transfer of business to Birmingham "WW" became responsible for the outworkers: craftsmen who worked at home instead of in a factory or communal workshop and who, at that time, formed a large proportion of the Birmingham gun trade. Although handicapped by defective eyesight he worked for some time on the boring bench and it was because of this type of work that he developed a very fine sense of touch which was to prove of value in later years. A good gunmaker was often said to have "eyes in his fingertips" and it is quite remarkable how imperfections can be detected by "feel" alone.

In 1851 a new factory was erected at Rifle Hill, Aston and son and father appear to have parted company. Certainly there were differences, the father viewed the introduction of the breechloader with scarcely concealed derision

W. W. Greener's famous "St. George Gun"

and the son would have nothing to do with the old-fashioned muzzle-loader. In 1864 W.W. Greener patented and started to manufacture an under-lever, pin-fire, half cocking breechloader and it is interesting to note that such was the rift that W.W. Greener was at pains to advertise that he had no business connection with his father. With the death of W. Greener in 1869, the Rifle Hill and St Mary's Works were again brought under one management. In the meantime, however, the son had patented a self-acting striker and in the same year, 1868, protection was sought for an over/under gun with laterally opening barrels, similar in concept to the later Dickson and Britte guns.

I have never seen a Greener side-opener but no doubt one was made. The famous Greener "cross-bolt" appeared and was combined with bottom holding down bolts in 1873 and in future years was to be widely employed, not only by gunmakers in Britain but also abroad, particularly in Germany and Belgium.

W.W. Greener followed in his father's footsteps, exchanging the tools of gunmaking for a pen, his first book "The Modern Breechloader" being published in 1871. "The Modern Breechloader" appeared in answer to numerous enquiries by sportsmen for the book "Gunnery in 1868" which had been promised by W. Greener and whose death occurred before the book could be completed. Encouraged by the reception given to his first book a second; "Choke Bore Guns" followed in 1876 and then in 1881 W.W. Greener published his magnum opus "The Gun and its Development". This book passed through nine editions and has recently been reprinted in facsimilie. Greener's later books include "Modern Shotguns", "The Breechloader and How to Use It" and books on rifle shooting.

Greener's name will always be associated with choke-boring, although he did not, according to present scholarship, invent this system of barrel boring. Shades of Manton vs Manton were evoked following the appearance of the Greener "Facile Princeps" gun. In 1880 a famous law suit took place in which the firm of Westley Richards claimed that Greener's invention was an infringement of their patent; Greener won his case.

By 1890 Greener claimed, with some justification, that his factory which fronted on St Mary's Row and had spread along Loveday Street to Bath Street was the largest in Britain and by 1923 the firm of W.W. Greener Ltd was to claim that the factory was the largest sporting gun factory in the world. W.W. Greener died at the age of 87 in 1921. The business was continued by his sons, Harry and Charles E. Greener, the firm having been made into a private limited company in the previous year. With the death of Charles Greener in 1951 the business was under the direction of H. Leyton Greener until it was sold in 1965 to Webley & Scott Ltd. The workmen, tools and expertise were subsequently dissipated and the factory pulled down, thus ending a business which made a truly great contribution to the art of making sporting guns.

W. & C. SCOTT LTD.

Not so long ago the future of W & C Scott Ltd appeared uncertain. Now it seems that a way has been found to keep this firm alive and so preserve some of the traditions of the past.

I have written in the past it is no exaggeration that Scott could lay claim to being the best known British shotgun manufacturer, particularly in the North American market and what we now refer to as "our former colonies". This was not based simply on volume of output, considerable though this was, but on the practical contribution to gunmaking and the high standard of the guns made for these markets.

By the turn of the century two guns were being offered, the "Premier" and the "Imperial Premier" at £82 and £112 respectively. Both were fitted with the Scott rectangular cross bolt and block safety bar-locks, while the quality of workmanship and materials was of the highest.

The "Premier" was in fact the first Scott gun I have seen and used. It belonged to my long-time shooting friend Alan Paton, but since it was not nitro-proved I suggested that it be submitted for proof, never thinking that it would fail — which it did. New barrels were fitted, but it was not the same gun and Alan sold it soon afterwards so I thought that that would be the last I would ever see of it. Some years later I spent some time in Italy gathering material for a series on the Italian gun manufacturers. With my Italian friend Mio Giannini I went to meet a well respected Italian clay bird shot, Piero Gualtierotti who had a gun shop in Castelnuovo. Piero shot with a British shotgun, a Scott, and this was shortly produced for my inspection. To the surprise of myself and everyone else I recognised the gun — Alan Paton's Scott. Certain features of the gun which I knew intimately could not have been faked and incredulity gave way to amazement and two old friends were momentarily reunited. Scott guns seem to have this ability to generate strong affection and this is particularly so in America.

For some time now I have been the recipient of catalogues and material

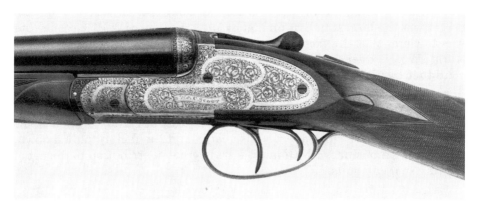

W. & C. Scott sidelock

from Dr. John A. Crawford of Oregon and recently he sent me a facsimile Scott catalogue of 1922. This was extremely interesting because I was able to compare what was on offer with the range described in an earlier catalogue of 1910.

John Crawford sent me a splendid photograph of one of the Scott guns in his collection. This Scott gun, Serial No 40534, was shipped round the "Horn" during the 1880s to Portland, Oregon where it belonged to Henry Winslow Corbett, a US Senator and one of the founders of Portland. The gun has the name, W C Scott & Son, the London address, 10 Gt Castle Street, Regent Circus, London and the name "Excellentia Triplex".

This name was new to me since it did not appear in the literature or in the catalogues I have.

John also sent me a photocopy of the E C Meacham Arms Co of St Louis, Mo, issued 1884, which shows a gun similar to the Scott No 40534 but the catalogue refers to the gun as the "Premier". So, we are left with the mystery of the "Excellentia Triplex". The answer to the name probably lies in the use of the Scott "Triplex" lever grip patented in 1875 and used on Scott guns until about 1914 having been replaced by Scott's "Improved" bolt which employed a rectangular cross bolt, the use of which was introduced in 1892.

Later research showed that the "Excellentia Triplex" was a back action gun made from 1884 until about 1888. The vast range of Scott, Webley and later Webley & Scott guns which were manufactured, most in a bewildering variety of styles and options must have been the very devil for the factory to keep track of over the years. The story has been partially covered by the book, W. & C. Scott, Gunmakers by Crawford and Whatley but much remains to be discovered and, of course, the history of the shotgun side of the Webley business has yet to be documented.

If you do have a Scott double sidelock please take a close look at the name on the barrel and also any names on the action flats. I would be very interested to find out if Scott guns bore any other names such as "Unique", "Reliance" and "Victoria".

Coming right up to date, guns by W & C Scott now bear the names "Bowood" and "Chatsworth". As mentioned above, the uncertainty concerning the future of this firm now appears to have been resolved. The name W & C Scott has been retained following a decision by Webley & Scott to cease manufacture of double shotguns. The people who would have been made redundant determined to remain in the shotgun business, and, financed by the Harris & Sheldon Group, a new company was formed under the name W & C Scott, with a factory bearing the appropriate name Premier Works. The factory is located at Tame Rd, Witton, Birmingham, not far from the Eley ammunition works.

The Birmingham gunmaker has over the years shown a remarkable resilience in the face of economic adversity, government indifference and the destruction of the foundations of the industry. The fact that Scott is a name still to be found on British-made shotguns is testimony to this rugged resilience and I wish them well in the years to come. Certainly, this wish is now more likely to be fulfilled following the recent take over of Scott's by Holland & Holland which augers well for the future of both companies.

JOHN HARRISON

This is a long story and a rather special one. John Harrison was born on October 26, 1905 and he died in April 1981. I met John but once, in 1969 when I was gathering material for a series of articles on the Birmingham gun trade which were published in Shooting Times.

When I had a long letter from another Mr Harrison, a reader, I thought I should try and put together as much information as possible on the working life of a man I had liked and admired. The letter followed our recent meeting at the 1982 Game Fair where I had learned that Mr F Harrison had bought a gun carrying the name Harrison Bros., Birmingham.

Mr Harrison was in a position to tell me quite a lot about his Harrison Bros. shotgun and after our meeting letters flowed between us and I received some photographs and historical data of immense interest and value.

The first item we should look at is the invoice for this gun. It was made for a Mr R S Morley and is described as a 12-bore boxlock ejector gun No. 9487 with 28in barrels and 2 3/4 in chambers. It is proofed for 1 1/4 oz of shot and the barrels are bored: right — 1/4 choke, left — 3/4 choke. A Churchill-type top rib is fitted with a secret head extension. The gun has an automatic rocker safe, Anson push-down fore-end rod and is decorated with "Best" engraving. A half-pistol grip and a horn tip finish the gun with the exception of an oval engraved with the owner's initials. The gun cost £62 with a further £2.50 (i.e. £2. 10s.) for the extra quality engraving. This, remember, was in 1954.

The gun case cost an additional £6. 10s. We now lose sight of the gun until it was bought by Mr F Harrison in 1978. He was that impressed with the gun that he wrote to John Harrison to ask if details could be provided. The letter he received was from 32b Lower Loveday Street, not from the Price Street address of the original invoice, and advised Mr Harrison that the gun had been made by the Harrisons, Albert and John, but Albert had retired, though John being "much younger at 72 year is still going".

John went on to say that the barrels for the gun were made up from the tubes by W. Pearce (now deceased). I had met Mr Pearce in 1969 when he told me that he had started work with Webley's when he was 14 years old and had set up on his own in 1956.

The barrels were bored by Mr T Yates, now retired. I had also met this gentleman on more than one occasion. Those with all the past articles will find him written up for he was quite remarkable with a very odd sense of humour. When bored, the barrels came back to John Harrison where they were jointed to the action, filed-up and finished. John was an action filer and

Harrison Bros. boxlock

he produced the action body on the "Regal Pattern" which was a copy of the boxlock then sold by Churchills. All this inside work — tumblers, sears, springs etc — was fitted by John as was the Scott lever-work and secret head.

Triggers, guard etc were made by Mr H Jones. This was yet another member of the gun trade I met in 1969. He had started by taking his father's dinner to him and running errands way back in 1912, working, as was often the practice, "half time".

The automatic ejector work had been made, fitted and timed by Mr E Smith, Mr J Mallen fitted the rough stock to the body of the action — "heading up" as it is called, and it was then finished to measurements and polished by Mr Eastwood.

We now are coming to the completion of the work. The gun was polished for engraving by the renowned Mr Woodward and it was then engraved by my very dear old friend Mr Harry Morris. After engraving it was then hardened by Mr Woodward. At this point it came back to John Harrison for the last time.

The gun was sent to proof before stocking and, as can be seen from the invoice, it was then proofed for 1 1/4 oz rather than the more usual 1 1/8 oz. The last job before the gun was ready to send to its new owner was to free, assemble and test the gun. This was done by John Harrison.

We don't know what the original owner thought of his new gun but we do know that when the second owner, Mr F Harrison, acquired the gun he was delighted. He went to see John Harrison in Birmingham in 1978 and spent the day in his workshop. This was a memorable experience and was evidently a great pleasure to Mr John Harrison who was delighted that one of his guns had come to light and was now in the hands of a man who very obviously appreciated it.

Let us just briefly re-cap on the chronology. The gun was made in 1954. We have seen HOW it was made and the people who did the work have been named. I then saw Mr John Harrison in 1969 and also I was able to meet quite a few of the men who had had a hand in the creation of gun No. 9487. Even after such a short time some had either retired or died and by the time Mr F Harrison bought the gun in 1978 very few of the original makers of the gun were still in business and those that were, were in the evening of their lives!

What might appear to be a fairly straightforward A & D type shotgun turns out to have quite a history. One which reflects much of the past of the Birmingham Gun Trade and which, on close examination, as we have been able to do, tells us something about the practices and the people who were once part of that close knit and rather special community.

G. E. LEWIS & SONS

Readers will be aware of my constant plea for old catalogues. One reader who has most kindly responded in a very practical way is Mr Shepherdson who sent me the Lewis catalogue for 1926-27.

A word about Lewis. The firm was founded by G.E. Lewis in 1850 and the address given on their 1926 catalogue was, 32-33 Lower Loveday Street, Birmingham. This is in the old traditional gunmaking quarter of Birmingham, around the old church of St Mary's where in the days before the ring road the streets were full of gunmakers; Weaman Street, Whittall Street, Sand Street, Bath Street, Price Street, St Mary's Row.

But, back to Lewis & Sons, makers of the renowned "Gun of the Period". Looking through the catalogue we turn over the pages of a past history. An ordinary gun in a stout cardboard box could be sent to any part of the British Isles for 2s 6d and this included the box! A gun could be sent to most parts of the world for 10s including packing and insurance.

Lewis produced their best quality sidelock hammerless ejector for £60. If Whitworth steel barrels were requested this cost an extra £10 as did a single trigger. Best quality locks with intercepting sears were used and the action body had carved fences, scroll and game engraving and all in the best of taste. A best quality A & D gun with Southgate ejector and treble top lever action was just £10 cheaper but all the extras could be had for the same price. A slightly cheaper sidelock was available at £50 but here the stock was not jointed up to the fences, but when we turn the page again we see another best sidelock with concealed extension and side clips at £60 and this would be a gun to be very proud of. Coming down the scale a sidelock ejector was to be had for £45 and here the purchaser had the option of a cross bolt action, either square or round instead of the normal extension. Some of the very wide range of guns offered were "named". The "Ariel", for example, was a best quality A & D actioned gun in a lightweight action with prices from £50 to a Third quality at £35.

It is of interest to read that the new model "Gun of the Period" which was a registered trade name, was offered with high grade steel barrels at £30 and with "Superior Damascus" barrels at £2 extra.

A double 12-bore of A & D pattern with top lever treble grip and steel

G. E. LEWIS'
"THE GUN OF THE PERIOD."
Has taken Honours wherever shown.
Paris, 1878; Sydney, 1879 and 1880; Melbourne, 1880 and 1881; and Calcutta, 1883 and 1884.

Price from **£15 15s.**

Cross-bolt or my Treble-grip Action.

The above is the latest development of **"The Gun of the Period,"** fitted with the newest and best Patent Ejector, combined with G. E. Lewis' Treble Grip.

We also make this Gun as a Non-Ejector, with treble-grip or cross-bolt action, at **12 Guineas** and upwards, or with top-lever and double-bolt, from **10 Guineas.**

Our stock of Sporting Guns and Rifles, Ready for Delivery, is the largest in England. Send for 200-page Illustrated Catalogue of finished Stock, giving bend, weight, and full description of every gun. We invite Sportsmen to come and inspect our Stock. Any Gun or Rifle may be Tested at our Range before purchase.

REPAIRS.—All kinds of Repairs by a Staff of the most Skilled Workmen in the Trade. Quotations Free.

Secondhand Guns by other Makers taken in exchange.

G. E. LEWIS, Gun and Rifle Works,
32 & 33, LOWER LOVEDAY ST., BIRMINGHAM.
ESTABLISHED 1850.

G. E. Lewis ad

barrels could be had for £8; this gun was, of course, of "Continental Make", but the prospective purchaser was reassured that "These are well made and reliable weapons".

Looking through the pages one comes across the helpful remark "that if you want to get within range of the wily duck and geese — order a Magnum at once". Firing the 3in 1 1/2 oz load Lewis built a magnum for as little as £18 and if you were prepared to have hammers on your gun then you could buy one at £10. Three inch 12-bore cartridges were then selling for 25s per 100. The magnum was tested to give 85 per cent patterns at 40 yards and was well reviewed by the sporting press of the time.

Pigeon guns were also offered firing the 2 3/4 inch case with 1 1/4 oz of shot. Both hammer and hammerless styles were available and, as usual, a wide range of prices suitable for all pockets could be had. The Lewis top lever treble bolt hammer gun was a very handsome weapon and, at £18, appears to have been good value. A cheaper version was available, the "Keepers' Hammer Gun" at £9. 10s. but with side clips and a percussion fence the price went up to £12. Slightly cheaper was the "New Model Keepers' Gun" at £9, but this model had back action locks instead of the bar locks of the gun which cost 10s. more.

The range of guns offered in the 1926 catalogue is truly amazing and it makes me annoyed that I was still in my pram at the time! A single barrel hammerless 12-bore magnum wild-fowling gun was £16. To give you some idea of values the 5 shot Browning automatic 12-bore shotgun was £9. Ball and shot guns were offered, double Express rifles from .303 to .600 and a range of bolt-action sporting rifles based both on Mauser and Lee Enfield military rifles. An interesting item is the Lewis "Cape Gun" with a rifle barrel and smooth bore shot barrel, the shot barrel on the right. Gun cases, cleaning equipment and a wide range of sportsmen's knives complete the range that was on offer to the sporting man in 1926. Cartridges are shown on the inside back cover, best quality, with deep brass heads at 21s per 100 and reliable smokeless at 14s per 100. If you bought 500 they could be sent carriage paid to any station in England and Wales. An interesting exercise in nostalgia if nothing else and for me a most useful mine of information on guns which were being made in the mid-twenties.

WILLIAM POWELL AND SON LTD.

The year is 1802. The place, Birmingham. Possibly the most important event in the lives of most of the inhabitants that year was the signing of the Peace of Amiens in March. So important an event was it that William Murdock illuminated the Soho Foundry of the world-famous firm of Boulton and Watt. What was so special about that you might ask? Well, it was done with illuminating gas, not oil lamps or candles!

Certainly not as spectacular but of importance to our story was the founding of the firm of Powell & Simmons. Joseph Simmons died in 1812 and some time after this William Powell appears to have moved to No. 3 Bartholomew St., from the original premises in the High Street.

At Bartholomew Street the firm was especially well placed for just across the way was the Birmingham Proof House, the foundation stone of which was laid in 1813. William Powell then moved to Carrs Lane. Earlier maps refer to Cares Lane. Although the gun trade was for many years one of the principal industries of Birmingham no complete history has ever been written. Certainly, the industry started on the south side of the city and William Powell's present premises are probably nearer to the original gunmaking quarter than those establishments still surviving in the area around St Mary's Church. Possibly the move north was to gain easier access to the Birmingham & Fazeley Canal, or more likely to the north lay available ground for building.

Without doubt Powell's must have taken part in the manufacture of firearms for the Napoleonic Wars for in the year following the firm's establishment war again broke out between France and Britain, not being concluded until Napoleon's defeat at Waterloo in 1815.

The premises at Carrs Lane must have been fairly typical of the gun trade throughout the second half of the 19th century. In the aftermath of the Wars in Europe, the gun trade suffered a slight recession but business picked

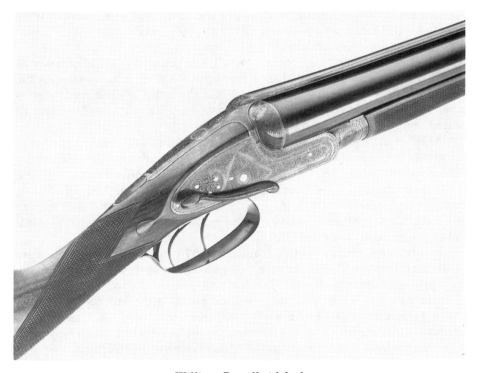

William Powell sidelock

up with the enormous demand for arms as a result of the American Civil War. Powell's were not, however, solely concerned with warlike weapons since, even if they didn't manufacture military weapons during times of war they would nevertheless be affected by shortages of skilled labour and materials. Before the end of this conflict, however, Powell patented the first of the inventions which formed part of their contribution to British gunmaking, for Powell's were not merely "makers of guns".

In 1864 the Powell Patent Snap-Action appeared, at first on hammer pin-fire guns, then on hammer guns and finally on both A & D and sidelock hammerless guns. The Powell snap action enjoyed a long period of popularity and many guns employing this system are still in use as readers of the Shooting Times & Country Magazine will know from our past surveys. The distinctive feature of the Powell system is that the top lever is lifted instead of being pushed to the side and the locking quadrant which it actuates bears securely against the top of the barrel lump. The system has the merit of simplicity and security and I would not be at all surprised to see it reintroduced.

In 1866 an ingenious half cocking mechanism was patented and three years later, in common with other progressive makers, Powell's invented a system to indicate when the gun was loaded. This may seem a little odd today but most shooting men had only just got used to pin-fire guns where the pin protruding from the breech could tell you whether or not there was a cartridge in the chamber and whether or not it had been fired. The ingenious gunmaker did away with pins and introduced central fire guns and, "damn me — you couldn't tell whether the gun was loaded or not without having to open the blasted thing". So, for many, until they got used to the idea, a device which told you whether cartridges were in the chamber or not was quite the vogue. Then, of course, people just got into the habit of opening the guns when they were not shooting them; this was quite simple with Mr Powell's patent snap action!

Another little problem was the removal of the fore-end to get the gun into these new fangled short cases. For this the fore-end had to be removed to take off the barrels and in 1873 a spring bolt fore-end fastening was introduced. In 1876 a transverse bolt locking system was patented and, of course, Powell's continued to build high quality "treble bolt top-lever A & D system guns" for "those sportsmen who may not find our Patent Action with Vertical Lever convenient to manipulate".

No further patents were taken out after 1876 but by this time there were enough well proven ideas to ensure that guns of the highest quality could be built and sportsmen on the whole are a pretty conservative lot. By the end of the century it must also have become pretty apparent that the guns bearing the name Powell which left the Carrs Lane premises possessed an important quality which must have pleased the owners but which may have given the makers' pause for thought — they lasted rather a long time if well looked after!

Even now, over a century later, this is still the case and among the lists of Powell guns which still survive, a surprising number remain in use in spite of damascus barrels and rebounding locks. One such hammer gun made in 1896 has a bar-in-the-wood action and the present owner told me that "it had fired many, many shots and is as good as ever". Other Powell guns have quite fascinating histories, guns made in 1893 being bought in 1922 as a 21st birthday present and still in use today.

One comment made against the vertical lever action was that the user of a loaned Powell "eased springs" by holding back on the lever instead of the hammer, fortunately nothing dreadful happened but the man got quite a fright.

Throughout the whole of the correspondence which followed the survey into surviving Powell guns one fact emerged time and time again — the affection and high regard that the owners had for their guns.

For any firm to have survived for over a century and three quarters is remarkable enough, in these days of constant and never ending change, that they should still be run by the same family is even more remarkable.

In 1977 David and Peter Powell completed the expansion of the premises and a thorough renovation of the outside of the building which has restored it to its former glory and provided a focal point of interest for the citizens of Birmingham, many of whom must be slightly tired of never ending concrete. That these changes have also provided ample facilities for new sales areas for both shooting and fishing equipment should do much to ensure the survival of the firm for the next 175 years. Today the firm service the guns they made in the past and also offer new sidelocks starting at £15,950 and boxlocks starting at £5,500. As with many of the surviving British gunmakers, you not only buy a gun but also a piece of history!

J & W TOLLEY

A question often put to me in letters from readers is — "I have a gun by Messrs 'X'; was he a good maker?" How does one categorise gunmakers? What makes a "good" maker? I suppose a "good" gun is the correct answer. The great gunmakers were something different. They did not just make good or even great guns; they altered the course of events by invention, innovation or style. As to the question — "Did the man who made MY gun make good guns?" the answer lies with the present owner. You have a gun bearing his name. What is YOUR VERDICT? Other words which crop up with regard to gunmakers are respectable, renowned, well-known, highly regarded and so on.

Not so long ago I received a letter from a reader telling me that he had a number of gun catalogues from the 1930 period and asking whether I would like to see them.

A "yes please" letter went off by return and in due course a parcel of

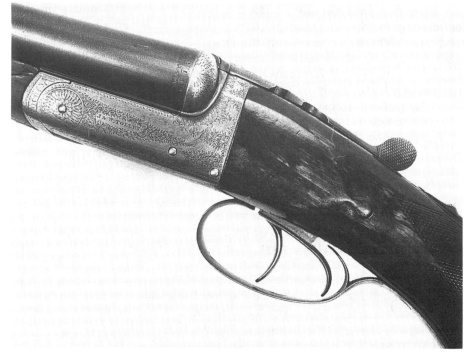

J. & W. Tolley boxlock

catalogues arrived.

I do not have a Tolley catalogue myself, although I have an early Tolley self-cocking gun, and in Shooting Times for April 10, 1971, I wrote about a Tolley double 8-bore rifle which a long time friend had been kind enough to let me photograph. The rifle was fitted with hammer back action locks and was stocked with a pistol hand and a cross bolt to the fore-end. Locking was secured with a rotary under bolt and I regret that I was not able to fire what must be quite a remarkable rifle. On the top rib is the address St. Mary's Square, Birmingham. The earliest address I have for the firm is 22 St Mary's Row and J & W Tolley appear to have started business there in 1859, moving to Loveday Street in 1878.

An advert of 1862 tells us that the firm were "Gun, Rifle and Pistol Makers, Contractors for Military Arms, Breech Loading Guns etc, also all guns suitable for the African Markets". In the ten years after 1862, production from the Birmingham trade was the highest ever achieved. Much was military; the American Civil War followed by wars in Europe did much to stimulate demand, but in the end many of these arms came back onto the market and, added to this, the development of mass production techniques in America meant that this country, for the first time, was capable of supplying much of its own requirements except for double shotguns which Birmingham and then Belgium continued to furnish for many years.

By the 1880s Tolley had moved again and acquired a retail outlet in London at 1 Conduit St, in the West End. In addition to their new "Perfection" hammerless gun Tolley also were able to supply wildfowl guns in all bores up to and including 4 and Express and Big-Game rifles up to and including double 4-bore.

Tolley were seen to advise their customers that they were "Makers by Special Appointment to the Persian Royal Family". The firm was also well known for its punt guns, specialising in Snider actions and a formidable weapon with a "screw-breech".

It is when we ask ourselves what is the exact category we would place the firm in that we come up against a problem. However, one patent appears against the names of J & W Tolley — that for a breech loading action which in 1879 was given only provisional protection. One of the mysteries is the relationship between J & W Tolley and Henry Tolley, also of Birmingham, who was by far the more prolific inventor. Henry Tolley was perhaps best known for his patent top extension. He worked in Weaman St, and appears to have ceased trading in 1892.

J & W Tolley continued in business with premises at 10 Vesey St, and their catalogue shows that they were "Late of 59 New Bond St". My records indicate that the firm was taken over by Holloway & Naughton, but when this was is at present unknown to me.

Tolley made some very interesting and unusual guns in their time. They also exported guns all over the world, and, although I don't think that they could be classed as "great" gunmakers, they certainly deserve to have something placed on the historical record for posterity.

WESTLEY RICHARDS

The firm of Westley Richards was established in 1812 and in June of that year the Americans declared war on Britain. Westley Richards supplied double-barrelled muzzle-loading pistols to cavalry officers who fought in the American War of 1812 and they also supplied weapons to Wellington's armies in the wars against Napoleon which ended in the Battle of Waterloo in 1815. William Westley Richards, the founder, was born in 1788 and he died in 1865. During his working life he was responsible for a number of inventions connected with the muzzle-loader; one was highly praised by no less an authority than Colonel Peter Hawker. Although founded in Birmingham, the firm was not typical of the Birmingham trade and its premises were in the old High Street quite some way from the gun quarter. A London retail outlet was established in 1815 at 170 New Bond Street, under the management of William Bishop, who was known to generations of shooting men as "The Bishop of Bond Street". The London end of the business grew in fame and fortune.

In Birmingham, Westley Richards, the son of the founder, took over the business from his father in 1840 and a further series of important inventions did much to influence the development of guns, rifles and revolvers. It has been said that the firm enjoyed the highest reputation of any Birmingham gunmaker and apart from the contribution made on the military side (the Westley Richards Monkey Tail carbine), sporting guns received attention; 1858, drop-down barrels; 1861, drop-down and slide forward barrels; 1862, the famous top-lever and "doll's head" extension, and, in the same year, patent rifle-sights. In 1864 the top lever design was modified to improve the operation and in 1866 the Monkey Tail capping breechloader was further improved. The stream of inventions continued until Westley Richards retired in 1872 and that year saw bolt-action and sliding breech-block designs. In 1878 his last patent covered the locking system for the drop-down barrel gun.

This remarkable man died in 1897 having lived through the most exciting period in the development of the British shotgun and, as we have seen, having made a notable contribution to that development himself.

With the retirement of Westley Richards, the firm was fortunate enough to find another outstanding man, John Deeley, to take charge. Deeley had joined the firm in 1860 and, between 1873 and 1907 he was partly or wholly responsible for some 17 patents. Of these, there is no doubt that British Patent No 1756, taken out jointly with W. Anson in 1875 is not only the most

Westley Richards sidelock

132

important of the patents associated with the firm of Westley Richards, but it can be said with confidence that it is one of the most important of all the 19th-century patents, protecting as it did the world famous boxlock Anson & Deeley action.

This was the first practical shotgun to be cocked by the fall of the barrels, and it was also the first practical re-design of the action of a double-barrelled shotgun and one which reduced the number of components considerably. It would be impossible to guess at the number of A & D and A & D type shotguns which have been manufactured since 1875 and the fact that guns of this type, similar in concept and design to the original, are still being made is more than adequate testimony to the brilliance of these two men.

The A & D action sporting shotgun quickly became very popular, and Westley Richards licensed others to manufacture it. Numerous "improvements" also appeared. Of the improvements to the original, two ideas were of significance, both patented by John Deeley. The first was an intercepting safety and the second, hand-detachable locks.

It is fortunate that the firm has managed to retain in its possession the first Anson & Deeley gun made. The remarkable thing about this gun is that it could be taken to any shoot today and used without comment well over a century after it was built. Unlike so many prototypes the Anson & Deeley looks "right" from the start. Possibly the only features which might betray its age are the shallow fences.

In 1896 the firm finally outgrew the premises in the High Street and moved not to the gun quarter but (again keeping to themselves) out to a factory in Bournebrook, on the south side of the city. This is where you will find them today. Things have changed but, once again, A & D guns and rifles are being built. Some 75% of the capacity of the works is concerned with the manufacture of highly specialised tools and dies. Some of the "space age" machine tools which are used in this side of the business are also used in the manufacture of the Westley Richards guns and rifles of today. There is a happy blend of the best of the old and new and the techniques employed for gunmaking are those best adapted to the kind of work involved.

The Westley Richards factory as it is today still builds the finest boxlock guns, but it should be placed on record that a fixed-lock 12-bore has a delivery time of about a year. Price is about £2,500. A similar gun, with the famous "hand-detachable" locks has a delivery time of 18 months to two years and the price is in the order of £6,500. Prices vary since each gun is made to the customer's exact requirements and an interesting aspect of having your gun made by Westley Richards is that, when you place your order, you are given the serial number(s) of the gun or guns. You can then visit the factory at any time until your gun is completed to watch its progress and talk to the craftsmen involved.

Westley Richards is rightly proud of its long and distinguished history and it is very pleasant to record that the company is not resting on its laurels, considerable though these may be. The firm is fully engaged in building what will undoubtedly be the heirlooms of tomorrow.

THOMAS WILD

The Definitive history of the Birmingham Gun Trade has yet to be written. Tantalising glimpses of the past are provided from time to time, but it is sad that as the years pass by more and more information is lost to us. The survival of gunmakers whose names ring down through the years are important to us and some have a longer history than at first might be expected.

One of the reasons for the lack of early documentation is that gunmaking in Birmingham was free from corporate restriction, although we know that a payment was made to the Birmingham gunmakers in 1690 by the Treasury on authorisation of the Office of Ordnance. The amount was considerable, £1,016. A further contract was obtained for the supply of muskets at the rate of 200 per month. The ability to carry out the work to the standards required and to manufacture the quantities mentioned leads us to believe that the Birmingham gunmakers were already well established, and certainly as the 18th century opened some 400 Birmingham gunsmiths petitioned Parliament to stop the persecution of the London Guild.

The 18th century saw an increasing demand for arms due to the Jacobite Rebellion, and in 1723 we find recorded the name of Benjamin Watson; later the name of Watson appears again with that of Ryan in connection with the formation of a committee for the erection of a Proof House, the firm of Ryan

4

The New T. Wild Featherweight Hammerless Ejector
DIRECT FROM MAKER TO USER.

A new production manufactured throughout in the usual T. WILD manner of aiming to give the very utmost possible value for money without sacrificing quality in the least degree. It is a proposition which must be considered by anyone thinking of purchasing a Best Quality Weapon of the Latest Lightweight Style.

Price - £35 0 0

T. Wild ad

& Watson being in business from 1777 to 1830. The style reverts to Benjamin Watson in 1830, and in 1857 the firm of Thomas Wild is first recorded, later to be bought out by a relative, Rowland Watson. Although today the firm of Thomas Wild is still in business, it is directed by yet another Watson, Mr R H G Watson.

The firm of Thomas Wild is important because it is one of the few Birmingham firms known to the public since most firms produced mainly for the trade. The manufacture of sporting weapons increased and the "birding trade" (as it is known) became more important as the Birmingham makers contributed not only to the numbers but also to the technical excellence of the sporting gun.

Exactly what the individual contribution of the firm of Thomas Wild was during the second half of the 19th century is unknown to us, but from their last catalogue issued in 1937 we can see the extent of their business. As well as the "Special" grade sidelock illustrated, with Anson fore-end, Southgate ejectors and Scott spindle, available in 12, 16 and 20-bore, Wild produced six grades of A & D ejector guns, some with ball fences, others with what the trade called Webley fences. The best grades had scroll backends to the action body and could also be had with "sunk" side panels. The prices varied from £60 for the sidelock down to just under £9 for a plainly finished A & D non-ejector. Top lever hammer guns were also offered with both bar and back action locks, the cheapest of which was £7 (the comparable Belgian gun being offered at just under £4).

Guns by Thomas Wild will be found to bear the name T. Wild on the action and T. Wild , Birmingham on the top rib. Today Wild do not issue a catalogue but "make to order", but it would be of interest to discover how many Thomas Wild guns are still in use for, as we have seen, the firm can be traced back to the earliest years of the gun trade in Birmingham.

CHARLES OSBORNE & CO. LTD.

Very few of the large number of gunmakers in these islands possess a recorded history. For most of them, the sole evidence that they ever existed, are the guns they made. From these we can tell what sort of work they turned out but many are unknown since little of what they made has survived.

One of the pleasures that I, and others like me, derive from our interest in firearms, is to discover a previously "unknown" maker and to delight in the skill and artistry of one of his masterpieces that fate has permitted to survive.

The larger gun makers issued catalogues and they also advertised, either in trade directories or in the sporting literature of the period. Others are known to us by surviving business papers; letter heads, invoices and similar ephemera. Others are known because they loaded their own cartridges and some of these have survived.

Charles Osborne of Birmingham was a large and well known firm founded in 1838 and we are fortunate that they did issue catalogues and some of these have survived as have examples of the very wide range of guns they manufactured. Their earliest address in Birmingham was at 1 Lichfield Street. In 1854 they moved to Whittall Street where, by 1889 they occupied Nos. 12, 13 and 14. As befitted an important 19th century gunmaker, they also had premises in London, first of all, from 1881 at 3 Broad Street, and then from 1885 to 1892 they were at 7 Whitehall Place, moving to Great Scotland Yard in 1893.

In the 1880's they had premises at 47 George Street, Edinburgh and at Blythswood, in Glasgow. The firm became a Limited Company in 1896 and they ceased to trade just after W.W.II.

We are fortunate in that a number of guns made by the company have survived and, indeed, many are still in use to-day. Of almost equal importance an early catalogue has escaped destruction and from this we can marvel at the wide range of shotguns offered by the company in 1889.

Even at this late date Osborne offered muzzle loading single and double barrel shotguns ranging in price from £1 to £6 for the top quality bar action double gun with damascus barrels. The only clue as to the quality of the gun is given by the statement that it has "Boxwood Furniture". The stock is of boxwood instead of walnut!

Single and double guns in .410 bore with side and top lever work are offered, these were known as "Collector's Guns" at the time and the name describes their intended use.

Osborne made a wide range of double, back action, hammer guns with side, top and underlever actions as well as a similar range of top lever bar action guns of better quality. The company also offered a very wide range of A&D guns with a variety of bolting and a wide range of finishes. A range of bar action hammer guns of high quality was also offered, two of these having their "Patent Concentric Wood Bar". This I have not been able to trace, but the style is what I have called "bar-in-the-wood". These two hammer guns look extremely attractive and I would very much like to see and examine any surviving examples.

The Osborne catalogue shows a very wide range of rook and rabbit rifles, also illustrated are Winchester, Colt and Bullard repeating rifles from America. A speciality of the house was the extensive range of double rifles which were popular in the South African and Indian markets. Also offered were wildfowling guns, both hammer and hammerless and a range of punt guns, one of which was built under their own patent, No. 11879 of 1888. The firm also specialised in making harpoon guns for porpoise and whale and the company's trade mark was, in fact, a representation of a whaling harpoon gun of the type which received a gold medal at an International Exhibition.

Even by the 1930's, Osborne continued to offer a very wide range of sporting guns and rifles and in fact added to the range of accessories by introducing a patent automatic turnover machine for cartridge loading.

One of the most interesting guns in the later catalogue is not their best London sidelock at £80 but their £36 A&D gun. This is not what it seems for this gun was made under a joint patent by Osborne and Ryland taken out in 1909.

Sadly, we know nothing of Charles Osborne and since the company appears to have been run by Ellis and Wilkinson it seems likely that the founder enjoyed but a brief relationship with the company that was to bear his name for well over a century.

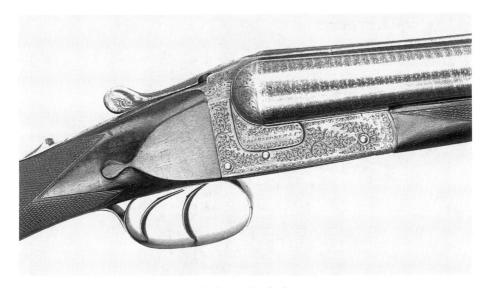

Osborne boxlock

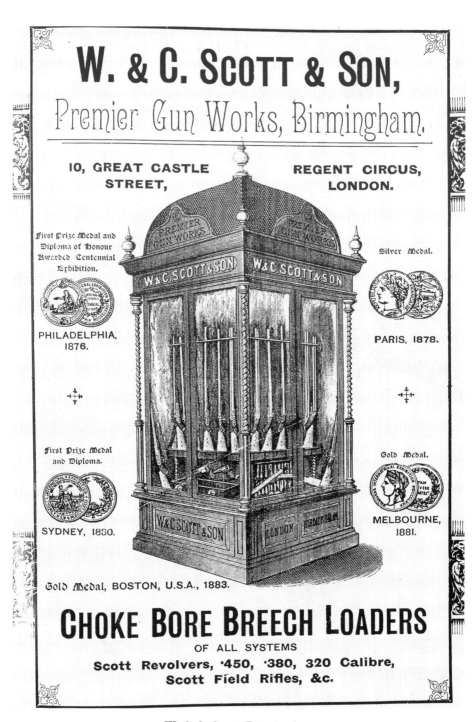

W. & C. Scott, Birmingham

WEBLEY & SCOTT LTD.

W. & C. Scott & Son's Specialities.
HAMMER PIGEON GUNS.

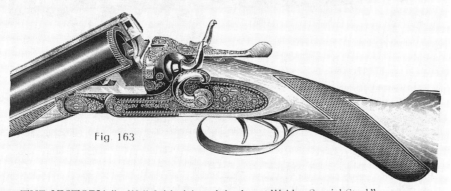

Fig. 163

" THE VICTORIA."—Well-finished breech-loader, "Webley Special Steel" barrels, choke or modified, circular hammers, with Scott's improved rectangular cross-bolt action £30 0 0

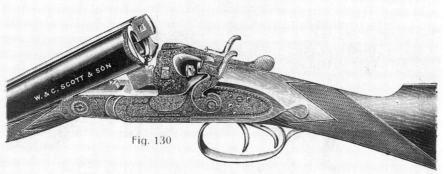

Fig. 130

"THE PIGEON CLUB GUN."—This well-known gun is strongly made, deep breech action, fine locks and barrels, choke bored in best manner, giving highest shooting power.   Specially built for Pigeon Shooters.   Marked between name and address—
THE PIGEON CLUB GUN. £38 0 0
Plainer quality £31 0 0

8

W. & C. Scott ad

139

THE WEBLEY DOUBLE HAMMERLESS GUN
EJECTOR OR NON-EJECTOR.

The design retains all the features of the Anson and Deeley system which has stood the test of time for reliability. Well balanced with graceful outline, each gun receives individual attention by the most highly skilled craftsmen making them comparable with guns of the highest grade.

This model can be confidently recommended to sportsmen requiring a hard hitting gun of sound construction at a moderate price.

Barrels 12 and 16-bore, 28in. and 30in., special steel, left choke, right cylinder. 2½in. chambers.

Action Box lock, hammerless, top lever, non-extension, solid tumblers, automatic Safety.

Stock Selected well seasoned Walnut, straight or half pistol hand.

Fore-end Push down rod " Anson " type.

Finish Superior finish throughout, chequered on hand and fore-end.

Engraving As illustrated, or more ornate if required.

Weight 12 bore, 28in. barrel, approximately 6 lbs. 6 oz.
16 bore, 28in. barrel, approximately 6 lbs. 2 oz.

Price :—**Ejector Model £45** Purchase Tax **£11. 5. 0** extra.
    Non-Ejector   **£40**   ,,   ,,   **£10. 0. 0**   ,,
Available for Export Only.

THE WEBLEY
SINGLE BARREL
SEMI-HAMMERLESS
EJECTOR GUN.

The Webley single barrel gun needs no introduction; thousands are in the hands of satisfied users in all parts of the world. It is a thoroughly sound and reliable general purpose gun, strongly built to withstand hard wear, with long range and hard hitting power.

The action has Webley's patent ejector mechanism and V. mainspring.

Barrel 12 or 16-bore, 28in. to 34in., special steel, full choke, 2¾in. chamber. 3in. chamber to order at extra cost.

Action Semi-hammerless, top lever, ejector.

Stock Well seasoned Walnut, half pistol hand.

Webley & Scott boxlock ad

140

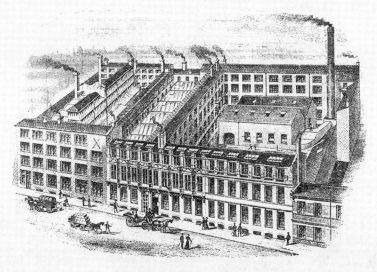

The Webley & Scott Revolver & Arms Co.

LIMITED.

Gun & Rifle
WHOLESALE CATALOGUE.

PREMIER GUN WORKS,

81 to 91, Weaman Street, & 8 to 22, Slaney Street, BIRMINGHAM.

Offices and Showrooms: 86, Weaman Street.

LONDON DEPOT: 78, Shaftesbury Avenue, W.

Telegraphic Addresses:
"ARMAMENTS," LONDON. "WEBLEY," BIRMINGHAM

Telephones:
3087 GERRARD, LONDON. 479 BIRMINGHAM.

ALLEN & JOSEPH, PRINTERS, BIRMINGHAM.

Premier Gun Works, Birmingham

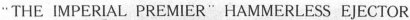

"THE IMPERIAL PREMIER" HAMMERLESS EJECTOR

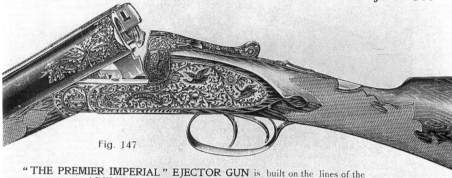

Fig. 147

"THE PREMIER IMPERIAL" EJECTOR GUN is built on the lines of the "PREMIER." The materials and workmanship are of the very finest quality possible; the stock of the finest walnut, and is artistically carved and chequered on hand and fore-end   The ornamentation and general finish of the gun is of the highest art ... £112 0 0

Sir J. Whitworth's Fluid Compressed Steel Barrels, £8 extra.

14

Scott's "Imperial Premier"

ESTABLISHED. 1857.

Telegraphic Address:-
"GUNNERY, BIRMINGHAM".

Telephone Nº 5593, CENTRAL.

19

MEMO FROM Thomas Wild

GUN, RIFLE & REVOLVER MAKER.

TRADE MARK.

Gun Works, 17-18, Whittall Street. BIRMINGHAM, 4.

PROPRIETOR:- R.WATSON.

WHEN REPLYING PLEASE QUOTE Nº

Thomas Wild ad

Vickers sidelock

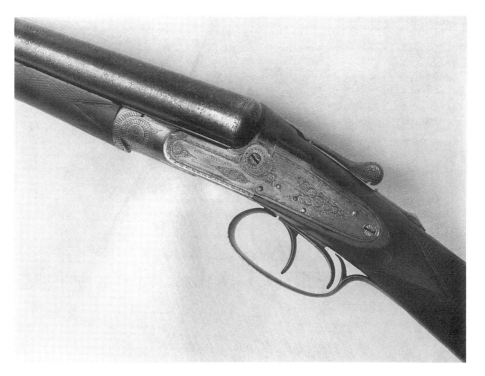

Tolley sidelock

J. & W. TOLLEY'S
"HANDY" PUNT GUN
WITH PATENT BREECH ACTION.
(PATENT, No. 2083.)

The above Sketch shows our latest contribution to Wildfowl Shooting in the "Handy" Punt Gun, for which the following advantages are claimed:—

HANDINESS.—The weight is about 35 lbs., as against 80 to 100 in the ordinary Punt Guns: a boy can carry it on his shoulder for miles, in removing it from one shooting to another.

STRENGTH.—The absence of a hinge or falling-stock gives it great stability, while the form and arrangement of the Breech Action are massive—very noticeable in so light a Gun. The amount of friction in this Action is reduced to a minimum.

SIMPLICITY.—No Gun could have fewer parts in its Action; there is simply one stout cross-bar, which contains the striker: this is the whole of the Breech Action. To load : pull out the breech cross-bar by the handle on the side—when the cartridge chamber is exposed ready to receive the cartridge—push the cross-bar back into its place, and the Gun is ready for firing. The empty cartridge cases are extracted quite clear of the Gun. In this action there are no delicate bars and rods to get disarranged.

SHOOTING.—This Gun is the first Punt Gun that has received in its boring the same delicate treatment as a Shoulder Gun. Hitherto Punt Guns have been very roughly turned out as respects the bore of the barrel, consequently the performance was poor compared with the Shoulder Guns, taking into consideration the resources in the Gun, its weight, bore, length and charge. We have now remedied this by giving to our barrel the same boring as in our long-range Shoulder Guns (*see* special sheet). The result is that, with this Gun, we get *vastly* improved shooting, and a much smaller, handier, and less expensive Gun will do the work for which punters have been in the habit of using the usual large and heavy Guns.

SPECIFICATION.—*Weight*, 35 lbs.   *Bore*, $1\frac{3}{32}$ in.   *Charge: powder*, 20 *to* 25 drachms.   *Shot*, 7 to 9 ozs.   *Length of barrel*, 5 *feet*.   *Price*, **£35.**   *Recoil Apparatus*, **£4.**

LARGE-BORE PUNT GUNS are made with the above Action at the following Prices:—

$1\frac{1}{4}$ in. bore, **£42.** $1\frac{1}{2}$ in. bore, **£48.** $1\frac{3}{4}$ in. bore, **£56.**   2 in. bore, **£66.**

Recoil Frames, **£5** extra.   Barrels over 7 ft. are charged £3 per foot extra.

J. & W. TOLLEY,
Pioneer Works, BIRMINGHAM, & 1, Conduit St., Regent St., LONDON.

ROBERTS & LEETE, Printers, Lime Street Square, E.C., and Southwark, S.E.

J. & W. Tolley punt gun

Tolley ad

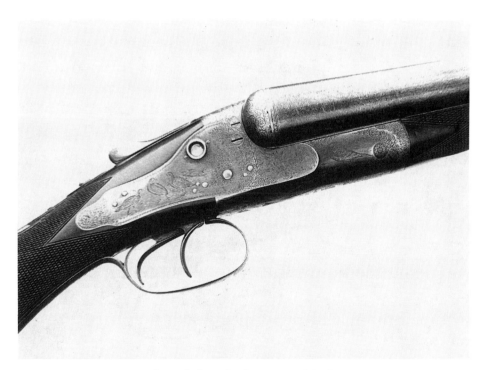

Scott 10 bore back action sidelock

145

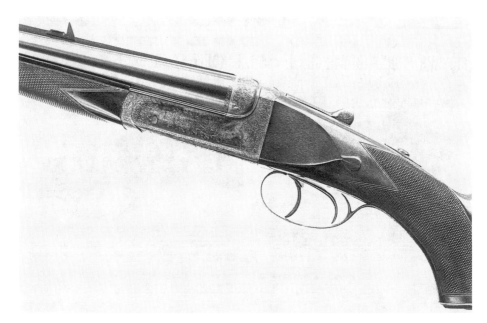

Westley Richards 460 boxlock rifle

8 bore Westley Richards

Westley Richards, Birmingham

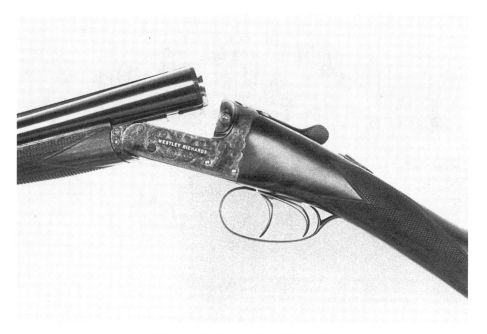

Westley Richards "Best" boxlock

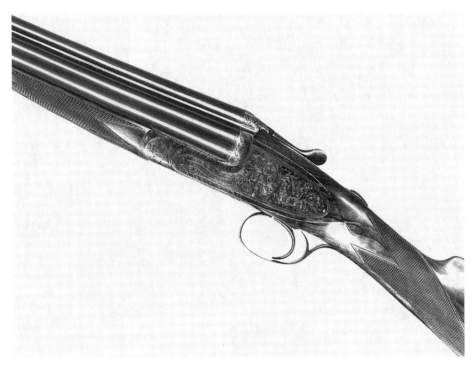

Westley Richards 3 barrel gun

William Powell label

PATENT TREBLE LOCK-FAST HAMMERLESS GUN

WITH

ANSON AND DEELEY'S PATENT LOCK AND COCKING ARRANGEMENT.

Fig. 1. Showing the Gun when open, in a position for Loading.

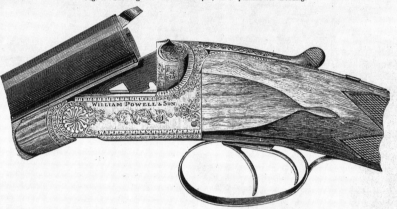

Fig. 2. Showing a Sectional View of the Gun when closed, the Action being Cocked, and the Safety Bolt on the Triggers.

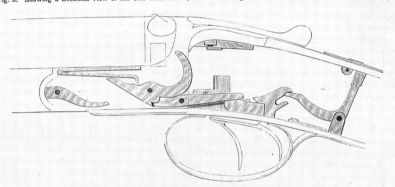

The above drawing represents our new Patent Treble Lock-Fast Snap-Action Gun, combined with the Anson and Deeley Lock and Cocking arrangement, which we recommend in preference to any other system.

Our Snap-Action, with Top Lever working horizontally, is exceptionally strong, and equal to withstand the most severe test to which a Gun may be subject. The Hammerless Lock mechanism is exceedingly simple, and not liable to derangement; the manipulation is rendered easy on account of the weight of the barrels, as they fall, effecting the cocking, and no extra or unpleasant pressure being required on the lever, when opening the Gun.

To lock the Triggers, it is only necessary to press back the Safety Bolt, which is placed in a convenient position behind the Lever, and they (the Triggers) remain securely locked until released by pushing forward the Bolt. The Safety Bolt may be made to lock the Scears and Tumblers if preferred, but the locking of Triggers is a more simple arrangement, and quite sufficient to render the Action free from accidental discharge.

The Safety Bolt may also be made self-acting if preferred, that is, in opening the Gun, the Safety acts on the Triggers, and they remain locked until the Bolt is pushed forward. We do not, however,

William Powell boxlock

149

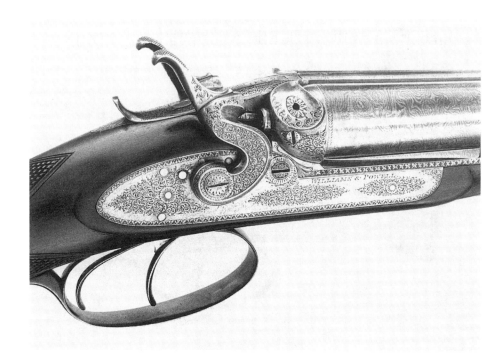

Williams & Powell hammer gun

Osborne ad

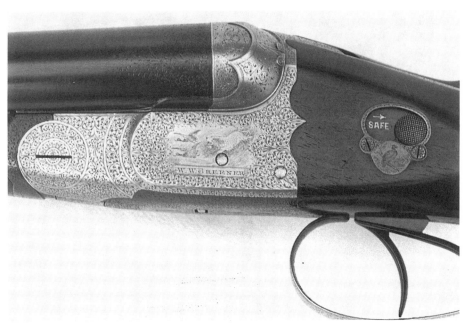

W. W. Greener boxlock

W. W. Greener boxlock

Current Birmingham engraving available

William Cashmore ad

THOMAS BLAND & SONS,

GUN AND RIFLE MANUFACTURERS,

LONDON, LIVERPOOL, AND BIRMINGHAM.

SPECIALITIES IN GUNS.

CAUTION.—In consequence of the unfair competition to which they have been subjected, and the way in which other makers have sold inferior arms under the name of "The Keeper's Gun," originally introduced into the trade by their Firm, Messrs. BLAND have been obliged, in self-protection, to adopt a trade mark for their "Keeper's" Guns, and for the future no "Keeper's" Gun will be issued by them without having the Trade Mark on the heel-plate.

The wording will vary so as to indicate the character of the Gun, whether a "Keeper's," a "Keeper's" New Model, or a "Keeper's" Hammerless, but in each case the Trade Mark will be the figure of a Keeper with his Gun under his arm, and accompanied by his Dog; in a circle, with the words, "THE KEEPER'S GUN."

An engraving of a specimen heel-plate so marked is appended.

"THE KEEPER'S GUN,"
A CENTRAL-FIRE BREECHLOADER
In 10, 12, 14, 16, and 20 bores.
PRICE 6 GUINEAS (WITH CHOKE-BORE BARRELS, 21s. EXTRA.)
STRONGLY RECOMMENDED.

From the Head Keeper to the Earl of Warwick, Grayfield Wood, High Littleton, near Bristol, June 24, 1880.—"'The Keeper's Gun,' No. 4535, stands its work wonderfully well, and is really the very best killing gun I ever had. I dare say I have fired 8000 cartridges from it during the time I have had it. I killed a carrion crow the other night with the left barrel (full choke) at 104 measured yards, measured by a witness present."

Addresses :—106, STRAND, LONDON, W.C.; 62, SOUTH CASTLE STREET, LIVERPOOL; and 41, 42, and 43, WHITTALL STREET, BIRMINGHAM.

Thomas Bland ad

153

Blands'
"Monte Carlo"
Pigeon Trap.

AS USED AT
MONTE CARLO

Highly Recommended

Automatic Action
Agitating Platform
=== No Springs ===

ALL THE ADVANTAGES OF GROUND AND
PLUNGE TRAPS ARE COMBINED IN THE
"MONTE CARLO," WITHOUT THE DEFECTS
OF EITHER.

"No Sluggish Bird can Sit on this Trap."

£1 15 0 each ;
OR SET OF FIVE—
£6 17 6

Thomas Bland pigeon trap ad

The WEBLEY & SCOTT REVOLVER & ARMS Co. Ltd.

WILD FOWL GUNS.

The Actions are all made **Backwork Double Grip.**

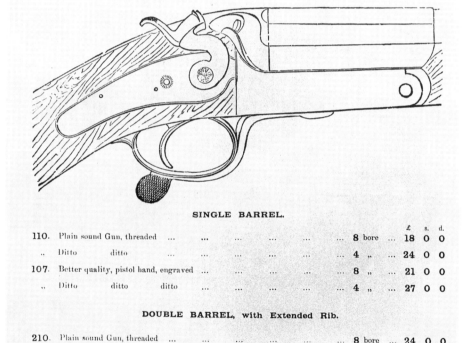

SINGLE BARREL.

			£	s.	d.
110.	Plain sound Gun, threaded ... ... 8 bore ...	18	0	0
„	Ditto ditto ... ... 4 „ ...	24	0	0
107.	Better quality, pistol hand, engraved ... ... 8 „ ...	21	0	0
„	Ditto ditto ditto ... ... 4 „ ...	27	0	0

DOUBLE BARREL, with Extended Rib.

			£	s.	d.
210.	Plain sound Gun, threaded ... ... 8 bore ...	24	0	0
207.	Better quality, pistol hand, engraved ... ... 8 „ ...	27	0	0

Webley & Scott ad

155

B.S.A. NON-EJECTOR MODEL

Double-barrelled Hammerless 12-bore

THE B.S.A. standard non-ejector model is specially manufactured for those sportsmen who require a shot gun sufficiently strong to withstand any amount of ordinary wear, but which is at the same time light and perfectly balanced for easy handling and for the quickest snap-shooting. It has crisp trigger pulls and is built on graceful lines.

Its wonderful killing power and consistently good pattern-throwing have evoked considerable praise from well-known shooting experts, whilst in workmanship and finish it conforms to the high standard for which all B.S.A. products are famous. In brief it is a highest grade gun at a very low price.

Price as specification

£15

Hand-made Stock to customer's measurements
£2 . 5s. extra.

A vulcanite Butt Plate can be supplied at 3 6 extra.

EVERY B.S.A. GUN OR RIFLE
IS FULLY GUARANTEED.

Always clean your gun with
B.S.A. Scientific Cleaners.

BARRELS.
28 or 30 inches. Jessop's special Sheffield fluid-pressed steel. Lumps formed solid with the barrels and the barrels dovetailed together. Right, improved cylinder; left, full choke. 2½ in. or 2¾ in. chambers

FORE-END.
Selected walnut, nicely checkered. Push rod type.

ACTION.
B.S.A. special pattern (Anson & Deeley type). Sears, tumblers, and other action parts of tough chrome-vanadium steel. Beautifully engraved body

of nickel-steel toughened by special method. This combination makes the action amazingly strong. Top lever; automatic safety.

STOCK.
Selected walnut, nicely checkered. Straight-hand or half-pistol grip. Bend at heel, 2 ins.; at comb, 1½ ins. Length, 14½ ins.

LENGTH.
46¼ ins. (with 30 in. barrels).

WEIGHT.
About 5¼ lbs.

Balance and trigger pulls have been specially watched to give this B.S.A. Gun the most superb handling qualities.

B.S.A. ad

156

THE PROVINCIAL GUNMAKERS

The introduction of the breech loader further restricted the ability of many of the smaller provincial gunmakers to compete with the Birmingham trade. The capital outlay involved in even the most rudimentary machine tools which were required to produce such things as the action body could not be justified by the scale of production normally associated with the country gunmaker. Increasingly the majority of the provincial gunmakers came to rely more and more on the products of the "gunmakers gunmaker" in Birmingham.

An additional problem was the constant attrition of the skilled labour force. The training of apprentices was expensive and the loss of the skilled craftsman, who could not be replaced, was, very often, the additional cause of the demise of the country gunmaker, though the proprietor of the "County" gunshop might still call himself a "Gunmaker" this was now becoming a mere courtesy title.

The larger industrialised cities of the north of England did make a significant contribution to the art and science of gunmaking. In the far north, Newcastle upon Tyne produced a number of highly skilled gunmakers whose fame spread beyond local bounds. Some, like Greener, left home and set up in Birmingham, others, like Pape, remained and prospered building up a devoted clientele whose support ensured their survival well into the 20th century.

Another important centre of gunmaking was Manchester. Like Newcastle, industry had produced a proud and newly rich indigenous population, sport was available, and socially acceptable on the moors of Northumberland, Yorkshire and Lancashire and the gunmakers were available to take advantage of the custom offered. In fact, a study of some of the history of the northern gunmakers showed that some, in fact, moved from Birmingham to Manchester to take advantage of the opportunities afforded.

Many of the makers are even to-day, little known outside their locality and others have only been identified in recent years because of the high quality of their surviving products.

To-day, with the benefits that can be made available to the smaller business gunmaking in the provinces is undergoing a revival and the output of the small, well organised workshop, often located in a county town is now of some consequence and may well result in the long term revitalisation of British gunmaking!

W. R. Pape, Newcastle

NICHOLAS ANDREWS & SON

Some time ago I had a letter from a reader, Mr H C Evans, asking for information about a 10-bore percussion muzzle loader with the name N. Andrews & Son on the lockplate and Gateshead on the barrel. A search through my records, recently augmented by yet another reader, John B Friedman, with names culled from American catalogues showed no N. Andrews. Not only was Mr N Andrews absent but also the name of Gateshead.

This happens quite frequently and serves to emphasize the quite large gap there is in our knowledge of gunmakers in the UK in spite of the painstaking work which has been carried out on this subject over the years. So often I am asked to comment on a gun when I have no description and no name. The next step in the process is to try and find someone with the records of the locus. The best plan is to try the local library. Some libraries have a special local study group and have made an effort to collect all the information on the locality in a manner which allows it to be used for research.

This was apparently the case in Gateshead since, when Mr Evans wrote to the library he received a letter which provided the following information. The Andrews family had a tallow chandlers in the 1780s which continued in business until 1834 when Nicholas Andrews retired. We learn from the directories that Nicholas Andrews is described as a "gentleman" in the 1838-1850 directories. Then we have more good fortune, the 1851 census tells us that Nicholas Andrews was 51 in that year and his son 28.

In 1850 Nicholas Andrews & Son took over the established business of J. Marshall, ironmongers and in 1852 they opened up a nail business, but the firm went bankrupt in 1856.

We have no information as to why, after three quarters of a century in business, the firm should fail. The founder, Nicholas Andrews the elder, retired early and over expansion may have been a contributing factor. The year 1856 saw the end of the Crimean War and the outbreak of war between Britain and Russia.

Neither of these events is likely to have influenced the fate of Nicholas Andrews & Son and we are left in the dark as to what happened to the firm and to the family in the years to come.

However, all is not lost for, from Gateshead, I have received a copy of the advert in the 1851 directory.

Underneath the advert for the Roker Baths Hotel at Monkwearmouth we find the advert for Nicholas Andrews & Son which tells us that they are in business at 16 Bottle Bank and at their Nail Manufactory at Sunderland Road End, Gateshead-on-Tyne. We have confirmation that they are wholesale ironmongers, offer stove and kitchen furniture, joiner tools, brushes, mops etc, and make cut and wrought nails. We also find that they are dealers in guns and every description of gun furniture.

NICHOLAS ANDREWS AND SON,

16, Bottle Bank, and at their Nail Manufactory,

SUNDERLAND ROAD END, GATESHEAD-ON-TYNE,

WHOLESALE IRONMONGERS,

CUT AND WROUGHT NAIL MANUFACTURERS,

STOVE AND KITCHEN RANGE MAKERS,

DEALERS IN

Guns, and every Description of Gun Furniture.

JOINERS' TOOLS, WARRANTED OF THE BEST SHEFFIELD MANUFACTURE.

BRUSHES, MOPS, ETC., ETC.

N.B.—The Public are respectfully invited to inspect their WHOLESALE PATTERN SHOW ROOMS, which contain the LARGEST ASSORTMENT of KITCHEN RANGES, REGIS-TERED and SHAM STOVES, at the most Reasonable Prices.

Country Orders punctually attended to.

PRINTED LISTS SENT TO ANY PART.

GENERAL SMITH-WORK DONE CAREFULLY TO ORDER.

Nicholas Andrews and Sons ad

The advert is of interest since it was published in 1851 but, according to the records, the firm did not take over the ironmongery and nail business of Marshall until 1852. From this we must assume that they were already in the ironmonger business before acquiring the business of Marshall.

I was also interested in "registered and sham stoves". A "registered" stove I understand to be one in which the air flow can be regulated by a sliding plate but I am at a loss to understand a "sham" stove. This incidentally illustrates one of the major hazards of research, getting sidetracked down fascinating by-ways and losing sight of the original goal, or at least mislaying things for a while; very interesting but very time consuming!

Since I haven't seen the gun myself I have to assume certain things about it, the most important being that Andrews did not "make" the gun but probably bought it from the trade in Birmingham. So from a very unpromising start we have quite a lot of useful information, and the gun now has "connections" which make it all the more interesting.

JAMES ADSETT

The introduction of hammerless, self cocking actions in the fourth quarter of the 19th century stimulated a flurry of inventive activity which makes this period of the history of shotguns one of the most fascinating.

The previous 25 years, from the middle of the century, had seen the

160

dominant position of the muzzle loader challenged and usurped, and then, the public having got used to loading the gun from the breech instead of the muzzle, the type of cartridge was changed from pin-fire to central-fire.

To many the under-lever hammer breechloader was the acme of perfection and, indeed, many preferred to use a hammer gun even when the hammerless action had become generally accepted.

Without doubt the significant development of the hammerless action was that due to W. Anson and J Deeley in 1875. This design represented a totally new approach to the problem and its elegant simplicity has ensured that this type of action has remained in world-wide use unchanged in its basic elements from the day of its inception over a century ago.

However, although the excellence of the A & D action is acknowledged today this was not self-evident in 1875 and no doubt many were distrustful of the quantum leap the design represented and preferred the more gradual development based on tried and true designs. Such a design was the Murcott of 1871 which employed conventional bar action sidelocks with provision for self cocking. This was achieved by an extension of the bolt which locked the barrels bearing on a stud on the tumbler carrying the striker. When the underlever was pushed forward, the barrels were unlocked and the strikers cocked. Similar to the Gibbs & Pitt of 1873 was the Scott of 1874 in which the locks were placed above the trigger plate. None of the mutant sidelock designs were particularly attractive, mainly because of the need to have an

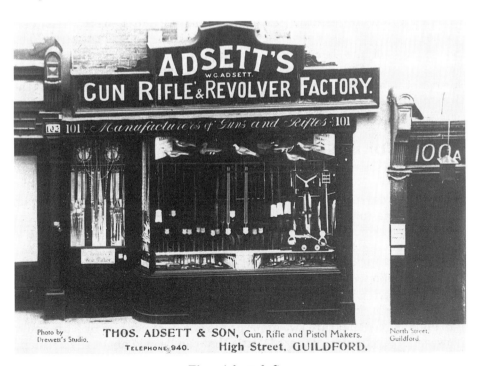

Thos. Adsett & Son

161

unsightly protuberance under the action, but by 1876 Scott had developed a pleasing sidelock design which was to become widely copied and used by other makers.

The search for a satisfactory self-cocking hammerless gun was not confined to the gunmakers of Birmingham and London. Interesting designs which could have developed further were placed on the market by a number of provincial makers and one of the most intriguing was that introduced by James Adsett of Canterbury some time after 1877.

James was in business at 4 Upper Bridge Street in 1869. We also find a James Adsett listed in Guildford from 1839 until 1866 and a Thomas Adsett in Faversham, Kent, in 1869. A Thomas Adsett survived in Guildford until 1900, and possibly longer, but at present the relationship of the various gunmakers bearing the name Adsett remains unknown.

The one Adsett I have seen is a hammerless, self-cocking design which employs the push-forward underlever to cock the combined tumbler and striker, and there is a safety or locking bolt which is pushed forward to prevent the gun being fired. Both James and Thomas Adsett were responsible for a further development of the shotgun action, for, in 1879, they patented an action which employed coil springs in a manner similar to the better known "Acme" action of Woodward.

After this the inventive genius of the Adsetts seems to have been exhausted and the literature is silent on their further activities. That I now know that at least one Adsett action has survived is due to Mr John Ashcroft who very kindly supplied me with details of his gun and even better, sent me the negatives. Are there any other similar Adsett actions in existence? The design may not have been stable so variants may have been made and may have survived. Are there any of the later Adsett actions with coil main springs still in existence and lastly, does anyone have any information on the firm of Adsett?

BURNAND OF NEWCASTLE

Articles which I have written on William Pape of Newcastle aroused a remarkable degree of interest and, if nothing else, this interest again highlights the immense contribution made to British gunmaking by the provincial maker. True, many sought the greater rewards which came to some by moving to London but others stayed in their home towns and established firms which endured and prospered for many decades. Amongst the people who wrote to me about their Pape guns was Mr E J Jackson of Ellesmere Port, Cheshire.

From Mr Jackson I received a splendid photograph of his Pape hammer gun and for good measure two other prints of a hammer gun by Burnand of Newcastle. Mechanically there is little that can be said about the Burnand gun, the locks are by Joseph Brazier, Ashes and since Brazier's name again

Hammer gun by Burnand

appears on the flats of the action it is not unlikely that this was a "Black Country" gun made by Brazier for the trade but made to special order.

As far as I can discover, the firm of Burnand was established in Newcastle about 1800 and probably by the time this gun was made, which could have been in the 1860s, the firm might have been in the hands of the second generation. Muzzle-loading guns were certainly made by the firm in the early days and one of the claims to fame is that W. Greener served his apprentice-ship with Burnand.

Burnand and his guns continue to intrigue me. I have the feeling that there were at least three Burnands and I would be interested to hear from anyone with a gun bearing this maker's name.

W GRIFFITHS

Every now and again I come across a new maker — new, that is, to me, since most are now long-since dead and gone. It is of particular interest to encounter a gun of superb quality by what is to me an "unknown".

Earlier in the year I received some prints of a gun by Griffiths from a gunsmith friend in America, Bill McGuire. I later asked for a loan of the negatives and Bill kindly sent me a set which I developed myself. Apart from the fact that the negatives were of a very high quality, it was obvious that here was a very fine gun by a maker whose work could stand comparison with

W. Griffith's hammer gun

that of the London trade.

Some of you will be familiar with the names of the provincial gunmakers whose work could stand alongside that of any gunmaker in the kingdom. Griffiths appears to be one of this select band of cunning craftsmen.

According to Bill McGuire the barrels are marked William Griffiths, late J. W. Edge. Bill wanted to know what Edge had to do with the gun and I was able to tell him that it was common practice for someone who had served his time or who had worked for a maker of repute to mention this fact on his products, at least in those early years before his own reputation was fully established.

J W Edge was to be found at 24 Ridgefield St., Manchester in 1848, certainly by the end of the century he was no longer in business and he was not listed in 1858. I have seen a very fine percussion shotgun by John William Edge and it is obvious where Griffiths learned his skills and perfected his craft. Edge had several patents to his credit but none has been discovered by Griffiths.

If Griffiths did not have the necessary technical innovative capacity to think up new ideas he was certainly a skilled and artistic craftsman.

If we were to ask where Griffiths worked we have a slight problem since there were three makers with the name Griffiths and all had the initial W. One worked in Birmingham, one in Worcester and one in Manchester. It seems likely that the Manchester Griffiths would be the likely man, but he is listed as W. J. Griffiths. This may have been a son of W. Griffiths or there may be some other explanation. Perhaps a reader in the Manchester area can come up with some answers. Certainly W Griffiths was a maker of very high-quality guns and we should know a little about him if at all possible.

MANTON & CO, CALCUTTA

Few people would dispute that the most famous name in the history of British gunmaking is that of Manton. The two brothers, John, the elder and Joseph made an extraordinary contribution to the development of the modern shotgun and, although John died in 1834, and Joseph a year later, the name Manton remains undimmed by the passing of the years and the artistry of their craftsmanship still has the power to delight and amaze.

Less well-known, perhaps, is the fact that the firm of Manton established a business in India in 1825. Frederick Manton left England for Calcutta and the business was established at 10 Lall Bazaar, Calcutta. The firm passed out of the hands of the Manton family in 1846 and, prior to moving to 13 Old Court House St, the firm was in business at 63 Cossitollah, Calcutta.

The first Manton & Co Calcutta catalogue that I have seen was shown to me by Gron and Chris Edwards during a recent visit to them. I have known both for many years and have learned a great deal from Gron Edwards' experience in gun collecting which goes back to the years before the last war

MANTON'S
Single-Trigger Hammerless Ejector Shot Guns.

PROVED FOR NITRO-COMPOUNDS.

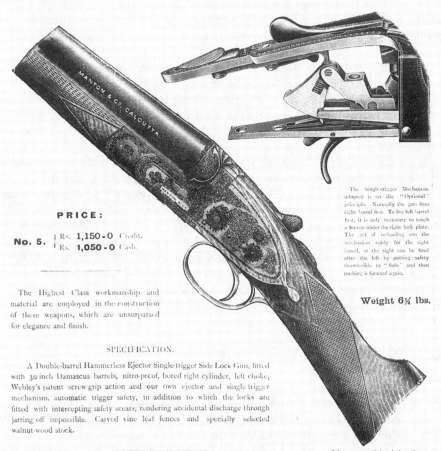

The Single-trigger Mechanism adopted is on the "Optional" principle. Normally the gun fires right barrel first. To fire left barrel first, it is only necessary to touch a button under the right lock plate. The act of re-loading sets the mechanism ready for the right barrel, or the right can be fired after the left by putting safety thumb-slide to "Safe" and then pushing it forward again.

PRICE:

No. 5. { Rs. **1,150 - 0** Credit.
          { Rs. **1,050 - 0** Cash.

Weight 6¼ lbs.

The Highest Class workmanship and material are employed in the construction of these weapons, which are unsurpassed for elegance and finish.

SPECIFICATION.

A Double-barrel Hammerless Ejector Single-trigger Side Lock Gun, fitted with 30 inch Damascus barrels, nitro-proof, bored right cylinder, left choke, Webley's patent screw grip action and our own ejector and single trigger mechanism, automatic trigger safety, in addition to which the locks are fitted with intercepting safety scars, rendering accidental discharge through jarring off impossible. Carved vine leaf fences and specially selected walnut-wood stock.

Advantages claimed for the Single Trigger.

1. The left barrel can be fired quicker.
2. The trigger finger cannot be bruised when firing the second barrel.
3. The length of the stock remains the same for both barrels.

Supplied in oak and leather case, with the following apparatus :

Cleaning Rod and Apparatus.	Powder Measure.	Loading Tube.
Turnover Machine.	Shot Measure.	Loading Rammer.
Recapping Machine.	Extractor	Oil Bottle.
Pocket Cleaner.	2 Dummy Cartridges	2 Turnscrews.
Disc Key.	Breech-cleaning Brush.	

Manton & Co., Calcutta

166

when one could not lift a book up to find the answers since there were hardly any relevant books then written! Gron told me of his delight in reading the books written by J.N. George which, for the first time, gave the gun collector an indication of the great scope of his subject.

The catalogue is 9in x 11in with 111 pages. Guns, cartridges and associated equipment take up 75 pages, the remainder being devoted to hog spears, knives, tennis, cricket, football, fishing and other pastimes. Manton's address was then "The Pioneer Gun & Rifle Works" and in the early days the firm sent guns abroad.

The 1909 catalogue identifies certain guns as being made by UK firms; for example, the "Standard" A & D 12-bore for use "with shot, ball or shell" was made by and bears the name of B. Woodward & Sons, London. Other guns in the very extensive range offered (with the exception of Holland & Holland and the products of gun factories such as Winchester, FN, and Mauser) are unnamed and one is left with the question — "Were any guns or rifles actually manufactured in Calcutta?". I think not and am of the opinion that the guns bearing the name Manton were probably made by firms in Birmingham and it would be interesting to see what sort of proof marks the Manton guns and rifles of the pre-1914 era bear. The terminology used by the firm is interesting. "Big Game" rifles are the 8, 10 and 12 -bores; the .450, .500 and .577 rifles are described as "Express Rifles" and the .400 and .470 rifles are known as "High Velocity".

Mention of "shot, ball and shell" is made above. The shell was the "Mead" shell which consisted of a hollow spherical core cast inside a spherical bullet. Other types of shells could be had including the "Forsyth" and the "Calvert". Rotary bullets were also advertised and I understand the term to mean the type of "vaned", cylindrical bullet such as the "Brenneke" or "Stendenbach". Duck guns in single 8-bore and guns for 3 1/4in paper or metal covered 12-bore are also advertised. In addition to the Browning 5-shot automatic shotgun the Swedish Sjorgen was also offered. Double hammer and hammerless rifles are shown together with the .275 and .350 bore "Mauser-Rigby" magazine rifles. A "Farquharson action" rifle for the .450-400 cartridge is advertised but this is in fact the Webley falling block action of 1902 and this lends further weight to my belief that Webley & Scott made most of the rifles and shotguns in the Manton catalogue.

BSA air rifles with both "Adder" and Lane's "Rotary" air gun pellets are the only air weapons to be seen in the pages of the catalogue but there is no lack of variety with the pistols. Colt, Webley, Browning and Mauser automatic pistols are illustrated together with a range of Webley revolvers including the "WG" Target Model, the Army Model and the "WP" hammerless .32 revolver. Webley Mark IV .455 revolvers as well as the Mark III .38 are to be had and at less cost the solid frame RIC and "British Bull Dog" revolvers together with the short barrel "Metropolitan Police Model" and the interesting .360 No. 5 Webley "Express". Smith & Wesson and "other American makes" complete the handgun section. A very wide range of shotgun cartridges, rifle cartridges, rook rifles and revolver and automatic pistol cartridges were also offered, a range wide enough to deal with most enquiries and a treasure house for the collector.

One comes to the end of the arms' section of the catalogue with the feeling that a very full and magnificent meal has been enjoyed and that for a brief period something of the grandeur that was Imperial India has lived again.

GILES WHITTOME

The manner in which firearms are made varies enormously. On the one hand we have modern, mass-production methods where required skill is built into machinery while at the other extreme it is possible for one man alone to make an entirely satisfactory gun.

Today, in this country, use of specialised machine tools is restricted to manufacture of military weapons and, to a lesser extent, the manufacture of simple bolt-action sporting rifles. However, the needs of the high-quality sporting shotgun market cannot be met by these manufacturing techniques. It is not that modern technology could not produce weapons of this type, but, quite simply, that because of the low demand it would be far too expensive to employ the highly sophisticated techniques that are now available for such low volume production.

Nor, on the other hand, is it possible for one man to make all the parts of a working shotgun himself, as part of an economically viable enterprise. It can be done as a "one-off" exercise and it has been done in recent years, though largely to satisfy the individual's sense of personal achievement.

For a commercial enterprise something different is needed. One cannot get a number of people who can all, as individuals, make identical things. It is expression of the individual's sense and feeling for craftsmanship which make the objects of their attention desirable.

The alternative is one which was adopted hundreds of years ago — specialisation. The advantages of specialisation from the production aspect can be readily seen in the manufacture of bows and arrows during the Middle Ages. Even today, many of the specialised skills developed are remembered in surnames such as Bowyer, Shafter, Fletcher.

In the manufacure of simple firearms the task was divided into those who made the locks, the barrels and the stock. In the North of Italy whole villages were "specialised" in this manner and the gun was subsequently assembled, tested and sold from a central point such as Gardone in the Val Trompia. In this country the gun trade developed along these lines in Birmingham, increasing specialisation along with the use of power for barrel making and for the forging of certain gun parts, which were then supplied to the trade.

By the mid-19th century the trade had become so highly specialised that even a relatively simple weapon like a muzzle-loader could pass through 50

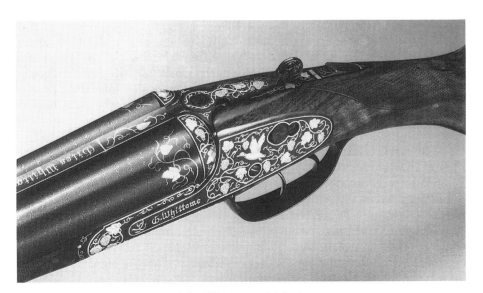

Giles Whittome sidelock

or 60 hands before completion. Obviously for the system to work well these skills had to be co-ordinated. Two broad classes of supplier emerged. The first was a time-served gunsmith with a general knowledge of gunmaking who set up on his own. He might employ journeymen whose skills and craftsmanship were known to him and to whom certain tasks were given. As an alternative he could own premises and let out space, a bench, light and even tools, to craftsmen who would work for him but also be free to offer their skills to others in the trade. This provided a very desirable degree of flexibility to cope with fluctuations in trade and could often mean that skilled men could be kept employed when otherwise they would have to be paid off or be idle.

So far, we have two methods of manufacture which were well suited to the production of sporting shotguns; the first where the entire operation was carried out under one roof by people employed by one man and the second where the operation was carried out by self-employed craftsmen, sometimes under one roof but often dispersed over a specific area. Some of the skills needed were of such a specialised nature that few "gunmakers" could ever aspire to having these operations under their own roof. Tube making, lock making and engraving are good examples.

The second means of co-ordinating manufacture differed from the first in that the man responsible, and whose name and address quite often appeared on the gun, was not a gunmaker in that he had special trade or craft skills. He was what we would call today an entrepreneur, contractor or even businessman. His skills lay in the co-ordination and organisation of the various skills, and purchase of raw materials perhaps, and his was the decision on what was to be made, quality, quantity, markets and methods of sale. He also had responsibility for the final firearm. His was the responsibility for ensuring customer satisfaction.

Some of the most commonly asked questions are, "Who made my gun?", "Did THEY actually make it?", and "Were they GUNMAKERS?" As you can see from what has been a somewhat lengthy preamble, the answers are not easy to find. The name on the gun might be that of a man long since dead, or a firm or, in rare cases, the gun might bear one name on the outside of the lock-plate, another on the inside, the engraving might be signed by someone else and the barrels bear yet another name.

The name on the rib and the outside of the lock-plate is the name of the manor firm responsible for the complete gun and, quite recently, I had the chance to meet someone whose name is on the ribs of some extremely fine quality shotguns and rifles, Giles Whittome.

Giles explained from the very first that he is not a "gunmaker" himself: that is to say his skills are not those of a barrel maker, lock maker or stock finisher. He is an accountant. This, when one looks at it is probably the most appropriate skill needed for survival in this age of government intervention and trade manipulation by tax law.

Giles solicits orders for the unusual, the unique, and the frankly mind-boggling in firearms and, providing that what the customer wants can be achieved by skilled craftsmen (within the constraints imposed by safety), Giles will endeavor to satisfy the customer's wishes.

Fundamental changes in the way the gun trade organises itself mean that no longer is it necessary for the craftsman to work in the gun quarter, within walking distance of the gunmaker. Probably the first to break the traditional 19th century mould was probably the engraver. Today, many engravers have reverted to what one might call a cottage industry. They live in pleasant rural surroundings and operate in a manner more in keeping with the 18th century than the 20th. With what can only be called the virtual demise of the manufacturing industry in many parts of the country who is to say that this will not be the way many things will be made by the end of the century?

Giles has a finger in many pies and the manufacture of "armes de luxe" is but one of them. He does not live in any of the "centres" of gunmaking but draws on the skills of many specialised craftsmen who do work for the London trade. Many of these people have also followed the lead of the engravers and no longer are cohabitants of a gunmakers' warren and the younger craftsmen (and their wives) appear to find this way of working more congenial. A co-ordinator is, however, needed for much of the work and it is here that Giles comes into his own.

I am delighted that we still have craftsmen in the gun trade of this country with the skills needed to produce what can only be described as a work of art and that we still have entrepreneurs of the stature of Giles Whittome who can "realise" armes de luxe to delight and astound present and future generations.

CHARLES ROSSON

A number of queries have been received on the subject of Charles Rosson. Since the information on files was quite meagre I asked for help from readers, and, as usual, this was forthcoming, for which my thanks. If we summarise the data contained in the literature we first of all look for facts about the firm in "English Gunmakers" by Bailey & Nie. Checking first of all in the Birmingham section we find a number of gunmakers by this name. The earliest listed is Thomas Rosson, 1838, 22 Lancaster Street. Charles Rosson is listed from 1840-1872 at 56 Hatchett Street and also for part of this time at 19 Livery Street. Charles Jnr is shown as being at 20 St Mary's Row from 1873-1882 and there is a G. Rosson at 1 Whittal Street from 1857 to 1861. During this period no firm by the name of Rosson is listed in the London directory so none of the firms listed above appears to have been sufficiently large to merit London agents or addresses.

In my own Birmingham gunmakers listings I have no mention of the Birmingham Rosson makers or any indication of the extent of their activities. No mention of any relationship, if any, between the various firms can be traced. In the provincial gunmakers list compiled by Bailey & Nie we find Charles Rosson in business in Warwick at 46 Market Place from 1859 to 1870. We ask the question is THIS Rosson any relation to the Birmingham

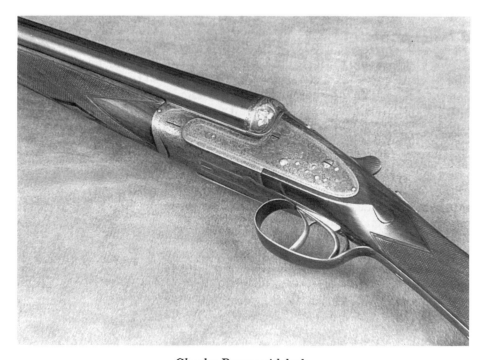

Charles Rosson sidelock

Rossons? — and, once again, we don't know.

If we then move into the 20th century, but only just, we find that Charles Rosson is listed at 4 Market Head, Derby and at 13 Rampant Horse Street, Norwich.

A further check is always advisable on the inventiveness of our quarry. In this case we come up with an answer, and another mystery. Charles Rosson of Market Head, Derby, Gun Manufacturer, obtained patent protection for a cartridge case ejector in 1889. This ejector could be applied to both hammer and hammerless guns.

Then we can have a look at the members of the Gunmakers Association where we find a Mr C.S. Rosson. The note I have against this name is Gunmakers, Norwich, sold out to Charles Hellis & Sons Ltd. But I have no date for this. This, then, is about the sum total of information available from the literature. However, Mr Wilson drew my attention to the fact that in the book *Experts on Guns and Shooting*, Teasdale-Buckell mentions that Charles Rosson of Derby was apprenticed to John Frasier and also worked for Hollis & Sheath in Birmingham. He is credited with the invention of a "try-gun" and a cartridge-loading machine capable of filling 2,000 cartridges an hour. Mr Hodgkinson of Derby told me that the original style of the firm was Dobson & Rosson. To prove the point I then received a photograph of the trade label which tells us that Dobson & Rosson were to be found at 4 Market Head, Derby and that the firm was "from Edinburgh".

A quick look at Bailey & Nie to see if they have listed Dobson & Rosson shows they have no mention. Mr Pember mentioned his Dobson & Rosson hammer gun marked 4 Market Head, Derby and bearing W. Anson's patent No 9454.

Mr Hodgkinson went on to tell me that he could just remember meeting Charles Rosson and that the style of the firm changed to Charles Rosson & Son at the turn of the century. "Young Rosson", as the son was known, continued the business until about 1950 when the stock was sold off and the firm ceased to trade.

Then from Mr Stoodley (who very kindly sent me a copy of the Charles Rosson patent) came details of his Rosson gun No 8097. Then we move to Stockholm where another Charles Rosson gun exists. This is a No. 33074 and the owner, Mr Ehrencrona, sent me details from which I learned that the gun was a side-by-side double finished in what we might call "London-style" stocked to the fences, and all-in-all a desirable gun. It is much later than Mr Stoodley's gun which is not stocked to the fences and has the earlier pattern of back-action lock with a bar-lock plate. The other Rosson, C.S. Rosson of Norwich, is also of interest since they sold a gun with a most unusual slide opening, but this is another story!

JOHN ADAMS SCOTCHER

The gunmakers of the second half of the 19th century can be placed in several categories. First, there were the "great" makers of the capital, the capital not only of a country, but of a rich and powerful empire. Then came the important makers of the great centres of population, many of whom enjoyed, and had earned, a reputation as great as the fashionable makers of London's West End. Then came the makers to the trade, the Birmingham makers who made guns to order and put someone else's name on rib and lockplate and last, but by no means least, were what I call the country gunmakers. Many of these made guns in their entirety, others did most of the work, but bought in locks and furniture from the suppliers in Birmingham and Wolverhampton.

As the years went by, fewer country makers actually made guns. More and more parts were made elsewhere, until at last the gun was made to their specification and bore their name, but all the work was done in Birmingham.

The history of many of these small country gunmakers is unknown. In their day they were an important part of the sporting scene and the owner or proprietor an important and respected figure in the community.

However, with the passing of the years, information and records of the history of such men became increasingly hard to come by. Old records have been lost and names and events forgotten.

It is therefore with some considerable satisfaction that I received a letter from Gareth Jenkins of the Moyses Hall Museum, Bury St Edmunds, giving me details of Suffolk gunmakers. A very complete list of the gun trade in Bury St Edmunds was provided, dating from 1782 to the present day. Details of the three present firms in the gun trade were also included, Horrocks, Clayton and Anglia Arms. The recording of firms at present or recently in business is important, since it is only by such records that the historian of tomorrow will have access to information we so sadly lack today.

One of the most important of the Bury St Edmunds gunmakers was John Adams Scotcher. From Mr Jenkin's researches it appears that Scotcher began business in 1864 at 17 Market Hill. In 1868 the name was changed to 17 Meat Market and the address was again changed to 4 The Traverse, from c1900. Without local knowledge, one might think that Scotcher had moved twice. This does not appear to be the case, he stayed where he was, but, as so often happened, the street name or number was altered. Again, as so often happened, Scotcher took over premises which were previously occupied by William Young, who had been in business as a gunmaker from 1823 to 1858. What happened in the intervening years from 1858 to 1864 is not known. Scotcher's business may have been established at an earlier date but not recorded.

In 1896 the style of the firm changed to J.A. Scotcher & Son, the son being John Gepp Scotcher. J.G. Scotcher apparently lived on the premises in 1912 and his father at 30 St Andrew's Street South, where the chimney pots bear

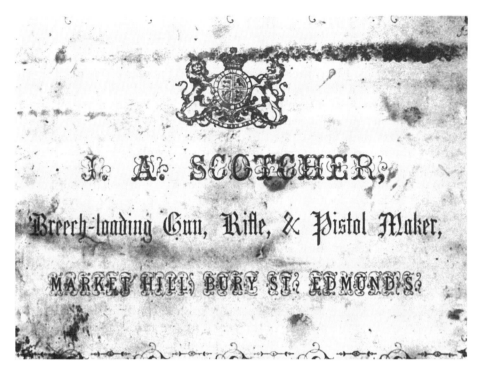

J. A. Scotcher label

the initials J.A.S.

Some nine Scotcher guns are known, all are breechloading, and those for which I have details are of good quality with a number of pleasant detailed touches to the finish which raise them from the ordinary to guns of quality.

One of the Scotcher guns in the museum collection is numbered 2375 and has a convential rotary under-bolt, whereas the other back action hammer gun is a top lever with J. Thomas's patent Vertical Grip of 1870.

Scotcher seems to have gone out of business in 1912, and in 1916 the premises were taken over by Henry Hodgson, who remained in business until 1952 at No 4 The Traverse. After a lapse of six years, we find Robert Horrocks and Violet Clayton at No 4A The Traverse and at the same address the style changes in 1971 to Robert M & D Clayton where, according to Mr Jenkins, they are still in business. So, from the available records, this part of Bury St Edmunds, in spite of several changes in name, remains firmly wedded to the gun trade as it has done since the first quarter of the 19th century.

JAMES WARRILOW

Not long ago I was searching through the thousands of negatives that have accumulated over the years and I came across two photographs of a rather nice boxlock "made" by Warrilow. Prints were made but before they could be marked the pencil broke and I made a mental note to place the numbers on the prints so that I could locate the negatives again and from the number perhaps locate some data on this gun.

The prints turned out rather well but of course I forgot to put the identification numbers on the prints. Half a day has been spent searching for the negatives; they are not on the card index so this time the system has slipped up.

The stock has sunk panels and drop points and fancy chequering. If one then has a look at the top of the barrels, one can see how the fences were finished, the file-cut broad rib and the words "Full Choke" on the left barrel and "Cylinder" on the right one. The name of the "maker", James B Warrilow, can just be seen in the panel on the rib and quite prominently the legend "Patent Clip Lump, May 31, 1884". The barrels are damascus and nicely engraved at the breech and we have a well made and interesting boxlock which belies its name, since it does not have the box-like look of many A & D actioned guns, the shoulders and rounded action appearing to reduce the length of the action bar.

One question always asked when one comes across a gun with a name

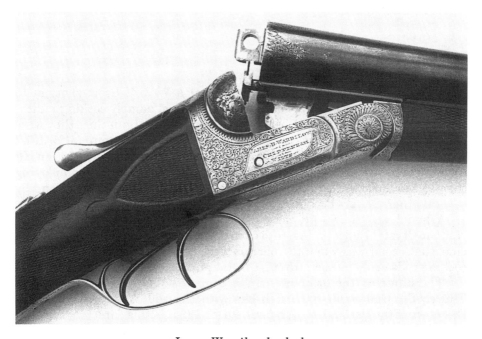

James Warrilow boxlock

that is not well known is "Did they make the gun? If not, who did?"

My feeling is that Warrilow did not make this gun. I have little or no evidence, I don't even have my notes when the photograph was taken, but the feeling is there. Perhaps it is because the name and address on the bar of the action do not exactly fit in with the panel, the space being left for this purpose.

If one then asks, "Who did make it?" my answer would be C.G. Bonehill, Belmont Firearms & Gun Barrel Works, Belmont Row, Birmingham.

To go back to the man whose name is on the barrel and action. I know that the firm was in business in 1908 and that the full style was "James Blakewell Warrilow, Railway Works, Chippenham, Wilts". Yes, the word "Works" does make me think a little but if the name is anything to go by Mr Warrilow made railway engines not guns, or perhaps the works was alongside the railway?

Why Bonehill then? The reason is that the patent date given on the barrel is for a boxlock action and a fore-end fastener. Another patent, taken out on the same day as Bonehill, protects his idea for a prolonged rib and a special web which provides not only the underlump but also the underflats. The breech end of the barrels is cut away to accomodate the "all through" lump which is described on the gun as a "Clip Lump".

So what appears at first sight to be an ordinary boxlock is shown even by simple visual examination to be something more and, on further investigation , a number of interesting features appear. Anyone with any information of Mr James B. Warrilow of Chippenham might perhaps drop me a line and if there is any information on what went on in the "Railway Works" this would be most welcome.

WILLIAM GOLDEN

Previously I have used a photograph of a W & C Scott shotgun to illustrate a feature of early hammerless shotguns, namely cocking indicators. I had hoped to be able to show an earlier Scott shotgun since they were of importance in the development of the sporting shotgun in Britain, representing as they did an alternative to the Anson & Deeley action. In addition to being made by Scott themselves in Birmingham, guns employing the Scott action were made by Holland & Holland as the "Climax", and by several other makers both in London and the provinces.

When I was shown an early hammerless gun recently I noticed the "Patent Crystal Indicator" set into each of the lockplates. This gave the first clue, the second was when the barrels were removed, the distinctive Scott cocking rods could be seen through rectangular slots in the action flats.

The name on the lockplate of this gun was Wm. Golden, 6-12 Cross Church St, Huddersfield; this checks with the address given in White's Directory of the Borough of Huddersfield for 1894. In this Directory will also be found Chas. Golden, 53 Tyrrel St. and the firm of Carr Bros., 4 Cloth Hall

Golden hammer gun

St., who bought the business of Golden in 1914 and who continued in business themselves as Ironmongers until 1949.

The hammerless gun by Golden presents several problems. It was made after 1879 but whether it was made by Scott or Golden under licence from Scott, is difficult to tell and only someone with knowledge of the facilities of Wm. Golden would be able to give any indication of whether or not they had the capability to manufacture themselves. From an examination of the gun I would be of the opinion that Golden made it themselves in Huddersfield. As a Yorkshireman by ancestry I should certainly like to think that this was the case. There are other problems requiring a solution. What was the relationship between Charles and William Golden, what was the respective size of the two businesses and did this Charles Golden have any connection with a C Golden who took out several patents relating to firearms between 1860 and 1870?

I have also been able to see a slightly earlier Wm. Golden hammergun. This one is marked on the top rib "Maker to His Majesty, the late King of Prussia". This, of course, poses even more problems!

How on earth did a relatively obscure Huddersfield gunmaker become "Hofrustmeister" to the Prussian Court and which King of Prussia does the legend proudly borne on the top rib refer to? Questions and yet more questions. It could have been Frederick William IV but this is unlikely since he became totally mad and on his death in 1861 the crown passed to his brother William I. William became German Emperor in 1871 and it is quite likely that the subtle difference between Konig and Kaiser may have escaped the attention of the engraver. If we disregard this possibility the gun could have been made at any time, since the inscription states to the *late* King of Prussia and this, of course, puts us back to Frederick William IV since William I would have been the late German Emperor!

The Golden family appear to have begun their gunmaking in Bradford since the patents taken out by Charles Golden give his address as Bradford, so we can assume that the William Golden and Charles Golden in the Directory of 1894 were the sons of Charles Golden of Bradford.

Much of this, of course, is conjecture. I would be most interested to learn of any other Golden guns and, in particular, to the inscriptions on the top rib. Did the King of Prussia visit Yorkshire during the mid-19th century? If not, how did Golden get his appointment? It is all very interesting and I hope that with the help of readers we might be able to add some fact to the fiction of Golden the Gunmaker of Huddersfield.

W. J. GEORGE

One thing which I have tried to do over the years is collect catalogues. To my intense regret I did not start doing this until the late 1940s when already the attrition of the gunmakers had speeded up due to the changed economic and social conditions and the former magnificence of the catalogues of more lordly gunmakers had degenerated into a typed listing of secondhand guns.

One of my early post-War visits to London resulted in my receiving one of Henry Atkin's last independent catalogues which whetted my appetite for more. I then tried to acquire older catalogues and I was fortunate enough to be given some by readers of this magazine and later to receive photostat copies.

One development was the introduction of facsimilie catalogues. Possibly one of the finest of these re-prints was that issued by Holland & Holland in July 1976. The original was issued 1910-1912. It was 8in x 11in and had 72 pages. The H & H Royal Hammerless ejector with detachable locks was 75 guineas and over half the catalogue was devoted to rifles and cartridges for rifles and the Paradox ball and shotgun.

Such pristine catalogues as the H & H reprint make one look very carefully at any "mint" catalogue from the period before 1914. So it was when some years ago I received a copy of a catalogue issued by W.J.George of 181 Snargate Street, Dover. The catalogue was the same size as the H & H one but with fewer pages — 24 instead of 72. The covers were in an attractive green with gold lettering and the whole was, as they say, "got up in a fine manner". The catalogue was in pristine condition but there was no indication that it was a reprint but on the other hand there was no evidence of use. It appeared to be unopened. I have seen one or two catalogues bearing the same name and from the same period and in the same condition.

A feeling of curiosity had been aroused but it wasn't until I received the offer of a reprint of this catalogue from Larry Barnes of Gunnerman Books, Auburn Heights, USA that I was motivated to delve more deeply.

How best to do this? A search through the literature had not produced any useful leads and the only mention of the firm I was able to find was in a list of 1908 which was given to me by Peter J Wilson. However, a clue was given in the catalogue itself. In the introduction one reads "W.J. George, Cycle and Gun Manufacturer" and the clue lies in the word "cycle". The local newspaper, the "Dover Standard" of December 19, 1896 refers to the firm and the fact that guns and ammunition are stocked and that cycles by all the best makers can be obtained together with repairs and the "riding is taught by experienced instructors".

Very possibly then Mr George has started in business selling and repairing cycles and was so listed in the directories. This would account for his absence in the current literature which is based largely on trade directories. Mr George offers for sale the "Excelsior Gun" at 50/- (i.e £2.50) and a similar top-lever hammergun but with bar action locks at £3. 5s. This is the "Eclipse" keeper's gun. The top of the range is an A & D action gun with ejectors at £21. The potential customer is warned to "Beware of Foreign Rubbish" but later in the catalogue customers are told that a few foreign made guns can be supplied at £1. 17s. 6d. which have been tested "but no further guarantee can be given". At even lower prices were the bolt-action

THE ECLIPSE HAMMERLESS GUNS.

These Guns I confidently recommend to those who require a Gun to use, and not to look at, the price has been kept as low as possible, without doing away with the very best workmanship and material. I am aware that there are plenty of Foreign and Carret-made Guns advertised at a lower figure, but is it policy to buy at a few shillings less and pay pounds to keep the same in working order?

No. 121.

No. 124.

No. 119.—Top Lever, Side Lock, Hammerless, Double Bolt Action, with Stirling Steel Extended Doll's Head Rib, Very Fine Twist Barrels, Choke Bore, Automatic Safety Bolt, Pistol Grip, Selected Walnut Stock, **£7 : 7 : 0.**

No. 120.—Ditto, Damascus Barrels, **£8 : 8 : 0.**

No. 121.—Ditto, but with Greener's Treble Cross Bolt, Superior Finish, and Locks Nicely Engraved, **£9 : 9 : 0.**

No. 122.—Top Lever, Anson and Deeley's System Action, Damascus Barrels, Choked Bored, or order, Greener's Treble Cross Bolt, Selected Walnut Stock, Pistol Hand, and Fitted with my Automatic Safety Bolt, Plain Finish, **£10 : 10 : 0.**

No. 123.—Ditto, Fine Damascus, or Steel Barrels, Shooting Carefully Regulated, **£12 : 12 : 0.**

No. 124.—Ditto, Ditto, but Extra Finish, and can be had as a Trap Gun, if required, to fire very heavy charge, **£15 : 15 : 0.**

ECLIPSE EJECTOR GUNS.

To meet the wishes of numerous Customers, I am prepared to supply either No. 122, 123, 124, Hammerless, Fitted with Patent Automatic Ejector, which ejects exploded Case only, at the extra charge of **£5 : 5 : 0.**

Any Goods not approved of I shall be pleased to exchange if returned in good order three days from receipt of same.

W. J. GEORGE, GUNSMITH, DOVER.

7

W. J. George ad

180

military rifles converted to 12-bore and for about £1 one could buy such a gun, carefully selected "which would not go off unawares". One cannot help but wonder who bought the rejects!

"Collector's Guns and Rook and Rabbit Rifles" were listed along with "Saloon and Garden Guns" at less than 50p. Walking stick guns in .320-bore and up to .410 could be had along with "Air Canes" complete with shot and rifle barrels, pump, wad cutters, bullet moulds and shot measures. Both single and double percussion muzzle-loading guns were still available together with several revolvers and some rather appalling single-shot pistols, loading tools, game bags and a range of cartridges.

At the end of the catalogue the reader is advised that George manufactures the "Dover" cycles. The office and showroom was at 181 Snargate, the works at 11 Snargate and cartridges were held at 3 Five Post Lane. I wonder if any W. J. George guns have survived and how long George remained in business?

THOMAS HEPPLESTONE

If you were to ask shooting men where the best British shotguns were made I suppose that most would answer, "London" and then "Birmingham". The more knowledgeable would probably add "Edinburgh" and those with deeper interests might include Newcastle and York, thinking about Pape and Horsley respectively.

It is becoming increasingly apparent that we must now add another name to the list, that of Manchester. The Manchester gunmakers rose to prominence in the 19th century, during this period some 50 or so firms and individuals described themselves as gunmakers and of this number about ten produced work of very high quality.

One could almost refer to the "Manchester School of Gunmaking", what is not known is whether this was a spontaneous outpouring of indigenous skills or imported skills attracted to Manchester by booming prosperity, based on the cotton industry and the proximity of the Lancashire and Yorkshire moors.

An examination of the census returns has shown that some of the gunmakers were born in Manchester, some in nearby Cheshire and others were born in Birmingham. Insufficient data has been acquired to arrive at any conclusion and, sadly, cutbacks in the library services will prevent further research in this direction.

However, guns continue to appear which reinforce the importance of Manchester as a centre of 19th century gunmaking. The latest gun to appear bears the name of Thomas Hepplestone.

Hepplestone was born in Butley, Cheshire, in 1826. I haven't been able to locate Butley on my maps but am assured that it exists. Then comes the strange part, the first Thomas Hepplestone in the Trade Directories for

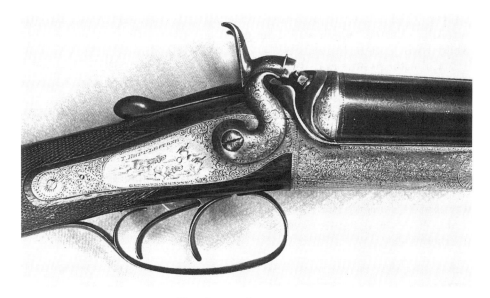

Hepplestone hammer gun

Manchester is listed in 1852. Thomas would be 26 years old by this time.

However, he is not listed as a gunmaker but as as silk plush manufacturer! He adds smallwares and hatter's trimming maker to his activities until in 1861 he adds "Patent breech loading gun maker"to his other enterprises. Then, in 1863, he concentrates on gunmaking and lists himself as a "Gunmaker". His address is 14 Thomas Street, Shudehill and then, four years later his address becomes 25 Shudehill. What appears to have happened is that his business must have prospered and he moved from a side street, Thomas Street, to a main thoroughfare and it was at 25 Shudehill that the firm remains, until it ceases to be recorded in 1910.

By 1880 he describes himself as a "Gun and Rifle Maker and Fishing Tackle Dealer" and in the 1881 census we find him living at 5 Whitlow Road with his wife Hannah and an elderly widow who is their general servant. He describes himself in the census as a Master Gunmaker.

If we go back a little to his earlier claim that he was a "patent breech loading gun maker" we find that Thomas Hepplestone patented breechloading systems in May, 1860, British Patent No. 1278. Three breech loading systems are described but I have never encountered an actual example, nor indeed, mention of one.

No advertisements or trade labels have come to light which might have shed further light on Hepplestone and we must turn to a contemporary account which advises us that the firm of Thomas Hepplestone was originally established in 1854. This contradicts the information we have already gleaned from the Manchester Directories. We do learn however, that the warehouse of the firm contains items of their own manufacture, "for the protection of which several patents have been taken out"and that there is an extensive stock of patent hammerless guns, double and single express rifles, small bore match rifles, military rifles and a wide variety of revolvers, including Webley's.

This then, was no small enterprise. However, only one patent in the name of Hepplestone has been traced and, as mentioned, no weapons to the design have so far been identified. Until we encounter more of his guns our knowledge of this Manchester gunmakers activities will remain scant. If you have a gun by Hepplestone or a trade label or an advert I would be interested to have details.

NIXON OF NEWARK

It is not often that we can lift a corner of the veil of history and see, with greater clarity, something of the shooting scene, a century and a half ago.

During research into the firm of Nixon of Newark, I was allowed to examine a small note book filled with graceful copperplate handwriting which recorded purchases made by T. B. T. Hildyard of Flintham Hall, Nr. Newark from 1849 until 1877.

In one year (1849) the estate bought 81 lbs of black powder, 44 bags of shot and 4,500 caps. Felt wadding was bought for 6d a sheet and the wads would be cut from the sheet with wad punches, as required.

A powder flask was bought for 8/6d and a new gun was bought for the Keeper at a cost of 10 Guineas. (10 pounds 50 pence) Loading rods (or ramrods) for muzzle loading shotguns were replaced at frequent intervals as were the "worms" or screws fitted to the rods to withdraw the charge from a muzzle loading shotgun. Keys to remove the nipples on these guns also got lost and required replacement as did the springs on the shot and powder flasks which seem to have broken quite frequently.

By 1864, changes were taking place. Breech loaders were now being used since we find that the estate bought a cartridge bag for 12s and 500 breech loading cartridge cases at a cost of 1 pound. A cutter was bought for trimming the case length to size, for it is evident that the estate was buying the components and loading their own cartridges. In 1865, 6,500 cases were bought and in 1867 a pair of guns was "converted" at a cost of 7 pounds and another gun was converted for 3 pounds 10 shillings in the following year. Whether these guns were converted from muzzle loading to breech loading (or "brich loading"as the accounts have it!) or were converted from pinfire to central fire is not known. Certainly in the 1870's both muzzle loaders and pin and central-fire guns were in use. What a splendid time this must have been!

It is, of course, possible that the keepers still used muzzle loaders and perhaps a member of the family continued to use a cherished pin-fire since, as late as 1877, 500 pin-fire cases were bought showing that a pin-fire gun was still being used.

The last entry in the book is March 26th 1878 and the receipt is signed "Nixon & Smith". The book has survived because it has been protected by a specially made metal case attached to which is a brass plate with the Nixon name.

I wanted to see the sort of gun that Nixon might have supplied to the estate during the period of the account book and I was able to see and photograph a 12 bore muzzle loading double gun by this maker at the 1988 Game Fair, Gun No. 1081. Two years previously, in 1986, I had the opportunity of seeing and photographing a 13 bore pin-fire gun No. 1275. This is a particularly fine example and one can see why Mr. Hildyard might have supported his local gunmaker!

The third Nixon gun is a conversion from pin-fire to central fire done very simply by inserting strikers through the standing breech which are struck by the existing pin-fire hammers. The conversion was not carried out by Nixon but probably by William Stovin of 4 Westgate, Grantham, whose name is on the barrels of the gun.

Nixon started business in 1829, the firm became Nixon and Lawton in the early 1870's and Nixon & Smith by 1878. Charles Smith served his apprenticeship with Nixon and then became a partner. He then acquired the business in the Market Place which continued to prosper under his guidance. Charles Smith died in 1908, aged 64 and the business was continued by his sons and, as Charles Smith & Sons Ltd., the firm is still trading to-day!

Nixon hammer gun

WILLIAM ROCHESTER PAPE

My first article on Pape was written nigh on twenty years ago and since then another six articles on this maker have graced the pages of *Shooting Times*. Chapters on Pape will be found in both my *Shotgun* books, based on information taken from these articles. However, although some readers do keep tear sheets and some have copies of the book, many do not, so I should start with a brief introduction to this well known, and to many, even famous, North of England gunmaker.

He was born in 1831, at Amble on the coast, north of Newcastle-Upon-Tyne. He was the son of James Pape and Dorothy Rochester. James had started a game dealer's and fishing tackle shop in Collingwood Street, Newcastle and young William Rochester started his business life with his father. He married Dorothy Crawford when he was 25 and, a year later, in 1857, he set up on his own at 44 Westgate Street, Newcastle. In 1863 he moved to No. 36, the former house of Sir John Fife at the corner of Collingwood Street and Westgate Road. Here, at the "North of England Gun Works" he had living quarters above the shop and he spent his weekends at Coquet Lodge in Warkworth where he was able to indulge in his passion for gun dogs, being renowned for his strain of black pointers. Pape is also credited with the launch of the first dog show held in Britain, in Newcastle in 1859.

His contribution to the art of gunmaking was considerable, taking out patents in 1866, 1867, 1870 and 1874. His patent No. 1501 of 1866 is considered by many to be the most interesting. The patent protects his ideas for a breech action but, more importantly, it also covers what was later to become known as choke boring, "the muzzle end of the bore is tapered inwards".

Many are the claimants to the honour of being the inventor of choke boring, almost as many as laid claim the the invention of the percussion cap! An American, Dr. G. G. Oberfell researched the subject very thoroughly and in his book, "The Mystery of Shotgun Patterns", credit is given to Pape and, in particular, for his successes in the London Gun Trials in 1858, '59 and '66. The first two were shot with Pape muzzle loaders and that of 1866 with a breechloader. His boring in that year produced patterns which to-day we would regard as "improved cylinder"and there is little doubt that he did not explain his ideas to the full for, in 1873, he allowed the patent to lapse.

He was awarded a purse of ten guineas in 1875 for his invention, the money being donated by Mr. A. Lane. As a result of this award Pape could claim that he was"the inventor of choke boring" and even many years later, the shop window of the premises at 21 Collingwood Street, where the firm had moved in 1903, bore the legend "Inventor of Choke Boring" and above a list of his successes in the London Gun Trials.

William Rochester Pape retired from active business in 1888, leaving it to his son Victor. William was injured in a road accident on April 5th 1923,

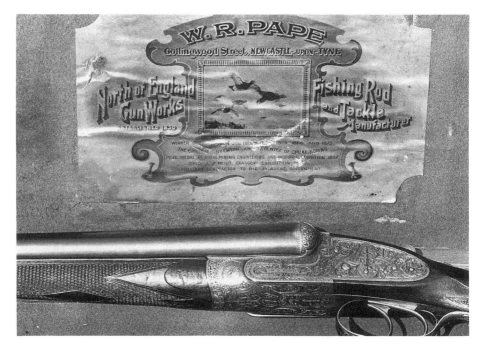

W. R. Pape sidelock

he died shortly after, aged 91.

I have seen a great many Pape guns over the years, many bearing minimal engraving.

I have one Pape catalogue dating from c1914 but by this time no sidelock guns are listed, although there are some very nicely engraved box lock guns. One cannot help but wonder if any other highly engraved Pape guns have survived? If you know of one perhaps you could tell me about it?

JOSEPH SMYTHE

Joseph Forrestall Smythe was a very successful provincial gunmaker who had greatly benefited from working for some of the most important gunmakers of the period. We learn that he worked for W. W. Greener of Birmingham, without doubt one of the greatest of the Birmingham gunmakers, but with north east connections, since the firm was founded in Newcastle in 1829 before moving to Birmingham in 1844.

We also see from the trade label that Smythe worked for Alexander Henry in Edinburgh. It was during his time with Henry that he came in contact with some of the great marksmen of the day, Horatio Ross and his son, and Lord Elcho, later the Earl of Wemyss. It was the Earl of Wemyss who bought the only three barrel Dickson gun I have encountered with two barrels above the third. All the others have all three barrels side-by-side.

After being with Alex Henry (the inventor of the rifling employed by the Martini-Henry British service rifle) Smythe moved to Dublin where he took over the management of the old established business of Trulock and Harris, of Dawson Street who were to acquire the Dublin business of the famous firm of John Rigby.

In 1885, J. F. Smythe returned to England and purchased the business of Francis Brebner who had established his business in the Bondgate, Darlington in 1866. When Smythe acquired the business it was in Blackwellgate and less than ten years later, in October, 1894, the premises were destroyed by an explosion possibly due to the inadequate storage of propellants since Smythe loaded his own range of shotgun cartridges.

By 1896, Smythe was back in business at 12 Horsemarket and by the turn of the century he had also extended his business to Stockton-on-Tees and later to Middlesborough. You will see that although Smythe did not have a Royal Appointment his label stated that he is "Patronised by His Majesty". This will refer to King Edward VII who, when Prince of Wales, had a pair of guns altered by Smythe and apparently the work was so well done, that his Royal Highness later "found an opportunity of tendering him his personal thanks".

Joseph F. Smythe died in December 1930 and I assume that the business ceased to trade in the thirties. If you have a gun by Smythe I would be interested to learn something about it if you care to write to me.

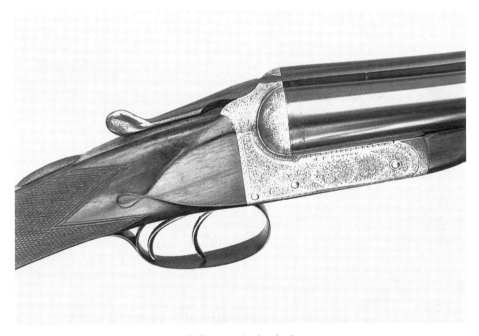

J. F. Smythe boxlock

THOMAS HORSLEY

The British Game Fair is an annual outdoor event, a cross between a County Fair and a Trade show. For me, it provides an opportunity to meet my readers and for them to bring along guns and goodies for me to see, comment upon and photograph and record. The year the Game Fair was in Yorkshire afforded a splendid opportunity for me to ask readers to bring along guns by what many consider to be the finest gunmaker the county produced, Thomas Horsley of York. I stress 'gunmaker', for Horsley was no mere retailer of Birmingham guns upon which his name had been placed. Thomas Horsley made guns and he also made a contribution on the development of the sporting shotgun as his several patents testify.

The story begins not in York but some miles south in Doncaster. Here Thomas Horsley was born on July 17 1810, the third son of Philip Horsley, a cheese and bacon factor. What took young Thomas away from the family business of cheese and bacon to gunmaking we will probably never know but we do know that he learned the art and craft of gunmaking in the York workshop of Richard Brunton, who was to be found in the Stonegate. Horsley is recorded as working in the Stonegate himself and since Brunton ceases to be listed as a gunmaker in 1830 it is just possible that Thomas acquired the business of his former master before moving to premises in Coney Street in 1834. In 1856 the firm moves from No 48 to No 10. In 1866 Thomas Horsley I, received an award at the Yorkshire Fine Art Industrial Exhibition for a 'Breech Loading Sporting Gun'. This is likely to be for a gun made under the 1863 patents — more of them later.

The second Thomas Horsley was born in 1844 and, as expected, he served his apprenticeship with his father in the Coney Street shop. When the founder died in 1882 Thomas Horsley II took over the business and it continued under his direction until shortly before his death in 1915. Four of his five sons continued the business, at the head of which was Thomas Horsley III, who was born in 1869. Like his father he had a keen interest in all shooting sports. His father was a particularly fine game Shot, and Thomas III had a keen interest in the breeding and handling of gun dogs as well as field shooting. It was during the time of Thomas II that the business returned to Doncaster where a branch of the firm traded as gunmakers from 1898 to 1892. After this the business was continued in the name of the former manager, who had been trained in York, D J Smithson. With the death of Thomas Horsley II in 1915, the business moved from Coney Street to 20 Blossom Street and then to 102 Micklegate Street in 1933. The third Thomas Horsley died in 1954 and the business was then run by Tony Horsley until it ceased to trade in 1959. You can still see the bench and tools used by the members of the firm displayed in the Castle Museum, York.

Some readers may wonder why so much emphasis is placed on changes of address? The reason is, that since the address of the maker is often engraved on the top rib of a shotgun it is often possible to date the gun from the address. It is of little use if the firm remained at one address for a century, but many gunmakers moved quite frequently and then the dates of such moves can assist in dating the gun.

These then were the men who founded the firm and who directed its activities through several changes in premises, during the golden days of game-shooting in Britain. But what of the guns which bear the name of Horsley? The earliest example we have of a Horsley breech-loader is No. 1456 which was sold in 1866. This is a double hammergun with bar-action locks and non-rebounding hammers. The interesting feature is the opening lever which is in front of the trigger guard with a 'button' inside the guard. When the gun is opened it reveals a single bite, sliding bolt-action, the bolt being withdrawn from the bite in the barrel lump by the lever in front of the guard. The patent for this action is No. 374 of February 1862. From the full specification we learn that the patentee, Thomas Horsley, is in fact the son of the founder, Thomas Horsley II who, when the patent was obtained, was 18 years old ! Since the apprenticeship at this time was six years it is very likely that he was still 'serving his time' and one wonders exactly how the labours of invention were shared. This was the first British 'snap-action', with the earlier examples all being based on Schneider and Daw patents.

Inventive genius was not exhausted by this, the first of the Horsley patents, since in the following year the single bite action with a top sliding

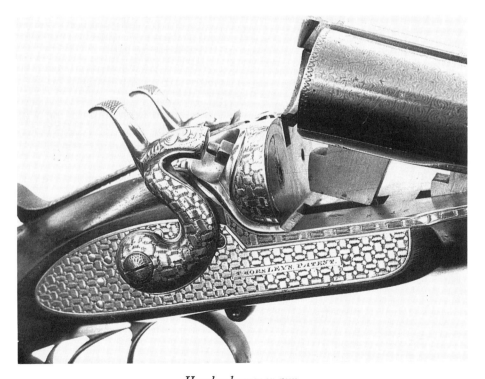

Horsley hammer gun

189

thumbpiece was patented, No 2410 of 1863. This, incidentally, was the same year that the famous Purdey bolt was introduced, the early versions being operated by a thumb-lever in the front of the trigger-guard. This action of Horsley's was fairly widely accepted, particularly in the county of its birth.

Horsley's built many types of gun and rifle and No 1833, made in 1870, has a double bite-action with the Jones type underlever. The same shape of fence, but 'loaded' indicators are not fitted although the striker withdrawal is still featured. Within two years the style of the standing breech and fences alters: the loaded indicators are no longer in fashion and gun No 2065 of 1872, although still 'bar-in-the-wood', now has ball fences and the lever for the striker withdrawal has been modified to operate vertically instead of horizontally, a much neater arrangement. It also has loaded indicators, but of a different type. The Horsley sliding thumbpiece is still used. When gun No 2203 (made in 1873) appears the loaded indicator pins have now vanished and there are minor styling changes to the style of the hammers and the thumbpiece.

Possibly the finest of the Horsley hammerguns, and certainly the nicest one I have seen, is gun No 2752. On this gun the Horsley sliding thumbpiece operates a double-bite bolt, there is a doll's head extension and the gun is 'bar-in-the-wood' — but by now the other two Horsley patents have been discarded so there is no striker withdrawal system and no loaded indicators are fitted. Horsley had, of course, to move with the times, and the earliest hammerless action I have so far encountered is the very Victorian looking No 2916, which dates from 1885. This gun employs an action based on Horsley & Pryse's patent No 3874 of 1883 and is a side-lever 20-bore.

By gun No 3301, the Horsley sidelock looks fairly conventional but once again, the York gunmakers manage to produce something which is elegant and very different from the 'run-of-the-mill' sidelock.

It is now a quarter of a century since this long established business in York ceased to trade. A surprising number of the guns the firm built, particularly in the great days when they were in Coney Street, have survived in spite of the twin scourges of rust and restrictive, nay draconian legislation. They have survived to remind us that the skills of the gunmaker were not confined to Birmingham and London and that the art and craft of gunmaking flourished in the north of England.

I hope that I have shown that the Horsley's of York and the craftsmen who worked for them built guns that any man would be proud to own and which truly reflect the heritage of the past.

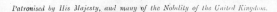

Patronised by His Majesty, and many of the Nobility of the United Kingdom.

J. F. SMYTHE,

(Formerly with " Henry, Edinburgh," and " W. W. Greener,")

Gun, Rifle & Cartridge Manufacturer,

N. Telephone Nos.—
Darlington - 0451.
Stockton - 0028.
Middlesbrough 0588.

Agencies—
Eley Bros.
Kynochs, Ltd.
U.M.C. Coy.

Maker of the
" VICTORIAN "
Ejector Game Gun.

Rifles for Home
and Abroad.

" Champion,"
" Field," and
" Durham Ranger "
Cartridges.

Fishing Tackle for
Loch, Lake and
River.

Author of
The Anglers' Guide
to the Tees.

General Sporting
Goods Outfitter.

Shooting and
Fishing Agency.

" The Sportsman's Repository,"

DARLINGTON,

And at Stockton-on-Tees and Middlesbrough.   ENGLAND.

J. F. Smythe ad

Telegrams—Adsett, Gunmakers, Guildford.   Telephone No. **940.**

Established 1800.

THOS. ADSETT & SON,

W. G. ADSETT

Gun, Rifle and Pistol Makers,

90, HIGH STREET, GUILDFORD, SURREY.

(BOTTOM OF PORTSMOUTH ROAD).

Extract from the " Guildford & District Outlook," August, 1924—

" Mr. Kenneth Bone, a son of Mr. W. J. Bone, of Agraria Road, is managing a farm
of several thousand acres in Rhodesia. Shooting with a retired English colonel, he
casually mentioned Guildford, " Ah ! Guildford ! " exclaimed the colonel. " I bought the
best gun I ever possessed at Adsett's, in High Street, Guildford."

Thos. Adsett & Son ad

William Golden engraving

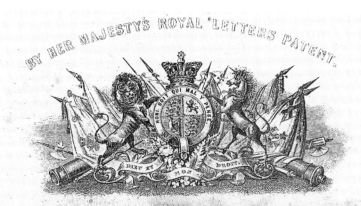

William Griffiths label

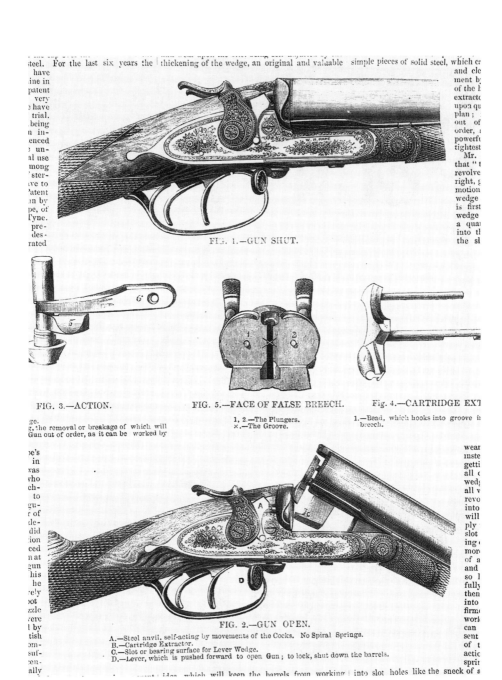

steel. For the last six years the | thickening of the wedge, an original and valuable | simple pieces of solid steel, which c...

have
ine in
patent
very
e have
trial,
being
n in-
enced
e un-
al use
mong
ster-
ive to
Patent
n by
pe, of
Tyne.
pre-
des-
rated

and cle
ment b
of the l
extracto
upon qu
plan ;
out of
order, a
powerfu
tightest
Mr.
that " t
revolve
right, g
motion
wedge
is first
wedge
a quar
into th
the sl

FIG. 1.—GUN SHUT.

FIG. 3.—ACTION.

ge.
g, the removal or breakage of which will
Gun out of order, as it can be worked by

FIG. 5.—FACE OF FALSE BREECH.

1, 2.—The Plungers.
×.—The Groove.

Fig. 4.—CARTRIDGE EXT

1.—Bead, which hooks into groove i
breech.

e's
in
vas
vho
ch-
to
gu-
r of
dle-
did
ion
ced
n at
gun
his
he
rely
oot
zzle
vere
l by
tish
om-
suf-
en-
ally

wear
inste
getti
all c
wedg
all v
revo
into
will
ply
slot
ing
mor
of a
and
so l
fully
then
into
firm
work
can
sent
of t
actic
sprir

FIG. 2.—GUN OPEN.

A.—Steel anvil, self-acting by movements of the Cocks. No Spiral Springs.
B.—Cartridge Extractor.
C.—Slot or bearing surface for Lever Wedge.
D.—Lever, which is pushed forward to open Gun ; to lock, shut down the barrels.

... idea, which will keep the barrels from working | into slot holes like the sneck of a

W. R. Pape ad

ROSSONS' GUNS·

The name on the gun is the safeguard of value. Every gun having our name carries with it a guarantee of reliability

"SPECIAL" Model Hammerless Gun.
12, 16 and 20 gauge.
£11-0-0.   5% cash.

A Gun with a Reputation

A well actioned Gun built on the box lock principle. The Boring and choking of the barrels is specially attended to, to ensure consistent patterns and great penetration. Straight or half pistol hand stock to order. Certificate of Proof supplied with each gun.
Made with 2 piece Ejector mechanism £5 5s. extra,

Repairs and Alterations:
New stocks ; new barrels; Re-jointing ; re-browning barrels; altering pull-offs, etc., etc.
Best workmanship. Lowest prices. Satisfaction assured.

G. S. ROSSON & Co.
Rampant Horse St.,
NORWICH.

C. S. Rosson & Co. ad, 1930's

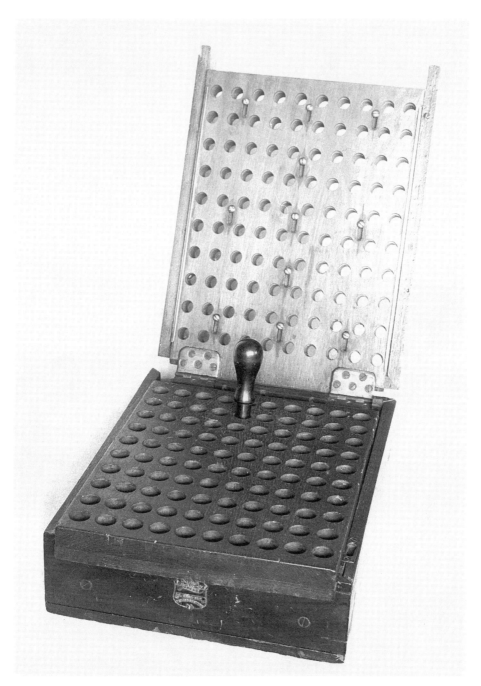

Erskine's loading machine

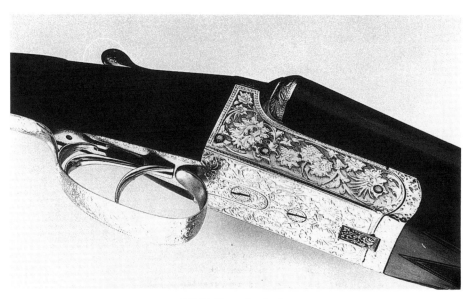

W. R. Pape boxlock

SCOTLAND

The manufacture of firearms in Scotland dates from the 16th century and the records of the Trades Incorporations such as the Hammermen Guild, Motto–"By Hammer in Hand all Arts do Stand", the names of gunmakers as far back as 1585 are recorded.

Throughout the entire period of their manufacture firearms of Scottish origin have shown an individuality in both design and decoration which has endeared them to generations of those who love the gun!

This is perhaps to be expected when one considers the almost barbaric exuberance of the early Scottish all metal "Fish Tail" pistols and the even more remarkable — and extremely rare — all metal long guns. One of the earliest surviving Scottish fowling pieces is now in the Tower of London, though formerly in the Cabinet d'Armes of Louis XIII of France. As was the practice, the lock plate is dated on the fence 1614 and it is signed with the initials R.A., a gunmaker, Robert Allison, of Dundee.

Scottish gunmakers produced conventional flintlock long guns, eventually discarding the distinctive Scottish locks with their unique mechanism and, of course, it must not be forgotten that one of the most important firearms inventions, the use of percussion powder instead of flint and steel was the invention of a Scottish Clergyman, the Rev. Alexander J. Forsyth.

With the coming of the breech loader the name of James Paris Lee, born in Hawick on the Scottish Borders, is associated with the rifles which bear his name, the British Lee Enfield and the American Lee Navy rifle.

We will encounter the products of the famous 19th century Edinburgh makers in these pages, Innes who was to make Forsyth guns, later to become Innes & Wallace, Gunmaker to his Majesty, Alex Henry, famous for his rifles and the British military rifle, the Martini-Henry. Another Edinburgh maker, famous for his rifles was Dan'l Fraser and for shotguns, the names of John Dickson, (who served his time with Wallace) James MacNaughton, Mortimer and Joseph Harkom are renowned for the high quality of their gunmaking and also for the distinctive styling and ingenious design which so ably continued the traditions established several centuries before.

Elsewhere in Scotland, particularly in Glasgow, famous gunmakers appeared, James Dalzell Dougall, the protagonist of the pin-fire and patentee of the famous Dougall "Lock Fast" action, Horton, an Englishman who moved to Glasgow, Charles Ingram, famous for his rifles, and Alex Martin, another riflemaker but also known for his famous "Ribless Shotgun".

To-day, the number of gunmakers has been greatly reduced but David MacKay Brown at Hamilton builds the Dickson Round Action and in the far north, by Inverness. the name of Dan'l Fraser will once again be found on rifles and shotguns made on the Black Isle. Guns made by the Scottish gunmakers of the past still survive and continue to give their modern owners sterling service and considerable owner satisfaction!

John Dickson III

JOHN DICKSON

The first John Dickson was born in 1794. We know nothing of his early life except that he served his time with J. Wallace whose shop was at No. 187 in the old historic High Street of Edinburgh. There is some evidence that Dickson entered into partnership with Wallace about 1830 but certainly John Dickson was in business in his own right in 1840.

Edinburgh in the mid-19th century was an important centre of gunmaking and competition must have been keen. Little is known of these early years and, in fact, the records of guns made starts with No. 1590 in 1854. The firm was then trading under the style of John Dickson and Son and John Dickson the second was already in business, having served his customary seven years apprenticeship.

The first double breechloader was sold in 1858 and although this gun No. 1928 has not been traced we have a good idea of what it must have looked like. From the records we know that it was a 14-bore and that it was intended to fire 1 1/4 ozs of shot in front of 2 3/4 drams of powder. It would, of course, be a pinfire and very likely was supplied in a two-tiered case with the bottom compartment arranged to hold 100 pinfire cartridges. The gun itself was a double and we again assume that back-action locks were fitted and that the lever would lie forward under the bar of the action. Cleaning rods, brushes, oil bottle and a full set of pinfire reloading tools would also be contained in the case.

A very high proportion, if not all the work associated with gunmaking would have been done in Edinburgh at this time. Not all would have been done in Dickson's shop but certainly Edinburgh supported enough outworkers to the gun trade for all branches of work to be carried out. The shop was now well established in Princes Street, a thoroughfare whose fame was to exceed that of the old High Street, and it was from this shop that a never-ending stream of shotguns and rifles was to pour during the golden years of gunmaking prior to the first world war.

In 1859 Dickson's made their first pinfire breechloader with the lever curved round the trigger guard. This was certainly keeping up with the London fashions but, at the same time, of course, muzzle-loading guns and rifles were still being made and in 1865 a pair were built for the Duke of Roxburgh which were bought in a pawnshop 32 years later for 50 s! The letter is still extant requesting information on these guns by the purchaser who also enquires as to whether or not they were built as breech-loaders, for they were bought as breechloaders in 1897!

The year 1865 saw the production of breechloading guns with snap actions. The first of these was made under Brazier's 1864 patent and shortly afterwards Dickson's built another double gun with the Westley Richards doll's head snap action.

Old John must have still been shopping about, or perhaps it was his son, for in the following year they built another snap action gun, this time on

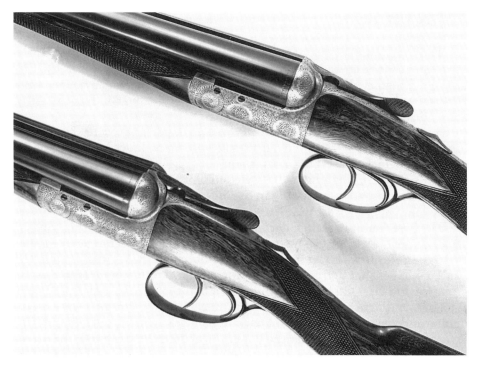

The famous Dickson Round Action guns

Horsley's patent and then later in the year the first double barrel breech-loader was made "of our own pattern". Unless gun No. 2683 comes to light we shall not know what their "own pattern" was, but it is likely that it would be a back-action pinfire with a double bite rotary bolt. All was not settled because towards the end of 1866 a 12-bore double was made with a "sliding action", and this would no doubt be a Bastin Lepage built to the order of a customer. Times were changing yet again, pinfire giving way to central fire and in 1867 several Lancaster pattern guns were produced for central fire cartridges, being followed two years later by guns with steel barrels and snap levers over the guard. Whether or not these were of the Purdey type is not known, but certainly Purdey actions of the 1863 pattern were made with back-action locks and the same year saw the first of the top lever snap actions manufactured.

The spirit of inquiry was still very much alive, for in 1871 yet another type of action was built, the Jones, which had been patented in 1870 and which was one of the earliest actions to have bolts at the top of the breech as well as on the lump.

To continue in business one needs customers to buy the guns and Dickson's had one of the most unusual customers a gunmaker ever had in Charles Gordon. He made his first purchase in 1875 and his last in 1906 and between these two dates Dickson's had made over THREE HUNDRED guns for their eccentric but valuable customer.

Dickson's themselves could also be accused of eccentricity, for in 1882 they brought out their three-barrelled gun and two years previously the foundations for their famous "Round Action" gun had been well and truly laid, to be further improved in 1887. With the exception of McNaughton's, yet another Edinburgh maker and a firm now incorported with Dickson's, no other firm ever made a gun like the Round Action and well over half a century later this unique shotgun is still being made.

Even more unusual was the Round Action over-and-under which opens to the side. With the exception of the Britt which shares the side-opening feature, but not the lockwork, no other O/U shotgun remotely resembles the Dickson. Beauty, as Dr Johnson remarked, is of itself very estimable, and should be considered as such and the Dickson Round Action is a really beautiful gun. It is also possessed of other qualities, one of which is longevity. The Round Action which advertises present production and which you will find on the cover of the current Dickson catalogue is the author's and this was built well over half a century ago. How many manufactured articles of today can be advertised by an illustration of one made 75 years ago? — very few I would think.

The last of the Dickson family left the firm in 1923 and shortly afterwards the premises were moved to Hanover Street, and then to the present premises in Frederick Street. Although this Edinburgh firm has a long and fascinating history, the people who work for Dickson's and those who guide its policy have their sights on the future and the shop in Frederick Street is modern and up-to-date. Possibly the only old-fashioned thing about Dickson's is their standard of sevice to sportsmen, a standard in keeping with their position as Gunmakers in the Capital of Scotland.

JAMES ERSKINE, NEWTON STEWART

I have referred to James Erskine once or twice in the past and recently requested information on him from readers. I mentioned that I had known of this man for many years and had made efforts to find out more about him since, by any standards, he was quite a remarkable man. Enquiries in Dumfries had produced several promising leads which on following up had suddenly dried up. I had become rather resigned to being unable to produce anything more on the Erskines and finally resolved to put down on paper what was available. I had spent time on research and talked to a number of people in Dumfries and Kirkcudbright, I had little expectation of anything more coming to light. I was wrong. Once again I underestimated the "power of the press" and, in particular of the sporting press.

At the end of September 1973 I received a letter from Mrs Mann. In her letter she told me that she had just seen my request for information in

Shooting Times and, as one of the surviving grandchildren of James Erskine, she felt that I might be interested in having some more information on the gunmaking Erskines. The story is a truly fascinating one because the Erskines can trace their family back to Charles Erskine, who, with his brother Robert, was with the Jacobite army of 1716. Charles went to live in Minnigaff, Galloway, where he married the locksmith's daughter and in due course acquired the business. His eldest son, Thomas, moved across the River Cree and set himself up in business as a gunmaker in Newton Stewart. His eldest son, James, left home and worked with Williams of Pool Lane, Liverpool, as a gun finisher. I think it likely that this Williams later became Williams & Powell in about 1840. James returned to Newton Stewart in 1830 and his younger brother John went to work for Williams in Liverpool in his brother's place. John stayed in Liverpool for 17 years finally rejoining the business in Newton Stewart.

James Erskine, on the death of his father, continued the business and with the help of his brother, who was accounted a first class gun filer, began to build up a reputation which was to be recognised by the award of a bronze medal at the famous Great Exhibition of 1851. The award was for a pair of muzzleloading shotguns with recessed hammers which were apparently given close examination by both Queen Victoria and Prince Albert. James Erskine was complimented on the high quality of the workmanship — it is to be regretted that the whereabouts of these guns is now unknown.

James Erskine is perhaps best known for the cartridge loading machine

James Erskine hammer gun

which bears his name, later to be improved by his son William so that the output of finished cartridges could reach 1,000 per hour. Later James invented a machine for loading military ball cartridges. This was tested at Woolwich Arsenal, approved and then rejected because it might cause a strike by workmen who were still loading by hand. Guns were made for HRH the Duke of Saxe-Coburg-Gotha, Prince Henry of Taxis and many other eminent people.

The business in Newton Stewart was at 62 Victoria Street, where, under the direction of the last male descendant of the Erskines, William, it remained until 1907, James having died in 1891.

William Erskine, who had joined the business in 1877 when he was 13, transferred it to Dumfries, buying up the old-established business of George Hume at 6 Loreburn Street where he remained until 1946. Then, the lease expired and the property was sold. William Erskine was unable to obtain another shop and, at the grand old age of 80, William the third son of James Erskine retired. I am indebted to Mrs Eleanor M Mann, the daughter of William Erskine. She tells me that she can remember filling the wad boards of the Erskine loading machine and that her father made these machines for export all over the world. In answer to my comment on the opinion of the period "that the Erskine machine was wholly unsuited to the private gunroom" Mrs Mann, as one who used the machine, tells me that her recollection is "that it was not bulky and that it could be easily operated". Your father and grandfather would be proud of you!

W. HORTON OF GLASGOW

Mr John Mullins directed my attention to this gunmaker. He told me he had just bought a 12-bore shotgun by a W. Horton of Buchanan St., Glasgow and that he was not able to find out anything about this firm. The gun was a boxlock ejector with an Anson-type fore-end and carried Birmingham proof marks. Mr Mullins went on to say that the gun handled nicely and that it had all the characteristics of an expensive gun. He also gave me a list of things he wanted to know; my attempt to answer some of his questions now follows!

The first thing to strike me was how little I knew about Horton. I had heard of him for nearly 30 years but although I had seen a 12-bore cartridge with the name Horton, Glasgow, I had not seen a gun or a catalogue of the firm and must admit that despite living in Glasgow I had not even looked for any evidence of the firm "on its home ground".

Mr Mullin's letter was to change all this. First of all, I remembered that I had a little bit of literature on Horton contained in a very early issue of *The Badminton Magazine of Sports and Pastimes* of November 1903. This was given to me by one of my oldest shooting friends, D.R. Pickup, the man indeed who might almost be said to have started me off on my long love affair with firearms. This magazine was given to me when I visited him in 1980 to renew an acquaintance disturbed by the passage of all too many years. However, that is another story for another time — back to the magazine! I recalled that it had an advert of the "Perfect Gun" by Horton and it was the work of a moment to locate the magazine and the advert. Except for Holland & Holland's it was the largest advert in the magazine and gave me a slightly different outlook on the importance of W. Horton.

I then put together the information I already had from various sources. From my old researches into Glasgow gunmakers done a quarter of a century ago I knew that William Horton was English and a gun stocker to trade. The firm had been founded at 29 Union Street, Glasgow in 1864 and the only information prior to this was a patent by a W. Horton of 1885 which dealt with improvements in percussion muzzle-loading guns. The firm moved to Royal Exchange Square, where they advertised as agents for Colt. By 1900 we find them at 98 Buchanan Street, Glasgow, one of the foremost shopping streets in the city. Today, this address belongs to the Royal Bank of Scotland, and though the staff was most helpful and polite my enquiries at the Bank about gunmakers did not bring forth any useful information. The firm moved to 199 Buchanan Street but this was only the works and today although the building still stands no evidence of a gunsmith's workshop remains although ample space and suitable buildings still exist at the back of the shop frontages.

The factory was interesting, one reason being because the firm was large enough to have a factory and another that while the shop remained in Buchanan Street for many years it was the factory that changed its location. The first and earliest information is that it was located at 11 Princes Square. This I found to be off Buchanan Street and convenient to the shop. The place itself is of interest since I was told that it had been a barracks but no remains of No 11 were to be found; the building is there but no No 11. This quite often happens, streets are renumbered and houses fall down, still no No 11. I then found that the works had moved to 64 Osborne Street near the Saltmarket. This was an area of Glasgow that had been completely rebuilt and No. 64 was a purpose built "flatted" factory so designed as to harmonise with the tenement dwellings round about. By some quirk of fate the whole of the building which houses No. 64 is still standing though many around it have been pulled down in yet another "city development plan", this one of recent origin. A thorough search through the building and its inhabitants brought to light no trace of Horton and so this avenue to further knowledge remains blocked.

Now about the shop; no one remembers this either. I know that the stock had been bought by the old established firm of Arthur Allen sometime in the 1920s and the present manager of the shop, John, had told me something of the takeover. A further call at Allen's produced the information that they had Horton's "try gun" but on examination although it well might have been used by Horton at their "private fitting range" mentioned in the advert, a minor problem is that the gun is marked Harkom, the famous Edinburgh gun-

W. Horton of Glasgow

maker. (It is, in itself, a very interesting gun.) John told me that Mrs Anderson, the former manager of the shop, was with Arthur Allen's when they bought the stock from Horton but from her I learned but little; as far as she had been concerned the "take over" of Horton's had "just been a lot of hard work". I felt a bit upset at this; here was someone "on the spot" who might well have been able to tell me much more about the Horton shop. Then I remembered that when I was a young man I lived in Birmingham; to this day I regret that I had not used my time properly in going round old gunmakers instead of drinking beer or chasing girls or both!

ALEXANDER MARTIN

The traditional gunmaker occupies a unique place in the scale of relationships between the shopkeeper and the customer. "Shopkeeper" you may say with some justifiable surprise, since YOUR gunsmith is certainly more than a shopkeeper, a mere vendor of packaged goods. For many of us the gunshop from which we purchased our first air pistol and supply of pellets was a magical place, and with the passing of time a warm and close relationship grew up, a relationship that transcended the shopkeeper-customer involvement; one in fact became a friend for the transactions were no longer restricted to goods and money.

I have, throughout my life had the pleasure of knowing many gunmakers, gunsmiths and gun vendors and my life was enriched by their knowledge, their wit and their concern for my welfare.

One such man was Sandy Martin who had taken over a business in the heart of Glasgow that had been in the family for several generations.

Most gunmakers of renown had something special for which they were well known and upon which their reputation was founded. This could be a special type of gun, a classic example would be the Powell with the vertical top lever, Dougall with his "Lockfast" action, John Dickson with the "Round Action", Greener's special actions, and Westley Richards with the A & D action. Martin's produced one special type of shotgun, the "Martin Rib-Less" which saved a quarter of a pound of metal and removed a potential source of rusting under the ribs. Martin's also offered their sidelocks with "Celtic" engraving but for most people the firm was pre-eminently concerned for the major part of its existence with rifles and rifle shooting.

It was founded in Paisley in 1837. I will remember a story told to me by Sandy Martin of those early days. Attempts had been made by Dougal to produce tubes for gun barrels and from what can be gleaned of gunmaking in those far off days, the attempts to produce tubes had not been successful. Sandy told me of a letter in his possession written by his grandfather. The letter had been sent from the Black Country, (that part of the Midlands, west of Birmingham, the centre of metal working), to the family in Paisley and recounted the trials and tribulations of a journey from Paisley to Port

Alex Martin sidelock

Glasgow by coach, then to Liverpool by ship and then on to the Black Country where a sack of horse shoe nails collected in Scotland was made into gun barrel tubes which would then be brought back to Scotland and used to build guns. This letter now seems to be lost but it is an important document since it does tell us something about the gun trade in the first half of the 19th century.

The firm prospered and moved to Glasgow. They were first established in the old Trongate, then moved to Argyle Street, and finally to Exchange Square.

In the 1880s the firm laid the foundations for its pre-eminence in regulating rifles for full-bore target shooting. Members of the firm had many successes at Bisley and produced Lee-Metford and Lee-Enfield target rifles and special Breech Loading Match rifles in .256 calibre. These rifles were built on Farquharson actions and also on the less well known Field action.

The firm offered sporting rifles of all types including Colt and Winchester rifles and a wide range of Colt and Webley target revolvers.

Yet another speciality was the range of sights and sight protectors. Even in the days before the first world war novelty items could be bought, and for a shilling (5p) penknives made from .303 cases could be bought and for a little extra, interesting pencils were also to be had. One of the most intriguing items that one could buy three quarters of a century ago was a "Burn's Patent Barrel Cooler" used for softening the fouling inside the barrel on hot and dry days. I have yet to meet anyone who used one of these devices or even anyone who ever saw one.

One of my last memories of Sandy Martin was of being taken by him into a warehouse not far from the shop which was filled to the roof with guns and rifles of all sorts. An Aladdin's cave of treasure. In those days I had no money to buy and had to be content with just looking; this in itself was a treat, for few outsiders ever crossed the threshold. To my regret I learned that all the contents were sold to an American dealer although many of the more important items had been gifted to the Glasgow Museum where, as the "Martin Collection" it delights the firearms enthusiast and serves to commemorate the name of one of the more important Glasgow gunmakers later incorporated in the firm of John Dickson & Son.

CHARLES PLAYFAIR

The craft of gunmaking appears to have reached its peak in Aberdeen in the 17th century. One of the earliest entries in the records of the town is for Thomas Gordone, Gunmaker who is noted for "keiping of the thre knok the zair bygane". This entry is for April, 30, 1591 and translated into modern English tells us that "Gordon has looked after the three town clocks during the past year". Some seven years later Gordon is mentioned in the town accounts for "mending the quheills of the towbuithe knok, and finding the oyle thairto". Gunmakers in Scottish towns appear to have had a virtual

Playfair "Farmer's Gun"

208

monopoly on the "rewling of the knokis of the burght" or the mending and regulating of the town clocks.

One of the later entries in the Aberdeen records is for Charles Playfair, who is recorded as being elected Deacon of the Incorporation of Hammermen in 1841. The number of gunmakers had fallen severely by the opening of the 19th century and Playfair is the sole survivor of the trade recorded in the old manner.

Playfair was a remarkable representative of what had become an almost extinct craft and had, in fact, in 1821 founded the firm which was to bear his name for well over a century. Little is known of the early years of the founder but we know that in 1842 the firm, with premises at 94 Union Street, was offering a wide range of fishing tackle, bows and arrows, cricket bats and balls and other sporting goods. By this time the second Charles Playfair must have joined the firm, for in 1845 the younger Playfair left Aberdeen for Birmingham and in 1846 entered into partnership with Mr Thomas Bentley.

The firm of Bentley & Playfair of Summer Lane manufactured all types of arms and one of the several mysteries which surround their activities is whether the name of Charles Playfair's partner was Thomas or Joseph Bentley. Certainly the establishment was one of some importance and a London office was opened at 60 Queen Victoria St. Charles Playfair the elder remained in Aberdeen and died there in 1876. The original firm appears to have been taken over by Messrs. Robb who continued the business. Charles the younger became Chairman of the Birmingham Proof House and he became a director of the Birmingham Small Arms Company of which he was also an original shareholder on the formation of BSA in 1861. Charles Playfair II died in 1898 aged 75 years and it is difficult to assess what contact, if any, he had with Aberdeen where the company, founded by his father, continued to trade.

Business in Aberdeen must have been good at the turn of the century since the firm adopted the style "Gunmaker to Prince Albert" and by 1876 the firm had become a private company at 138 Union Street where they had been forced to move, the original premises being acquired by the Town & Country Bank Company.

In Birmingham the third Charles Playfair, later Lt. Col. Playfair, presided over the amalgamation of Bentley & Playfair with Isaac Hollis & Sons and continuing the family association with the Birmingham Proof House, Lt. Col. Playfair established the laboratory facilities in 1912 and two years later he was appointed Proof Master, a post he held until his death in 1941.

Meanwhile, in Aberdeen, the firm of Charles Playfair & Company continued to be patronised by the sporting fraternity until, in 1955, the business was sold to the firm of William Garden Ltd. who continued to carry on the business until reorganisation had been completed.

No patents have been traced to members of the family nor, indeed, was the contribution to gunmaking such that the name of Playfair was widely known, yet a contribution was made and it would merit further work if only to bring to light the activities of but one of the many Birmingham gunmakers, Bentley & Playfair, since, like many of their contemporaries their role in the industrial life of Birmingham has been neglected.

JAMES LAWSON

The title might well have been "James Lawson, Gun Maker, Cutler & Ironmonger, Fishing Rod & Tackle Manufacturer". This information is culled from the receipted invoice dated October, 19, 1900. The invoice was given to me by my old friend Alan Paton but regrettably it does not tell us anything about the goods which Mr Robert Paton purchased in that first year of the 20th century.

We have what might be James Lawson's signature and an indication of how business was conducted — "many thanks, most humbly" (all very Dickensian!).

In over 30 years I have encountered just one firearm which bore the name of Lawson. This was a Royal Irish Constabulary revolver from the Kater Collection, at ICI, Ardeer, and, although not MADE by Lawson, it was sold by him and so engraved on the top strap.

Records tell us that the firm was established in 1872. Then Lawson was described as a "Gunmaker, Cutler, Edge Tool and Mathematical Instrument Maker". From my own records I know the firm was still in business when the First World War broke out.

But did Lawson make guns? The answer, very probably, is that he did not.

So, at this stage of our enquiries what do we know about the firm? Very little, I'm afraid. All we have is one revolver, one entry in "Scottish Arms Makers" by Charles E Whitelaw, a number of notes taken from the Glasgow Directories by me over the years, and, of course, the invoice.

James Lawson was but one of a number of similar businesses which did not restrict themselves to selling firearms and ammunition but sold quite a selection of other items as well. Not far away was the firm of William Landell which lasted well into my lifetime and where I spent a very happy day with the old retainers of the firm who told me stirring tales of riot and insurrection in Glasgow, of the militia being called out and the mob being pursued across the bridge into the then warren of the Gorbals.

Arthur Allan was also described in 1855 as a "Gunmaker, Cutler and Edge Tool Maker", whereas Hugh Brown, also to be found in Argyle St. spread his net even wider — "Sawmaker, Ironmonger, Cutler, Plane, Edge Tool and Gunmaker". Thomas Campbell reminds me of the Birmingham trade where gunmaking and dealing in spirits so often went together. By 1857 Thomas Campbell had a shooting saloon in Glasgow's Saltmarket and I wonder if this was a shooting saloon or a saloon bar with shooting instead

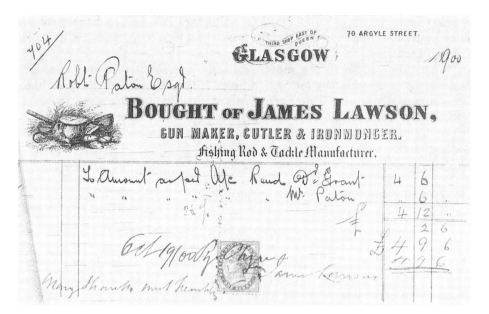

James Lawson invoice

of, perhaps, darts! The famous John Dougal started his business life as a fishing and fowling tackle maker, later to specialise in needles and fishing hooks. The business was established in 1808 and recorded as a gunmaker in 1837.

From the list of ventures described which merely scratches the surface we cannot help but get a picture of a busy, bustling commercial life, where opportunities come and go and where the people are ready to seize an opportunity whenever it is presented. Also it can explain how at times a gunmaker's name on a gun cannot be located in the records. Only this week I have had to tell two readers that I couldn't help with their queries. One was about a gun by Cufflyn of Folkestone, the other J Carr & Son, Gun & Rifle Makers, London. The latter might be the London retail outlet of a Birmingham firm but with regard to Cufflyn of Folkestone the only recourse is to local records in Folkestone. This is why any scrap of paper that has anything to do with guns or gunmaking is important. James Lawson was just a name in the directories, two lines on a Birmingham-made revolver, until that important bit of paper appeared and then, to me at least, he came to life, momentarily, the obscuring mists of time swirling aside to let us see, briefly, a little of the business life of Glasgow and of John Lawson.

Guns themselves are fairly robust; their chief enemies are rust and politicians. Trade labels in guncases, where these have been preserved can often provide much needed historical data, but here oil, physical damage and various nibbling creatures which eat paper have taken their toll over the years. Next of course we have catalogues and adverts. The latter can be single sheets or printed material in newspapers, magazines, books, etc. In later years cartridges and cartridge boxes can also help, as can entries in trade directories.

Lastly, we come to the most neglected source of information of all, business correspondence, letter headings, invoices, bills etc. Where these have survived all sorts of items of interest are likely to be uncovered. So when you are clearing things out of the attic and come to a pile of old papers, look through them please. There might be an old bill or invoice that could answer some questions. Don't forget, will you?

JULIUS COSTER

My interest in Julius Coster goes back many years to the start of my collection of Winchester rifles. The Model 76 lacked some parts and I needed metal to make them. I had asked in the tool room of a factory I used to visit and was told by one of the toolmakers that I should get in touch with his father, George Coster, who was a gunmaker, now retired and he would help me.

This was done and I met one of the most remarkable characters I have had the pleasure of knowing. As the years rolled by and our friendship grew I eventually got part of his history and then aided by a member of the family this grew into a search for more details.

George was the son of George Ernest Julius Coster, who we shall call Julius for simplicity. Julius, was also the son of a gunmaker, Johann Christoph Coster. Julius was born in 1850, in Niedermeiser, near Kassel in

J. Coster hammer gun

Germany. His father is recorded in Stockel as working from c1850 to 1870. We can assume that young Julius learned his trade from his father and in 1869 he left the family home and the business and came to Britain. After spending about a year in London he started work with Alex Henry in Edinburgh and prospered, rising to the position of Foreman. Henry had about 40 gunmakers working for him at this time and Julius would probably be described to-day as the Works Manager. He left Henry's employ in 1886 and went into partnership with Hunter, trading as Coster & Hunter from 18 Frederick Street. In 1890 the partnership was dissolved and Julius Coster continued in business on his own moving just round the corner, to 108 Rose Street in 1897.

In 1898 he closed the premises and moved across Scotland to Glasgow where he worked for Charles Ingram in Union Street until 1920. Father and son, then established a business in Glasgow at 145 West Nile Street. Julius died in 1927, his son George continued in business until 1930 when the shop was closed and George went to work for Alex Martin until he retired.

Julius Coster must have been a remarkable man, surviving photographs show him with a small white beard, known as a goatee, and he favoured the very large floppy caps which I recently discovered were known in Scotland as "doolanders". The only explanation I can think of for this name is that perhaps they were large enough for a "doo"(pigeon)to land on!

Over twenty years ago a Mr. Cossar who then lived in Kelso told me that his father, a gamekeeper, had been friendly with Julius Coster from whom he had bought his first gun, at the turn of the century. Julius used to come and stay with the family on his holidays. I was told that after a weeks holiday, Julius would have mended all the guns and clocks in the family and those of the neighbours also!

All I need now is to find a J. C. Coster of Niedermeiser and then I will have a record of guns made by three generations of the Coster family. I did write the story of the Coster family of gunmakers for the German magazine, Deutsches Waffen Journal in April 1967 but I received no response from the German readers but, who knows, a J. C. Coster gun may be brought along for me to see at a future Game Fair; let us hope so!

DAVID McKAY BROWN

Of the many mysteries which often shroud the old gun trade two stand out. The first is "Who made what?", and the second is the intriguing appearance of superb, distinctive sporting guns with little-known names that come from places well outside the established areas of gunmaking.

One expects to find quality guns being made in London, Birmingham, Edinburgh and Dublin because, until recently, these places had the necessary skills, but what is puzzling is how an unknown maker, like William Golden of Huddersfield, became established away from any centre of gunmaking.

213

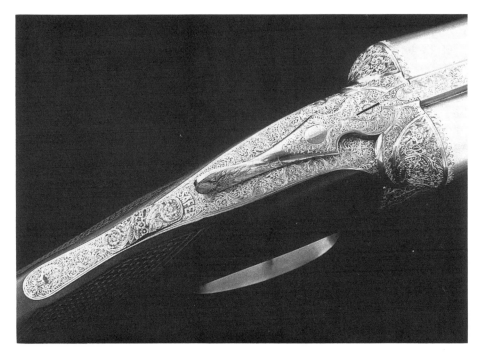

David McKay Brown round action

Men like Horsley of York, Pape of Newcastle and Griffiths of Manchester, built guns of superb quality and distinctive finish.

You might think that such men no longer exist, but you'd be wrong. They do and one such is David McKay Brown of Bothwell, near Glasgow.

David started his working life in the heavy engineering industry in the West of Scotland, as a draughtsman. Although he was fascinated by the techniques of metal working and forming, his interest in guns and how they were made grew until, against all the advice of family and friends, he left heavy engineering for an apprenticeship with the old established firm of Alex Martin of Exchange Square, Glasgow. Martin's had been established in 1835, moving to Exchange Square in 1844. It was here, in the workshop under the pavements, that David started to learn the art and craft of gunmaking.

Before David's apprenticeship ended, Martin's were brought by the Edinburgh gunmakers John Dickson & Son, a firm with an even longer and more illustrious history. As patentees of the famous Dickson round action shotgun their fame can truly be said to be world wide and, following the takeover, David Brown was transferred to Edinburgh where he came into close contact with the men who had built the round action.

When his apprenticeship was completed David decided to start up on his own. Premises were acquired in Hamilton and it was here, in 1967, that he started repairing guns. He sought work for his shop by canvassing the trade and soon built up a connection much as he would have done had he been in Birmingham.

He made Anson & Deeley-type shotguns from trade actions and then built double rifles for the London trade. Problems were many — raw materials, the need to train craftsmen (since it had proved impossible to lure skilled men from the south) and, of course, running a business in an age of ever-increasing bureaucracy.

The urge to build best guns remained and such time as David could spare from the bread and butter business of trade work was devoted to the task of finding out how to establish a gunmaking workshop that could build guns to the standards of the Victorian gunmakers.

What type of gun should he build? For David the choice was simple. In Edinburgh two quite unique actions had been developed, the MacNaughton and the Dickson. Both were what we call today 'trigger-plate actions'. The MacNaughton was the first; its patent dates from 1879 with a later introduction of an ejector mechanism in 1890. The cocking system employed by the Dickson dates from 1880 with the lockwork patented in 1882, followed by an ejector system in 1887 which, when coupled with modifications patented in the same year resulted in the Dickson round action. David Brown's association with the old Edinburgh gunmakers finally led to his decision to build this type of action. Five years were to pass before the first trigger-plate action gun was completed. Many of the old techniques had either been lost or could no longer be employed. Special tools, jigs and fixtures had to be made and the job of building such a special action had to be critically examined to see how best the many operations required could be done.

Modern practice was closely examined to see where techniques unknown to the Victorian gunmaker could profitably be employed. In fact, with the production envisaged, the traditional methods of gunmaking were not only more cost effective but the results were also better. In short, for many of the operations there was just no substitute for skilled hands.

Bigger premises were acquired in the historic town of Bothwell, and here the operations involved in building the round action gun were broken down into units so that the initial machine operations could be carried out to create a stock of part-finished components that could then be drawn on to reduce the time from placing an order to receiving the finished gun. The waiting period is now about eighteen months.

Douglas Proctor joined the firm direct from school as lockmaker and is responsible for locks, springs, lever work, spindle and bolt. Jim MacDonald deals with the work involved in barrel filing and boring and Robin Moir is the actioner. Brian Sinclair makes the gun stocks.

David McKay Brown has overall responsibility and all the work is carried out under his direct supervision. He also works at the bench himself, jointing barrels to the action, filing and finishing off.

Each gun is a 'one off' — a *sculpture* in metal and wood. Materials employed are of the highest quality and strength and functioning of the gun are above reproach. In my view the Edinburgh trigger-plate actions are among the sleekest and best-looking shotguns ever made.

You will need to draw about £15,000 from your piggy bank for a McKay Brown, but you will then have a gun that will perform faultlessly in the field. You will also have a superb investment.

Engraving provides the finishing touch and the customer has a wide choice of styles of engraving from some of the acknowledged masters of the art who do the work for David McKay Brown.

John Dickson "Round Action"

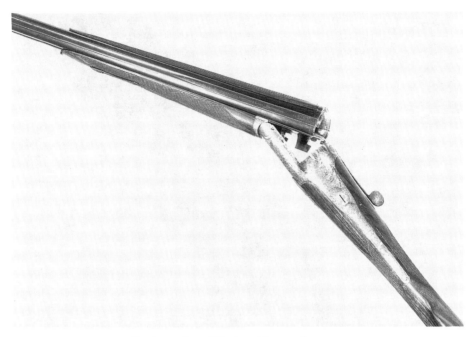

Dickson Over/Under side opening gun

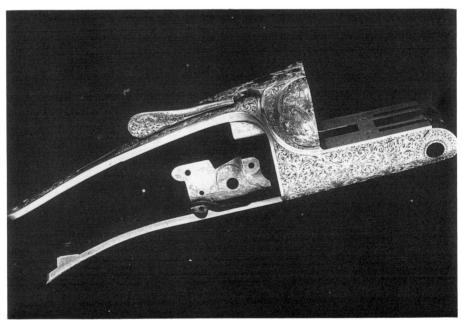

David McKay Brown's engraving

218

David McKay Brown's shop

David McKay Brown discussing gun with John Amber

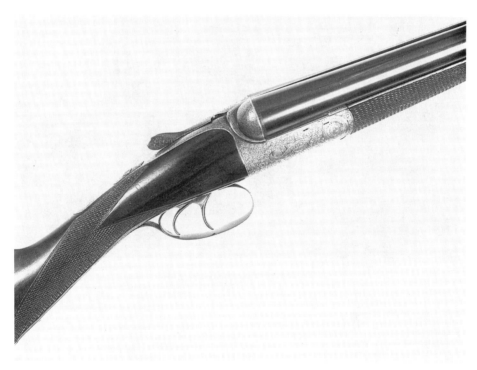

Dickson "Round Action", made in 1911

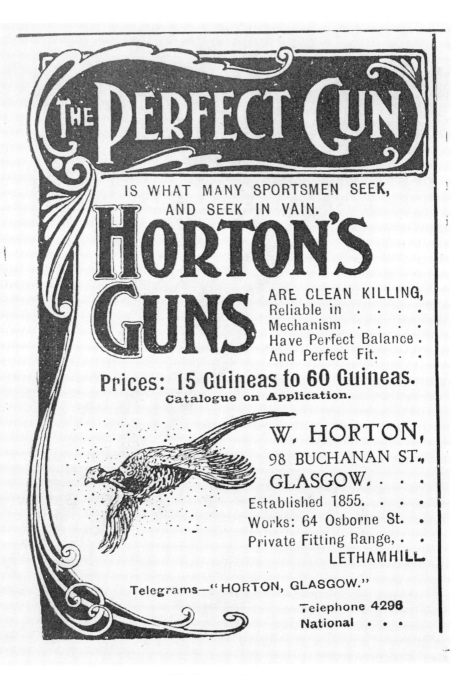

W. Horton, Glasgow

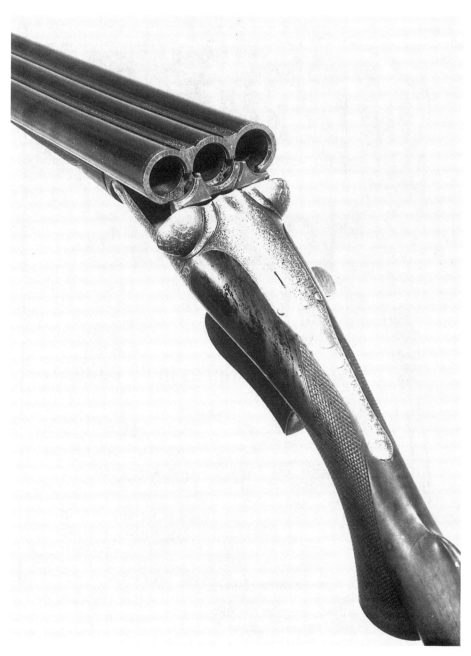

Dickson three barrel gun

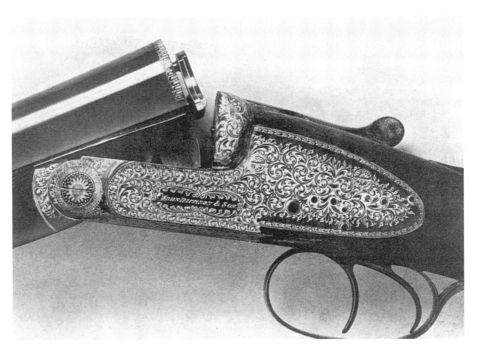

Dickson sidelock

Engraving a sidelock

LET'S BUILD A "BEST" GUN

You may have bought it, you may have inherited it, you may, on the other hand, have purchased that "Best" gun secondhand either through a gunmaker or at auction. New, the price you paid could have bought a very nice new car, second-hand, in good condition, a "Best" gun will still cost a lot of money, say up to £20,000.

Here we are not only paying for the highest quality; at these prices we are also paying for the "name."

To establish a "name" is not easy and with the exception of competition shooting where at the turn of the century names such as Churchill, Grant, Boswell and Lang became well known because of their successes at Gun Club meetings — no such easy way of quickly establishing a reputation is now available in this country.

Today the reputation is either there and has to be maintained (for it can be quite easily lost) or it has to be built up quite gradually by recommendation and word of mouth.

Not all the best guns were made by the famous London or even provincial makers. The best gun has about it an air which is recognizable whether it is built in London, Liege, Birmingham or Brescia.

Many best guns were built by gunmakers whose names are unknown except to the gun trade itself. Sometimes, in spite of the name on the lockplate and top rib, the name of the *maker* of the gun will be revealed by a few initials discreetly impressed into the metal, more often than not, since the livelihood of the gunmaker depended on his anonymity the true maker of the gun will not be discovered. This practice is now affected by the provisions of the Trades Description Act. This happened to be the way the gun trade was organised and in some respects it is not dissimilar to the motor trade. One could ask "When was the last true Bentley manufactured?" The purist might well answer "The day before the firm was bought by Rolls Royce Ltd." The same questions could be asked about any number of marques, some both the name and quality have survived, others, just the name and no more. Much the same applies to today's builders of quality guns.

Since we are talking about "best" guns, what do we mean by the word "best" particularly as used by the gun trade?

Let us first of all have a look at the dictionary definition. The most appropriate appears to be "excelling all others in quality". I have just done a quick search through my gun library to see if anyone has been bold enough to give a definition with reference to guns. The indexes of most of the books on shotguns do not include "best gun", that is, with the exception of *Shotguns* by Pollard. Even Pollard does not define the term so we are left with the dictionary one. That is until we have looked at how these "best" guns are made.

Who are the makers of "best" guns? Boss have always *said* they were since in the advertisement section of Pollard's book we find their advert with the statement "Builders of best guns only". Stephen Grant & Sons are not quite so dogmatic, they merely state "Makers of Best Quality Guns and Rifles". James Purdey comes close but avoids the term "best", their statement is "Manufacturers of the Highest Quality Weapons Only". This was in 1923. Today their advertisement might merely state "Purdey — London", such is the power of prestige.

I could have gone to one of the famous name firms and asked for two or three days of their time and access to all their secrets. Two firms have indeed offered these facilities and I shall be taking advantage of their offer later in the year. To start with, however, I want to show you how a best gun is made by a firm you may not have heard of — A. A. Brown & Sons of Alvechurch. You may not have heard of them but their roots go deep into the history of gunmaking in Birmingham.

The first recorded member of the gunmaking Browns was John Joseph born in 1853. He was one of eleven sons, five of whom became master gunmakers. One of the sons, George, was an engraver, Sidney was a stock finisher and three others were action filers. John went to work for Webley & Scott and he met and married Maria Chapman who was a cartridge loader at Webley & Scott. They had two sons who survived, John and Albert Arthur, both of whom entered the gun trade.

Albert Arthur worked for the firm of F. E. & H. Rogers of Loveday Street. He married Minnie Davis in 1911 and they had two sons, Albert Henry and Sidney Charles, born in 1913 and 1916. By the thirties we find the firm of Albert Arthur Brown at 27 1/2 Whittal Street and in the years just before the war the firm becomes A. A. Brown & Sons at 35 1/2 Whittal Street.

Until the outbreak of war the firm made gun actions for the trade. During the war armourers tools and gun components were made and the firm was also bombed out. They moved to the outskirts of the city until the war ended when they re-established themselves in the heart of the old gunmaking quarter at 4 Sand Street. In the post war years materials for building quality shotguns were difficult to come by so Brown made an air pistol, the "Abas Major" of which some two thousand were produced from the Abas Works in Sand Street.

With the easing of restrictions A. A. Brown went back to making high quality box-lock guns for the trade and a few sidelocks as well. They bought the machinery and tools from the old established firm of J. Asbury & Sons which had closed down and were then able to manufacture guns complete from rough forging and bar steel. The firm specialised also in the production of top ribs for double shotguns and these were made for the trade, a very much more complicated job than one would at first imagine!

A. H. Brown joined the Board of Guardians of the Birmingham Proof House in 1946 and during his membership, which lasted for twenty two years, he was Chairman for five. In 1946 the next generation of gunmaking Browns appeared, Robin who is now a partner. In 1957 Mr A. A. Brown retired and three years later the firm had to move once again. This was due to the redevelopment of the centre of Birmingham and along with many other firms their premises were demolished. Well over half of the gun trade was affected by these changes and many smaller firms went out of business at this time. Browns moved into premises which were offered by the firm of Westley Richards where they were to remain for fourteen years. In 1961 Robin Brown joined the firm to serve his five years apprenticeship as a gunstocker, learning his craft from one of the best men of his day, Mr Albert Thompson. Robin became a partner in 1967.

During this period one of the foremost engravers in the country, Les Jones, started to work for the firm full time. The emphasis during this period was on high quality sidelock guns for the home and export trade. As had happened many years ago with the firm of Webley & Scott it was decided that all the guns made by the firm, regardless of the purchaser, would bear the company trade mark "ABAS", a mark still in use today.

A move was made to Alvechurch, a pleasant village some 14 miles south of Birmingham, in 1974. Premises at 1 Snake Lane were purchased and alterations carried out to make them suitable for the manufacture of guns.

With the move to Alvechurch also came the decision to concentrate on the manufacture of guns for private customers (with a few exceptions). This represented a distinct change in marketing policy and this was to be followed by another important decision, that to manufacture one quality of gun only, the best.

The family has a tradition of well over a century of gunmaking behind it, the knowledge and the skills are there. New and modern premises are available and over 95% of the work is carried out "in house", to use current jargon.

The locks, which formerly were made by specialist lock makers, as was the practice in the trade, are now made "in house". This had already been considered but when the lockmaker which they used went into liquidation "in house" manufacture was a sensible choice. Many of the internal parts of the gun are gold plated — not because this looks nice — indeed most of the plated work can't be seen, but because gold plated components are less liable to corrode. This work is also done "in house" both the copper and gold plating. It is better to have control over these processes and it also saves a lot of time since jobbing platers can well lose the odd small lock component, not realising that the work needed to replace that one small part is quite high since the item is not stamped out by the thousand on a press.

Gold plating has other advantages, the work required for overhaul is very much reduced when the gun is returned to Alvechurch for servicing. This also means that the cost of such work is reduced!

Bought in items include the tubes, bar or chopper lump for the barrels, special forgings for the action body, one forging is used for 28, 20, 16 and 12 bore guns, a special forging is used for the .410. Bar stock is also bought in, the fore-end is now made from case hardening steel and, of course, the high grade timber for the stock is purchased from specialist suppliers.

Machining of the forgings and bar stock is all carried out in the workshop by Harold Scandrett who has been with the firm for thirty three years. Some of the operations are done by outside specialists such as chequering and barrel blacking. Case hardening, on the other hand, is done in the traditional manner in animal charcoal on the premises. Known also as "bone meal" to the old time gunsmith today this comes from Scotland where it is used in the making of whisky!

Emphasis is on traditional methods of manufacture, not merely because it is traditional but for the simple reason that these techniques suit the present volume of production and the fact that each gun is an individual creation. The term "custom gun" has become somewhat debased and as an alternative to "best" gun one can use the term "bespoke gun". This means

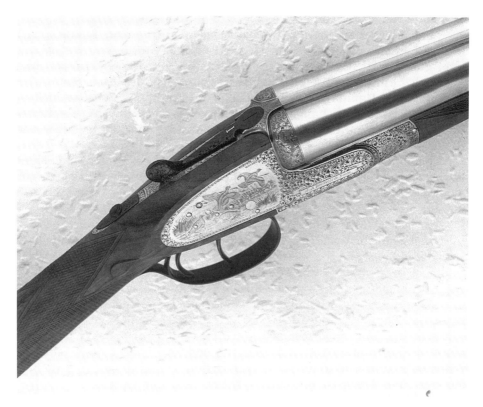

A. A. Brown & Sons "Best" sidelock

"made to the customer's exact requirements" and it is an alternative to having several grades of gun on the range none of which suit your precise needs.

The standard specification is for the "best" gun and the options available, in general, are to provide a lower cost alternative.

The guns are sidelocks and can be built in 12, 16, 20, 28, or .410 bores. Barrels are "side by side" and can be made from 24" to 30" long. There is a choice of chamber length, choke, weight, balance and stocking.

Chopper lump tubes are standard but dovetailed tubes can be provided at lower cost. The gun is a self-opener, but this unit can be removed or the gun can be made as an easy opener with the option to have no self opening device at lower cost. Locks have intercepting safety sears and can be hand detachable if required. Trigger pull weight to suit the customer's requirements with the option of a single trigger, the guard has a single bead on the finger side of the bow. Ejectors are Southgate and the fore-end is secured by the Anson push rod fastening. The safety is automatic and has a gold inlaid "SAFE". The action is bolted by a top lever operating a hardened steel bolt with double bites on the barrel lump. Disc set strikers are fitted and the action has beaded fences with fluted sides and double bars on the underside. On lightweight guns the action body can be rounded.

Stocks are made from specially selected French walnut and customers can have a choice as to figure and colour. The finish is hand rubbed oil and a gold oval is fitted which can be engraved with initials or a crest. The grip is straight with a slight diamond shape and drop points but a pistol grip can be made if required.

Engraving is to the customer's requirements and can vary from standard fine English scroll to any type of special engraving. The action can be colour hardened or "brushed silver" and the barrels, guard, top lever etc., are finished in deep black.

Measurements for the stock can be taken from an existing gun, from details provided by a shooting school or the measurements can be taken at Alvechurch. Guns can be made as matched pairs, triples or sets and any type of gun case can be provided. The cases can be provided with outer covers and accessories and the guns are proof tested at the Birmingham Proof House.

This is not merely the specification of the A. A. Brown & Sons "best" gun it indicates in fairly precise terms the extent to which guns of this quality can be made to suit the customers exact requirements. For this reason, although it is possible or order a gun or guns from a gunmaker by post or telephone, nothing serves as well as does a visit in person. One of the pleasures of buying a gun of this quality is the discussion with the gunsmith. This serves many purposes, it means that you are more likely to get exactly what you want and of possibly even greater importance you feel that you have had a hand in the building of the gun, since, of course, you have if your ideas and wishes have been incorporated in the final end product.

We learned something of the history of the firm of A. A. Brown & Sons and why I chose them to illustrate how one goes about making a best gun.

It was during a visit to the factory at Alvechurch in 1977 that the idea of taking a reader through the various stages of building a best side-by-side double first came to mind. The first positive steps were taken following a 2 day visit by Robin Brown when we discussed all the aspects of their operation.

This is not as easy as it sounds. I first followed the manufacture of a shotgun by modern techniques at the F.N. factory in Herstal, Belgium. This was the renowned Browing O/U and, with the aid of a number of F.N. officials who gave me much of their time, I was able to follow the manufacture of the O/U from the forge to the finished product. Because of the volume of production I was able to see guns at all stages of manufacture but where the output is measured in tens rather than in thousands this cannot be done. All too often with the small volume of output it is very often impossible to see a finished gun let alone guns in various stages of production.

With Browns, the first part of the manufacturing process is to break down the various operations into specialist areas and allocate these to the members of the production team. Since all the people in the workshop are working gunmakers we find the tasks split up as follows. Harold Scandrett is responsible for most of the machine operations, he also part files-up the gun furniture, trigger plates, triggers, guards. All of these items are made from forgings, none are castings. Harold is also responsible for most of the work in connection with the production of the sidelock mechanism which is based to a large extent on the Holland and Holland design, possibly one of the most widely used sidelock mechanisms for "Best" guns. The lock components are jig machined from bar stock, the steel being chosen for each component to give the most desirable characteristics. In addition, Harold does the barrel work, boring, choke regulation, making the extractors and top ribs and blacking work. He also does machining work for the trade and barrel repairs such as raising dents, polishing bores etc. Mr A H Brown and Mr S C Brown are responsible for the critical work of joining the barrels to the action, this is known as jointing. They also fit the disc set strikers and prepare new guns for submission to proof. Both craftsmen work on the locks and they fit and finish the fore-end and finish the stocks. In addition they are responsible for freeing and finishing all work after case hardening.

Mr Sidney Brown also does the repair, renovation and overhaul work done by the firm on both their own and other high quality English guns. His son, Robin Brown, who, following the retirement of Mr Albert Brown in 1978 looks after lock fitting, the cocking and ejector work, fore-end fitting, furniture fitting and the final filing up of triggers, guards etc. Also included in this section is the safework, preparation for stocking, marking the wood off to the customer's measurements and the machining of the fore-end wood. Robin does the fitting of the self opening mechanism, he makes the single trigger mechanism and is responsible for colour case-hardening and the

Stock work

copper and gold plating. He also stocks screws and part finishes all new guns.

The test firing of the gun, patterning etc. is also done by Robin and, with the help of his wife, he looks after the office work.

The work of making the gun is split into sections and each one of the gunmakers has his own specialist responsibilities.

There is one other gunmaker, Albert, who retired in 1978. He, as we have seen, continues to work on a part-time basis on jointing, lockwork and smoothing actions ready for the engraver.

Because of the manner in which the work is organised it is not possible to see all the operations being carried out in one day. I might have to stay in the workshop for a month or more before it would be possible to say that *all* of the operations have been seen. To add to the difficulties much of the work is done in batches. This is very important where work is machined since special jigs and fixtures are employed and the machines have to be set up to do a specific operation. It would obviously be time wasting and grossly expensive to set up a machine to carry out an operation on one component so a batch will be machined and then put aside to be drawn upon as guns progress through the shop.

It would, of course, be possible to make the whole of the gun by hand but this would be inordinately expensive. Equally expensive, if not considerably more so, would be to make the gun entirely by machinery and modern metal forming techniques. One only has to look at the complex beauty of an aircraft jet engine blade to see that the techniques employed to manufacture this small, but extremely intricate item could be used to make shotgun actions and components. One could, no doubt, produce "The Venus de Milo" by computer controlled machines but a "one off" would be more costly than the original and if made in large numbers it would no longer be "unique". This is where some of the expense of the best gun is to be found. The high quality of the raw materials cost money, one has only to look at the price for best quality stock blanks. The major expense is time. The machines employed are really only power driven files. They are used to shift the metal from the 3 1/2 lbs. weight of body forging. Other machines have some measure of "built in skill". This is because the skill went into the design and making of the jigs and fixtures. The skill that is used to finish the gun is where most of the money goes. Each gun is unique, no other gun is exactly like it, it is, if you like, sculpture in wood and metal.

You will have noticed that there is no quality control department at Brown's, it is not necessary, each man who works there is his own quality control, his own critical inspection department. In spite of this pride of craftsmanship it has to be emphasised that each gun and each part of the gun is unlike any other made before or after. Each is an individual creation and is subject to critical evaluation by both partners, Sidney Brown and Robin Brown. Not only do they examine the work of the rest of the team they also comment on the work of each other. This means that the critical analysis of all the work is continuous and very thorough. The work on even a simple item such as a trigger is not finished because the time allocated to its manufacture has run out or because it's five o'clock, the work finishes when the craftsman is satisfied that the trigger is as near perfection as he can make it. Each man will have his own standards, the firm will have its own rules, "this is how we like our triggers to be made, this is how we like our actions to be filed up," (in the case of Brown's, with fluted sides to reduce the width of the action and with double bars.) It is at this point that we move into the area of opinion and matters of personal taste. One might like the way one man files up the fences, not all are alike, but on a best gun whilst the style might vary the quality does not. Within limits the man who buys a bespoke gun can have things made the way he wants them (having regard to safety — a painting or a piece of sculpture does not have to undergo a proof test!) and if the customer's wishes clash with what the gunmaker considers to be appropriate it is the task of the gunmaker to alter the standards of his potential customer. The man might well want gold inlaid nude females pursued by satyrs frollicking along the action. The gunmaker may not wish to have his name on a gun so ornamented and if he can't change the views of the customer he can decline to make the gun. I have often wondered if this has ever happened!

Today, even with the benefit of ample funds it is not an easy matter to have the things you want made exactly as you would like them to be. Clothes, shoes and the binding of books come to mind as being some of things that can

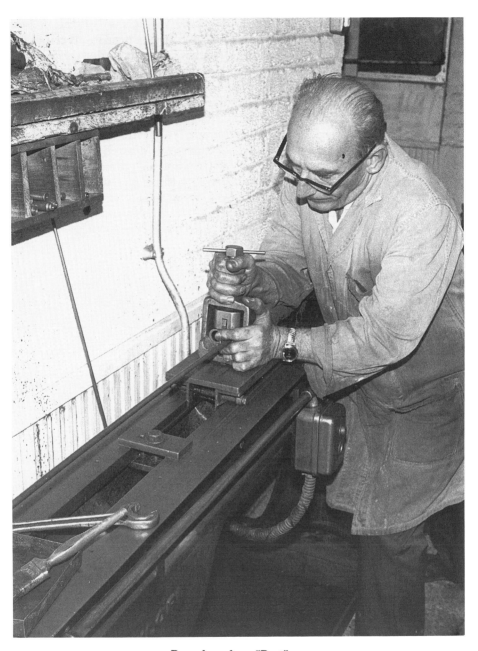

Barrel work on "Best" gun

be made in small numbers to suit precisely the wishes of the critical customer. Into this special category of individually produced items comes the best gun. If you merely want a tool to be used and then discarded the best gun is not for you. If you wish to own something that is intensely personal, that is part of you and in which you can take both pride of ownership and pride in using then a best gun has to be considered. You may be fortunate enough to have the considerable pleasure of discussing with the gunmaker exactly what you think you need. If you can't wait up to two years and don't have the money for a new gun then perhaps a used gun can be altered to suit you. You could, of course, say that a firm like Brown's and the guns they make are totally irrelevant in today's society. In this I think you would be wrong. Without the ultimate we have no standard of comparison and in any case the world would be a sadder and less enjoyable place to be if you and I could not take pleasure and delight in looking at what we consider to be perfection — the best gun.

THE GROUSE GUN

Let us play a game of pretend, you and I! Let us pretend that we have been invited for a day out, a day at driven grouse, some time just after the 12th!

Let us also pretend that we have a Fairy Godmother who has granted us our wish that we can have exactly the right type of shotgun for the occasion.

She has also promised to outfit us sartorially and with a sprinkling of pixie dust we have been blessed with the necessary skills needed to deal with Lagopus lagopus scoticus on his native heath. Probably more has been written about red grouse than any other game bird, questions have been asked in the House of Commons and in the opinion of many of the 19th century pundits "grouse shooting is not only the most laborious of all shooting but is a science in itself!"

That there is magic I will not dispute. I remember, as though it were but yesterday, a day out, not thirty miles from where I live now, but twenty years or more in the past, a day which started with all the elements of a total disaster since most of the beaters did not turn up. This task was taken over by the wife and daughters of a retired R.N. Admiral. Never have I seen more enthusiasm, more raw energy, more sheer delight expended by human beings, of either sex, it was a delight to watch the girls at work and their efforts produced a day of true and lasting enchantment. The bag was minuscule compared with the mega-bags of N. Yorks in the great Edwardian days, but every bird of ours was a well won trophy of the day, to be discussed over dinner and the evening's wee dram!

The appeal of driven grouse has attracted many to the famous moors of the North of England and Scotland for well over a century. If we were to go to a gunmaker in the first half of the 19th century and ask his advice he could well agree with Hawker and tell you that the best gun to use is the largest single gun you can manage and nothing smaller than No. 3 shot. Some years later, Captain Lacy complained that "grouse are becoming generally more scarce every year in the Northern Counties of England, where, formerly, they were wont to abound." Lacy also advises a single gun, but it must be stout with a large bore and nothing smaller than No. 3 shot to be used. Preferably, we are told, the shot should be contained in one of Mr. Eley's "cartridges". These were specially made to load in muzzle loading guns with the shot contained in a small wire basket, complete with wads etc., so that the charge was concentrated. This accounts for another name that may be encountered in the literature of the period, "wire cartridges".

Those who pursued "muir game" with muzzle loading guns were advised to alter the shot and powder loading dependent upon conditions and, in the afternoon, change to a lighter gun!

One cannot help but wonder exactly what did happen on the shoots in the days before breechloaders and railway trains. Again we lack a Samuel Pepys of the gun, to record what did happen and what guns and loads were actually employed, rather than the recommendations and advice laid down by the experts. The obscuring curtain of time is drawn back briefly on occasion for we are told of a drive in 1836 in the days of the muzzle loader, on a shoot where the guns had changed to the percussion system. An old cock had come down the length of the line, having been shot at by everybody, only to be brought down by old Sir William Cooke with a flint gun. Sir William took off his white hat and called out "There's your copper caps gentlemen!"

Certainly the changes wrought by the coming of the breechloader and the facility of travel afforded by the railways were significant both as regards to the guns employed and the social climate in which they were used.

By the closing decades of the 19th century the general recommendation for a game gun was that it should be of 12 bore with a weight of 6 1/2 lbs regulated to fire 3drs of black powder and 1 oz. of shot. For those who wished for a lighter gun, the 12 bore could be made as light as 6 lbs. but if used with the normal charge the recoil was excessive and the general recommendation would be to use a 16 bore.

By the 1880's the game gun as we know it to-day had evolved. With the exception of the single trigger and the re-introduction of the O/U barrel arrangement little has changed in the last century. In fact one could, to-day, take out a pair of Purdey's bought new in 1887 by one's grandfather and no-one would notice except perhaps to pass an envious look.

Holland & Holland "Royal" sidelock

Have in fact things stood so still? To find out I asked a few friends in the gun trade and here are their comments. For driven grouse our fairy godmother would have to provide a pair of guns. Even she could not reduce the lead time, which for new guns would be in the order of two years. And, of course, with the pair of guns the lead time might well increase slightly over the two years, much would depend on what was wanted and how busy the gunmaker happened to be.

For the average Grouse Gun the weight would be about 6 1/2 lbs, 28" barrels to fire an 1 1/16th oz of shot. With a pair of guns the ideal boring for some folk would be for the No. 1 gun, — choke and Imp. Cylinder and for the second gun, Imp. Cyl. and half choke. Using guns bored in this manner requires that there is a close relationship with the loader. One has also to bear in mind the resale value of sporting guns. If you have unusual ideas incorporated to suit yourself these ideas may not suit a prospective purchaser when the guns have to be sold and for this reason having both guns bored the same might be prudent. There is now a movement to have Imp. Cylinder in all barrels and to rely on a variation in the type of cartridges used to modify the pattern. As a guide, one can always take out excess choke if field experience shows that this is desirable but it is not easy to put it back again!

If we also were to consider walked up birds, there is now a case to go down to a 20 bore. Such a gun firing 7/8ths of an ounce of shot has much to commend it on a hot day with the midges biting.

Certainly, things have changed from our large single muzzle loader but whatever gun we use, and whatever the size of the bag, the magic remains from anticipatory first light to the evenings reminiscences with the bird steaming on the plate in front of you!

London's Best

GLOSSARY OF TERMS

Action — The heart of any gun, consisting of the receiver, bolt or breech block, feed mechanism, and firing mechanism. The most complex portion of any firearm.

Anvil — In a Boxer primer, the separate portion of the primer which rests against the bottom of the primer pocket and against which the firing pin crushes the priming compound. Stamped out of thin sheet metal (usually brass) in the form of a cone with the sides notched to form two or three legs, the anvil is seated friction tight in the mouth of the primer cup, after charging and foiling. In a Berdan primed case, the anvil is the conical projection rising from the case metal itself.

Automatic Safety — A mechanical safety on any firearm which is automatically engaged either by cocking or by reloading the gun. Safeties of this type are considered desirable on guns used by those with little firearms training. They are generally simple in design, opening the breech or cocking the firing mechanism acts through a push-rod to cam the safety into its fully engaged position, preventing inadvertent firing until one deliberately disengages the safety manually. Most safeties bolt the triggers only allowing the gun to be discharged by accident if there is wear or a malfunction in the lock, for this reason better quality guns are fitted additionally with intercepting safeties.

Anson rod fore-end — Patented by W Anson, in 1873, this is possibly one of the most popular fore-end fastenings on double guns.

Automatic Selective Ejector — In any single-shot or break-open action, a device which ejects only FIRED cases clear of the breech when the action is opened. Most common is the type of ejector found in double-barrelled shotguns, in which a system of hammers, rods, and springs act upon the ejectors to eject the case. The automatic ejector is activated only by the firing of its companion lock, this device is intended primarily as an aid to rapid reloading. An rare alternative is the optional ejector where the ejector mechanism can be switched off.

Arcaded fences — Style of decoration on a shotgun fence. Characterised by a series of engraved arches.

Base wad — In a shotshell, the circular plug which fills the head of the case and surrounds the battery cup primer. Base wads have been made variously of moulded fibre, compressed paper pulp, compressed layered paper, and plastic, with or without a plastic, paper or metal overlay.

Ball fence — British shotguns have distinctive fences. This is mainly because the shape of the fence is created by hand, and not by machinery so allowing for individual expression. A Ball fence as the name implies, is rounded as opposed to the flatter type of fence, which characterises, for example, Holland & Holland shotguns.

Back action — Back action locks have the mainspring behind the tumbler, instead of in front. This avoids the need to house the mainspring in the bar of the action. (See back action lock) A hybrid type of lock is the use of back action mechanism on a bar action lock plate. This can often be detected by the position of the holes for the pins in the lock plate.

Bar action — The bar of the action is that part to which the barrels are hinged, and which extends in front of the breech face. Guns with sidelocks can have Bar action locks or back action locks. In the case of the bar action lock the mainspring of the lock is in front of the tumbler, and lies along the bar of the lock plate, which fits into the bar of the action.

Bar-in-the-wood — The alternative name here is "wood covered action". In this type of action, popular in the late 19th century, the metal of the bar is recessed and the wood of the butt stock is carried forward over the metal. A classic example is the McNaughton "Edinburgh" action. This can be visually very attractive but the reduction in the amount of metal tends to reduce the strength of the action.

Bolt — This term is used on shotguns for the means of securing barrels in a closed position. Examples are -: The Westley Richards Bolt which locks the gun in the closed position, by engaging the "bite" or notch in the barrel extension. The best known example is the Purdey Bolt, which lies below the barrels in the bar of the action and locks into two bites in the barrels lumps.

Bore, (alternatively Gauge) — The term identifying bore diameter of a shotgun. It originated in firearms antiquity when all guns used a spherical lead ball, and represents actually the number of balls suitable for a given bore that could be cast from one pound of lead.

Bead fence — A type of fence with the addition of a narrow decorative beaded edge.

Beavertail F/E — Most often on a shotgun, a forend of greater width than normal. It serves two purposes : a better grip for the forward hand, and to protect the hand from hot barrels during fast shooting. On British shotguns a metal, leather covered guard is the preferred alternative.

Black Powder — The oldest small-arms ammunition propellant, consisting of a mechanical mixture of charcoal, sulphur and saltpetre (potassium nitrate). The exact formula varies, but a common one is 15 parts charcoal, 75 parts saltpetre and 10 parts sulphur, by weight. Early black powder was a simple mechanical mixture of the various ingredients, finely ground. So named because of its colour, black powder is considered a "low explosive" and will — unlike smokeless powder — detonate if ignited unconfined. For this reason, both its manufacture and its use are generally considered hazardous. Black powder mills are always subject to periodic explosions and, consequently, as much of the work as possible is done by remote control. The major use for black powder today is in modern muzzle loading guns.

Bar lock — The type of gun lock developed during the muzzle loading period, in which the mainspring (which drives the hammer) is situated forward of the tumbler and hammer so that it, and the lock plate upon which it is seated, extend forward alongside or under the barrel. The bar lock is usually the most robust and durable of the several types, and is generally simpler to build or maintain than other gun locks. When the basic bar lock is found on relatively modern breech-loading shotguns (with or without exposed hammers) it is generally referred to as a "side lock".

Breech plug — In a muzzle loader, the plug that closes the breech end of the bore. Drilling, reaming, and rifling must be accomplished through the entire length of the barrel blank, which is then threaded to receive a plug that is screwed in to seal the breech. The breech plug often contains an integral upper tang for securing to the stock, or some form of hook or other patent breech system that assists in securing the entire barrel assembly to the stock.

Butt Plate — Any protective plate, metal, horn or plastic, attached to the butt to protect the wood, of particular value on muzzle loading shotguns. Best guns have the butt chequered without a protective plate, although metal tips have sometimes been fitted to the heel and toe of the butt providing some protection without excess weight. An alternative are the "skeleton" plates, where the Heel and Toe tips are connected by a thin metal band.

Ball and Shot — A special type of shotgun designed for use with both shot and ball cartridges. A particular variant is the "Paradox", patented by George Vincent Fosbery, V. C, in 1885. Fosbery's invention consisted in forming, in the choked part of the gun barrel, a number of spiral grooves which provided improved accuracy when used with ball without seriously affecting the shot

241

pattern.

Bites — The notch cut into the lump or barrel extension into which a bolt enters.

Bridle — The metal plate found inside a sidelock which provides additional bearing for the tumbler and sear.

Back action — A common gun lock during the percussion period. The mainspring and attendant gadgetry of the back action lock are located to the rear of the hammer, permitting a shorter lock plate and eliminating the forward extension found in the bar lock.

Best Gun — The term "best" when applied to shotguns is a term employed by the London trade, to indicate that the gun is of the finest quality. Some makers, Boss for example, advertised that they were makers of "best" guns only, and the use of descriptions such as this, probably gave rise to the term "best" gun.

Chamber — That portion at the rear of the barrel of any gun that is enlarged to accept the loaded cartridge and support it during firing. The chamber must be large enough in all dimensions to accept the largest standard cartridge of a given calibre, yet small enough to permit smooth operation while providing strong support to the relatively weak cartridge case.

Chopper lump — A method of construction of barrels for double barrelled, side-by-side shotguns in which the "lump" extending beneath the breech is forged as an integral part of the barrel. When the barrels are assembled, the two lumps are carefully fitted on their mating surfaces and brazed solidly together into a single unit, into which locking and other functional recesses are cut.

Cocking indicators — Any device which the act of cocking a gun moves into a position where it may be seen or felt in order to notify the shooter that the gun is cocked. Typical examples are the pins found on some high-grade hammerless shotguns which protrude slightly when they are cocked and the gold inlaid line on the external portion of the tumbler visible on sidelocks. See also "Window"

Cross-bolt — One of several additional types of bolting through the barrel extension. The most popular is the Greener "Round Bolt" but also to be found is the Scott square cross bolt.

Conversion — During the 19th century, labour costs were low and material costs high. This was long before the "throwaway society" and Conversions which today would be ruled out, on the grounds of expense were feasible. Conversions which took place were from percussion muzzle loading to breech loading, pin fire to central fire and from non-ejector to ejector.

Case harden — A method by which steel and iron parts are given a very hard, thin, wear-resistant surface, while the interior portion of the parts retain their original properties. Parts to be treated are brought to a high heat and are packed in case hardening compounds or molten cyanide salts rich in carbon, this is absorbed by the surface of the metal. Case hardening often produces a pleasing pattern of red, blue and grey colours — traditional on action bodies and lock plates. To preserve the colours the surfaces are often varnished.

Cross eye stock — A butt stock bent or formed to allow the gun to be mounted on one shoulder of the shooter while his opposite eye aims the gun. Also at times called a "bent" or "goose neck" stock.

Chequered side panels — The side panels on the A & D boxlock guns were thought by some to be rather plain. It became the practice of certain makers to sink the panel and chequer the sunken portion. An extension of this was to fit an engraved metal plate into the sunken side panel instead of chequering the surface.

"Crab joints" — Patented by Westley Richards in 1862, the "crab joint" is a tongue in the stock which enters a recess in the fore-end to protect the hinge.

Concealed extension — A special type of top extension which when the gun is closed, is concealed by the top of the standing breech.

Damascus barrel — A form of barrel construction once considered superior to all others, particularly for thin-walled shotgun tubes. At a time when the cheapest barrels were formed by welding a strip of flat metal longitudinally around a mandrel, (solid bar) Damascus barrels were made by twisting and welding small pieces or rods into larger ones, which were then coiled around a mandrel and forge-welded into a spiral. The main problem with Damascus barrels is that in forge welding the multitude of seams by hand, it is inevitable that slag and other inclusions weaken the structure, and that some of the welds are poorly done, even by the finest craftsmen. Many old Damascus-barrelled guns are still in almost daily use with modern ammunition. Because it is difficult to tell the difference between the best damascus barrels and the cheap and therefore weak barrels it has become the practice to regard all damascus barrels with suspicion. The only true test is to submit the barrels to the Proof Test with the risk that they may fail and be destroyed.

Doll's head — A form of auxiliary locking device on a double barrelled shotgun wherein an extension of the rib or barrel breech is shaped like a ball on a post, and seats into a recess in the standing breech. It is of little real value in strengthening the action unless absolutely perfectly fitted, and even then useful only when the main locking system begins to wear.

DB Gun — Any gun consisting of two barrels joined together along their length, either side-by-side or one over the other. The term "double" when used alone usually indicates the former, while the latter is designated "over/under" or "superposed". In general, double-barrelled guns are of the break-open type. Both barrels may be chambered for shotshells, or both for rifle cartridges. A type of double barrel gun made during the late 19th century was the Cape gun which had one barrel smooth bored for shot and the other rifled. Double-barrelled guns are generally more costly than their repeating or single-shot counterparts because they require two separate, independent firing mechanisms, and , of course, two barrels which require some skill in their assembly.

Drop — The measurement of the slope of the top of the buttstock from the line of sight of any gun, though generally applied more to shotguns than to rifles. Drop is generally measured at the front of the comb and also at the heel of the butt. The simplest method of measuring drop is to invert the gun and place it on a table top and then measure from that surface to the proper points on the stock. Drop is necessary in any gun to bring the sight line up to eye level when the butt is against the shooter's shoulder.

Drop points — Decorative feature on the stock, to the rear of a lockplate on the sidelock gun and at the rear of the side panel on the stock of an Anson & Deeley.

Double grip action — Known generally as the Double Screw Grip Under-lever, this action which will be found on all grades of guns was patented by Henry Jones, a Birmingham gunmaker, in 1859. The barrels are provided with two lumps, each of which is provided with opposing slots, into which a rotating bolt engages by what can best be described as an interrupted screw thread. Sadly, Henry Jones is today almost forgotten, and he also failed to reap the financial reward which was his undoubted due.

Engine turned rib — File cut rib. Distinctive anti-glare pattern produced on the shotgun rib, available in a variety of patterns.

Forcing cone — That portion of a shotgun barrel directly ahead of the chamber, where the relatively large diameter of the chamber is reduced to bore diameter. It is, in effect, a short cone segment. When a shotshell is fired, the shot charge and wads exit the case, they expand radially to fill the mouth of the forcing cone, and are then squeezed down to bore diameter as they pass through the cone.

Fore-end fastener — The original type of fastener for the fore-end of a side by side double gun, was a flat cross bolt passing through a loop under the barrel. If the bolt is easy to remove it is generally insecure and if tight, makes it difficult to take the gun apart. One of the first successful alternatives was patented in 1866, and consisted of a short lever which was turned to one side to release the fore-end. The most popular of many patent fore-end catches is known as the Anson, patented in 1873, and consisting of a short push rod, which protrudes from the tip of the fore-end.

French lever — Lever under the fore-end which the Belgians referred to as the "French lever".

Fence — Those parts of the standing breech which close the end of the barrels.

"Fancy back" action body — The term used in the Birmingham trade, the back of an Anson & Deeley box lock action body is finished in a series of curves or scrolls which, of course, requires careful fitting of the stock.

Gauge, see bore — The term identifying bore diameter of a shotgun.

Grip Safety — A separate mechanical safety, spring-loaded and protruding from the grip or stock usually found located in the trigger guard tang.

Greener Safety — A form of safety generally found on double-barrelled shotguns, situated on the left side of the buttstock just below the top lever. Introduced by W W Greener, the famous Birmingham gunmaker, on guns of his manufacture during the middle 1870's. Now more frequently encountered on German three barrel guns since they employ the tang safety to select the third barrel and erect the sights.

Gold Oval, Crest plate, Thumb plate — The small oval which may be Gold or Silver, inlet into the stock either at the hand or underneath the stock at the toe and which can be used to carry the initials or crest of the owner.

Hammer- In any gun, a pivoted, spring driven member which rotates with force to strike and drive forward the firing pin to fire the cartridge. Hammers usually have an extension spur for manual cocking.

Hammerless — Any gun not fitted with an exposed hammer, such guns are divided into two classes: those with the hammer (or tumbler) enclosed by other parts of the gun, and those in which a reciprocating striker is used in lieu of a hammer.

Hand — A term employed for the grip or small of the stock.

Half cock — A position of the hammer in a hammer-actuated firing mechanism that serves as a manual safety. In most instances, the half-cock notch in the hammer is cut deeply so that the nose of the sear cannot be forced out of it by pressure on the trigger. Generally, the sear can be disengaged from the half-cock notch only by drawing the hammer back toward the full-cock position.

Heelplate, see butt plate — Any protective plate, metal, horn or plastic, attached to the butt to protect the wood.

"Intercepting sear" — The standard safety on a double gun, merely bolts the triggers. The gun can still be discharged accidentally, by jarring the sear out of bent. Accidental discharges of this nature are possible due to damage or wear on the sear, or the build up of oxidised oil or dirt. An additional possibility is that the sear is not fully engaged at full cock, due to wood binding because of dimensional changes in the stock. To avoid the hazard of accidental discharge, some locks are provided with an additional sear, which if the sear is jarred out of bent, the safety or intercepting sear will be engaged and prevent the lock from accidental discharge. Secondary sears are fitted to both sidelocks and boxlocks.

"Keepers guns" — A general term to describe a low cost, but soundly constructed gun, suitable for rough working use.

Lock — Originally, the complete firing mechanism of a muzzle loader consisting of the hammer and the complete mechanism necessary for cocking it and driving it forward to fire the gun. Today, a more general term referring to any type of firing mechanism.

Lapping — A method of polishing the interior of a gun barrel (or other metal surface), by passing a tight-fitting, soft-metal plug coated with very fine abrasive powder and oil through it.

"Lockfast" action — Patented by James Dalzell Dougall, a Glasgow gunmaker, the Lockfast system employed forward moving barrels, actuated by an eccentric hinge pin operated by a lever lying along the bar of the action. The action face had disc shaped projections which, when the barrels were closed, entered recesses at the breech and so ensured positive locking. An extremely robust action used for both shotguns and rifles during the 19th century.

Matt top-rib — see engine turned rib.

Metal toe plate — see butt plate

Non-ejector- Normally a break-open shotgun in which the extractor only frees empty cases from the chamber and raises them sufficiently to be plucked out by the fingers.

Oil finished Stock — Traditional finish for gun stocks based on the use of linseed oil, usually referred to as London Oil Finish.

Proof — In Britain, Proof is the compulsory testing by law, to ensure, as far as practicable, that the gun has adequate strength to withstand the stresses and strains which it will be subjected to in use. Proof of shotguns involves pressures some 70% higher than the service pressure, which, in a 12 bore game gun may be taken as 3 tons per sq. in.

Pull — The pressure required to cause the trigger to fire, can be accurately assessed by a spring balance.

Pinfire — An early type of self contained cartridge of French origin, where the cap is ignited by means of a pin, which passes through the rim of the cartridge. The barrel has a small cut out at the top through which the pin passes, so that it can be struck by an external hammer.

"Pendulum systems" — A type of single trigger mechanism.

Quadruple grip — A type of action which would combine a double grip beneath the barrels with additional bearing surfaces on the barrel extension. As the number of locking surfaces is increased the difficulty of ensuring that locking is effective on all of them, is also increased.

Rebounding Hammer — A gun in which the hammer or firing pin automatically draws back after striking the primer and is held in the retracted position.
See "Half cock".

Rib — A raised portion on top of the barrel which may serve as a sight base, and on double guns the metal strip which is laid between the barrels.

Round action — The Dickson Round Action, invented and manufactured by the old established Edinburgh firm of John Dickson and Son. This is one of the most famous of the "Round Actions", others should more properly be described as "Rounded Actions". An alternative name for the Dickson action is a trigger plate action where the mechanism is mounted not on side plates, nor in the body of the gun but on an extended trigger plate. One of the most graceful, and strong shotgun actions. The Dickson is a "special" action with its own unique ejector mechanism.

Receiver, see Action

Rotary bolt system — Bolt system used extensively on all calibres of shotguns, one of the strongest breech closures ever invented for hinge barrel actions. (See Double Grip.)

Sear — The part or device which serves to engage the hammer, striker, or other firing device and hold it in the cocked position until firing is desired. A sear must be of good design and manufacture since loads imposed on it are quite high. The sear is disengaged to cause firing by trigger movement.

Sidelock — A form of firing mechanism used primarily in side-by-side, double barrelled shotguns, but found occasionally in other types. The side lock is simply a refined version of the traditional bar lock but with the hammer transferred to the inside of the lock plate. Advantages are ease and care of cleaning, the main disadvantages that it requires a great amount of wood to be cut away at the weakest part of the stock.

Smokeless Powder — The modern propellant for all small arms ammunition, invented in the middle 1880's. Smokeless powder is a fuel which burns efficiently without external oxygen. Single base powder is composed basically of nitrated cellulose, this material is mixed with nitric acid and solvent and converted to a stiff dough to which is added very small amounts of other components. Double base powders however, require the addition of varying degrees of nitroglycerine. Before powder is ready for packaging, all traces of solvents and acids must be removed before it is dried to a specific moisture content.

Snap action — A type of locking mechanism on hinge barrel guns which is automatically operated merely by closing the gun, as opposed to "inert" actions which require some manipulation before the gun can be closed.

Solid pin action — The cross pin about which the barrels of a side-by-side shotgun are hinged is machined as part of the action body and is not removable.

Sliding breech — A type of action typified by the French Darne.

Spindle — Connection between the top lever and bolt invented by William M Scott and patented in 1856.

Striker — The separate firing-pin which is struck by the internal tumbler on both side lock and box lock guns.

Scroll — Type of engraving usually classified as large, medium or small.

Side clips — Small extensions at the side of the fences designed to eliminate lateral movements of side by side shotgun barrels.

Southgate ejector — A special patented ejector system, dating from T. Southgate's patent of 1893.

Stub-twist barrel — One of the many types of shotgun barrel, made by welding strips of iron and steel together. (see Damascus)

Tumbler — The component in the interior of the lock by which the mainspring acts on the hammer causing it to fall and explode the cap. It also accommodates the sear at half or full-cock.

Try Gun — A fully adjustable stock, probably of British origin, and widely used by British custom gunmakers. Consists of a stock which is made in several parts and fitted with clamps, screws and sliding members so that virtually all dimensions may be quickly altered to fit the gun to any individual. Once the proper dimensions are finalized , they are used to make a custom stock to fit the shooter accurately.

Tube locks — A special container to hold priming powder, the best being patented by Westley Richards in 1821.

"Three Ring Mark steel" — Special barrel steel, made by Friedr. Krupp, Essen. Trade Mark — "Dreiringmarke". British shotguns will be encountered with barrels made from German barrel steel and so marked.

"Thumb Hole" snap action — The second method of operating, the Purdey bolt patented in 1863, was by using a short lever in front of the trigger guard, operated by passing the thumb through a hole in the bow of the guard, thus giving rise to the name for this type of action.

View — To examine a firearm very closely to determine any defect prior to going to proof. If the firearm passes then it will be stamped with the View Stamp, normally a 'V' .

Ventilated top rib — Rarely used on side by side double game guns, more likely to be encountered on Clay Pigeon guns.

Windows — These are the crystal cocking indicators, patented by William M Scott in 1875. They consist of a small circular window fitted to the lock plate, and allowed the position of the tumbler to be seen. Their use was discontinued in 1905.

Whitworth Fluid Compressed Steel — A patented method of producing steel for gun barrels, devised by Sir Joseph Whitworth, and accomplished by applying pressure to the cooling ingot to reduce flaws to the minimum. Barrels made from this type of Steel will bear the Whitworth "Wheatsheaf" trademark.

Wedgefast action — Barrel bolting mechanism patented by W W Greener in 1873, which employs an extended rib which shuts into the false breech when closed and is secured by a round cross bolt working in the false breech. Used in conjunction with a double grip snap-action.

BRITISH MAKERS

Atkin, Grant & Lang & Co.
6 Lincoln Inn Fields
London, England
WO2
Phone: 0707 42622

Bailons Ltd
Bath St
Birmingham, England
B44 6HG
Phone: 021 236 7593

Boss & Co. Ltd.
13 Dover St.
London, England W.1.
Phone: 071 493 1127

David McKay Brown
32 Hamilton Rd.
Bothwell
Glasgow, Scotland
G71
Phone: 0698 853727

A. A. Brown & Sons
1 Snake Lane
Alvechurch
Birmingham, England
B48
Phone: 021 445 5395

E. J. Churchill Ltd.
Ockley Rd., Beave Green
Dorking, Surrey, England
RHS 4PU
Phone: 0306 711435

John Dickson & Son
21 Frederick Street
Edinburgh, Scotland
Phone: 031 225 4218

William Evans Ltd
67a St. James Street
London, England
SW1
Phone: 071 493 0415

HS Greenfield & Son
Upper Bridge Street
Canterbury, Kent
England CT1 2NB
Phone: 0227 456959

Hellis, Beesley, & Watson
132 White Lion Rd.
Little Chalfont
Amensham, Bucks
England HP7 9NQ
Phone: 0494 76 2370

James Purdey & Sons
Audley House
South Audley Street
London, England
W1
Phone: 071 499 1801

John Rigby & Co
5 King Street
Covent Garden
London, England
WC2 HN
Phone: 071 734 7611

W. & C. Scott Ltd
Tame Rd
Witton
Birmingham, England
B6 7H8
Phone: 021 328 4107

Arthur Turner
33-35 West Bar
Sheffield, England
SR 9PQ
Phone: 0742 22560

Holland & Holland Ltd
33 Bruton Street
London, England
W1
Phone: 071 499 4411

William Powell & Sons Ltd
35-7 Carrs Lane
Birmingham, England
B4 79X
Phone: 021 643 06899

Westley Richards & Co
40 Grange Rd
Birmingham, England
Phone: 021 472 1701

Thomas Wild
32 Lower Loveday Street
Birmingham, England
Phone: 021 359 1830

Benjamin Wild & Son
55 Price Street
Birmingham, England
B4 6J2
Phone: 021 359 2303

John Wilkes
79 Beak Street
London, England
W1
Phone: 071 437 6539

F. J. Wiseman & Co
3 Price Street
Birmingham, England
B4 6JX
Phone: 021 359 1256

"The Workmanship is Faultless"

Quote on the Dickson 'Round-Action' gun from The Modern Shotgun (1931).

"Nothing has changed"

Quote on the new availability of the same gun from John Dickson

We are pleased to announce that our famous Patent 'Round-Action' hammerless ejector gun is once again available to order.

We also offer an extremely comprehensive range of new and used guns and rifles, clothing and accessories.

John Dickson & Son

GUN, RIFLE AND FISHING TACKLE MAKERS. ESTAB. 1820
21 Frederick Street, Edinburgh Tel: 031-225 4218.

Fine English Shotguns

from a Fine English Gunsmith.

On October 21st 1805, the battle of Trafalgar was fought off the coast of Spain. Fifteen enemy ships were destroyed but not a single British vessel was lost. No doubt Lord Nelson, commander of the British fleet, was largely responsible for this victory but it must surely also say something for the quality of our guns.

In the same year, a gunsmith was establishing himself in the historic City of Canterbury. Today, the third generation of Greenfields offers the same caring service from the same premises, but with a much wider range of facilities in our Shop, Shooting Grounds and Workshop.

We have good stocks of second hand English shotguns and rifles, as well as clothing and accessories for sale or export. Please telephone or write for details to:–

Gun making and repairs in our workshop

Country clothing

New and second-hand shotguns

GREENFIELDS
of Canterbury

H S Greenfield & Son
Upper Bridge Street,
Canterbury, Kent,
England CT1 2NB
Tel: (44) 227 456959

THE WILLIAM POWELL SIDELOCK EJECTOR

The Supreme Example of British Craftsmanship

MAIL ORDER CATALOGUE $5

featuring Shotguns, Accessories and Country Clothing

WILLIAM POWELL & SON (GUNMAKERS) LTD
33/37, CARRS LANE, BIRMINGHAM B4 7SX
ENGLAND
Telephone: 021-643 0689/8362

BY APPOINTMENT TO HRH THE DUKE OF EDINBURGH
RIFLEMAKERS. HOLLAND & HOLLAND LTD. LONDON

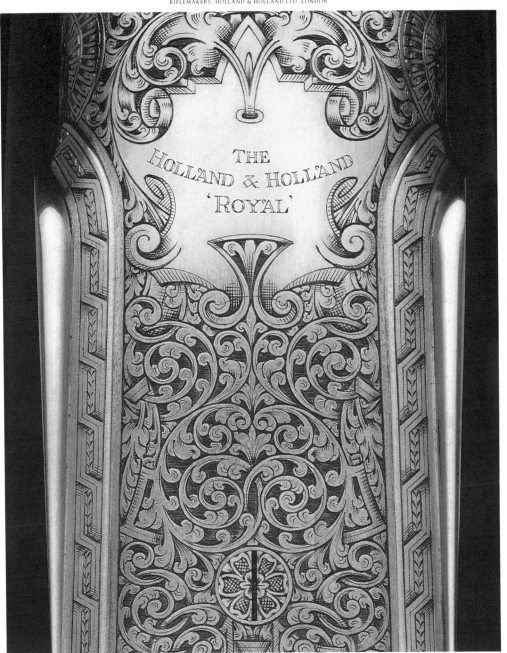

THE
HOLLAND & HOLLAND
'ROYAL'

HOLLAND & HOLLAND LTD

31 & 33 Bruton Street, London W1X 8JS   Telephone 071-499 4411. Facsimile 071-499 4544. Telex 269021 GUNNER G

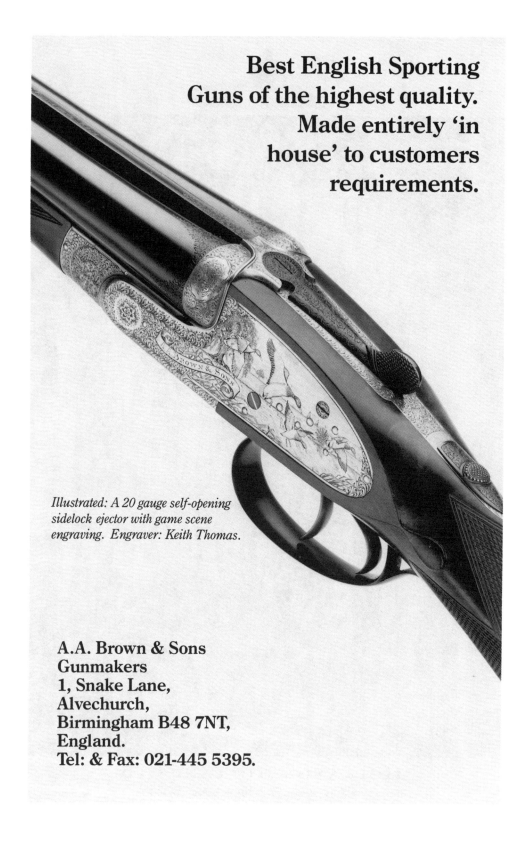

Best English Sporting
Guns of the highest quality.
Made entirely 'in
house' to customers
requirements.

*Illustrated: A 20 gauge self-opening
sidelock ejector with game scene
engraving. Engraver: Keith Thomas.*

A.A. Brown & Sons
Gunmakers
1, Snake Lane,
Alvechurch,
Birmingham B48 7NT,
England.
Tel: & Fax: 021-445 5395.

JONATHAN LAWRENCE
Fine English Guns

MATCHED PAIRS AND OVER/UNDER WOODWARD, BOSS, PURDEY GUNS A SPECIALITY.

We are noted for handling the Best of "Best" British guns.

Guns usually in stock include hammer guns, wildfowl magnums, and English game guns in small bores.

We ship guns world wide and have had many customers in the United States and Canada for several decades.

Jonathan Lawrence
Park Farm House
Waterstock, Oxfordshire
ENGLAND OX9 1JT
Phone: 0844 339469
Fax: 0844 338890

INDEX